Rigged:

How Globalization and the Rules of the Modern Economy Were Structured to Make the Rich Richer

By Dean Baker

Published by the Center for Economic and Policy Research
Washington, D.C.

Published by the Center for Economic and Policy Research
1611 Connecticut Ave NW, Suite 400
Washington, DC 20009
USA
http://cepr.net

Cover design by Justin Lancaster

ISBN: 978-0-692-79336-7

Contents

Acknowledgements

This book brings together much of my writing and thought from the last decade. It has benefited from input from many friends and colleagues, especially John Schmitt, Eileen Appelbaum, Jared Bernstein, Helene Jorgensen, and Mark Weisbrot. I had much great research assistance in compiling and analyzing data from Cherrie Bucknor, Nick Buffie, Evan Butcher, Tillie McInnis, Michael Ratliff, and Rynn Reed. Kevin Cashman also helped with research and more importantly did great work with editing and layout. Our copyeditor, Pat Watson, did his usual outstanding job of translating economic nonsense into normal English.

This work benefited from support from a number of sources including the Ford Foundation, the Ewing Marion Kauffman Foundation, the Arca Foundation, the Stephen M. Silberstein Foundation, and the Bauman Foundation. The chapter on the financial sector is derived in part from a paper that was funded by the Century Foundation's Bernard L. Schwartz Rediscovering Government Initiative.

Alan Barber, Dawn Niederhauser, and Matthew Sedlar did much to keep this book moving forward.

I would like to thank Biscuit, Noodle, Fender, Harrison and especially Helene for their endless patience and unconditional love.

Chapter 1

Introduction: Trading in Myths

In winter 2016, near the peak of Bernie Sanders' bid for the Democratic presidential nomination, a new line became popular among the nation's policy elite: Bernie Sanders is the enemy of the world's poor. Their argument was that Sanders, by pushing trade policies to help U.S. workers, specifically manufacturing workers, risked undermining the well-being of the world's poor because exporting manufactured goods to the United States and other wealthy countries is their path out of poverty. The role model was China, which by exporting has largely eliminated extreme poverty and drastically reduced poverty among its population. Sanders and his supporters would block the rest of the developing world from following the same course.

This line, in its Sanders-bashing permutation, appeared early on in Vox, the millennial-oriented media upstart, and was quickly picked up elsewhere (Beauchamp 2016).[1] After all, it was pretty irresistible. The ally of the downtrodden and enemy of the rich was pushing policies that would condemn much of the world to poverty.

---

1   See also Weissman (2016), Iacono (2016), Worstall (2016), Lane (2016), and Zakaria (2016).

The story made a nice contribution to preserving the status quo, but it was less valuable if you respect honesty in public debate.

The problem in the logic of this argument should be apparent to anyone who has taken an introductory economics course. It assumes that the basic problem of manufacturing workers in the developing world is the need for someone who will buy their stuff. If people in the United States don't buy it, then the workers will be out on the street and growth in the developing world will grind to a halt.

In this story, the problem is that we don't have enough people in the world to buy stuff. In other words, there is a shortage of demand. But is it really true that no one else in the world would buy the stuff produced by manufacturing workers in the developing world if they couldn't sell it to consumers in the United States? Suppose people in the developing world bought the stuff they produced raising their living standards by raising their own consumption.

That is how the economics is supposed to work. In the standard theory, general shortages of demand are not a problem.[2] Economists have traditionally assumed that economies tended toward full employment. The basic economic constraint was a lack of supply. The problem was that we couldn't produce enough goods and services, not that we were producing too much and couldn't find anyone to buy them. In fact, this is why all the standard models used to analyze trade agreements like the Trans-Pacific Partnership assume trade doesn't affect total employment.[3] Economies adjust so that shortages of demand are not a problem.

In this standard story (and the Sanders critics are people who care about textbook economics), capital flows from slow-growing rich countries, where it is relatively plentiful and so gets a low rate of return,

---

2   As explained in the next chapter, this view is not exactly correct, but it's what you're supposed to believe if you adhere to the mainstream economic view.

3   There can be modest changes in employment through a supply-side effect. If the trade deal increases the efficiency of the economy, then the marginal product of labor should rise, leading to a higher real wage, which in turn should induce some people to choose work over leisure. So the trade deal results in more people choosing to work, not an increased demand for labor.

to fast-growing poor countries, where it is scarce and gets a high rate of return (**Figure** 1-1).

FIGURE 1-1
Theoretical and actual capital flows

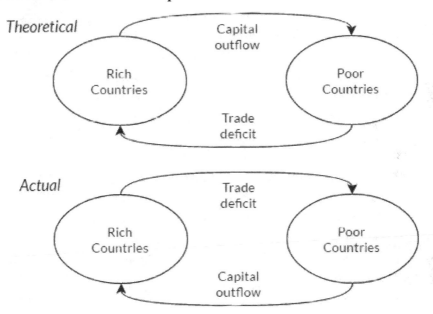

Source and notes: See text.

So the United States, Japan, and the European Union should be running large trade surpluses, which is what an outflow of capital means. Rich countries like ours should be lending money to developing countries, providing them with the means to build up their capital stock and infrastructure while they use their own resources to meet their people's basic needs.

This wasn't just theory. That story accurately described much of the developing world, especially Asia, through the 1990s. Countries like Indonesia and Malaysia were experiencing rapid annual growth of 7.8 percent and 9.6 percent, respectively, even as they ran large trade deficits, just over 2 percent of GDP each year in Indonesia and almost 5 percent in Malaysia.

These trade deficits probably were excessive, and a crisis of confidence hit East Asia and much of the developing world in the summer of 1997. The inflow of capital from rich countries slowed or reversed, making it impossible for the developing countries to sustain the fixed exchange rates most had at the time. One after another, they were forced to abandon their fixed exchange rates and turn to the International Monetary Fund (IMF) for help.

Rather than promulgating policies that would allow developing countries to continue the textbook development path of growth driven by importing capital and running trade deficits, the IMF made debt repayment a top priority. The bailout, under the direction of the Clinton administration Treasury Department, required developing countries to switch to large trade surpluses (Radelet and Sachs 2000, O'Neil 1999).

The countries of East Asia would be far richer today had they been allowed to continue on the growth path of the early and mid-1990s, when they had large trade deficits (**Figure 1-2**). Four of the five would be more than twice as rich, and the fifth, Vietnam, would be almost 50 percent richer. South Korea and Malaysia would have higher per capita incomes today than the United States.

In the wake of the East Asia bailout, countries throughout the developing world decided they had to build up reserves of foreign exchange, primarily dollars, in order to avoid ever facing the same harsh bailout terms as the countries of East Asia. Building up reserves meant running large trade surpluses, and it is no coincidence that the U.S. trade deficit has exploded, rising from just over 1 percent of GDP in 1996 to almost 6 percent in 2005. The rise has coincided with the loss of more than 3 million manufacturing jobs, roughly 20 percent of employment in the sector.

There was no reason the textbook growth pattern of the 1990s could not have continued. It wasn't the laws of economics that forced developing countries to take a different path, it was the failed bailout and the international financial system. It would seem that the enemy of the world's poor is not Bernie Sanders but rather the engineers of our current globalization policies.

FIGURE 1-2

Per capita income of East Asian countries, actual vs. continuing on 1990s growth path

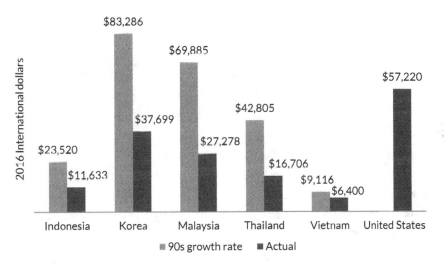

Source and notes: IMF (2016) and author's calculations.

There is a further point in this story that is generally missed: it is not only the volume of trade flows that is determined by policy, but also the content. A major push in recent trade deals has been to require stronger and longer patent and copyright protection. Paying the fees imposed by these terms, especially for prescription drugs, is a huge burden on the developing world. Bill Clinton would have much less need to fly around the world for the Clinton Foundation had he not inserted the TRIPS (Trade Related Aspects of Intellectual Property Rights) provisions in the World Trade Organization (WTO) that require developing countries to adopt U.S. style patent protections. Generic drugs are almost always cheap — patent protection makes drugs expensive. The cancer and hepatitis drugs that sell for tens or hundreds of thousands of dollars a year would sell for a few hundred dollars in a free market. Cheap drugs would be more widely available had the developed world not forced TRIPS on the developing world.

Of course, we have to pay for the research to develop new drugs or any innovation. We also have to compensate creative workers who produce music, movies, and books. But there are efficient alternatives to patents and copyrights, and the efforts by the elites in the United States and other wealthy countries to impose these relics on the developing world is just a mechanism for redistributing income from the world's poor to Pfizer, Microsoft, and Disney. Stronger and longer patent and copyright protection is not a necessary feature of a 21st century economy.

In textbook trade theory, if a country has a larger trade surplus on payments for royalties and patent licensing fees, it will have a larger trade deficit in manufactured goods and other areas. The reason is that, in theory, the trade balance is fixed by national savings and investment, not by the ability of a country to export in a particular area. If the trade deficit is effectively fixed by these macroeconomic factors, then more exports in one area mean fewer exports in other areas. Put another way, income gains for Pfizer and Disney translate into lost jobs for workers in the steel and auto industries.

The conventional story is that we lose manufacturing jobs to developing countries because they have hundreds of millions of people willing to do factory work at a fraction of the pay of manufacturing workers in the United States. This is true, but developing countries also have tens of millions of smart and ambitious people willing to work as doctors and lawyers in the United States at a fraction of the pay of the ones we have now.

Gains from trade work the same with doctors and lawyers as they do with textiles and steel. Our consumers would save hundreds of billions a year if we could hire professionals from developing countries and pay them salaries that are substantially less than what we pay our professionals now. The reason we import manufactured goods and not doctors is that we have designed the rules of trade that way. We deliberately write trade pacts to make it as easy as possible for U.S. companies to set up manufacturing operations abroad and ship the products back to the United States, but we have done little or nothing to remove the obstacles that professionals from other countries face in trying to work in the United

States. The reason is simple: doctors and lawyers have more political power than autoworkers.[4]

In short, there is no truth to the story that the job loss and wage stagnation faced by manufacturing workers in the United States and other wealthy countries was a necessary price for reducing poverty in the developing world.[5] This is a fiction that is used to justify the upward redistribution of income in rich countries. After all, it is pretty selfish for autoworkers and textile workers in rich countries to begrudge hungry people in Africa and Asia and the means to secure food, clothing, and shelter.

The other aspect of this story that deserves mention is the nature of the jobs to which our supposedly selfish workers feel entitled. The manufacturing jobs that are being lost to the developing world pay in the range of $15 to $30 an hour, with the vast majority closer to the bottom figure than the top. The average hourly wage for production and nonsupervisory workers in manufacturing in 2015 was just under $20 an hour, or about $40,000 a year. While a person earning $40,000 is doing much better than a subsistence farmer in Sub-Saharan Africa, it is difficult to see this worker as especially privileged.

By contrast, many of the people remarking on the narrow-mindedness and sense of entitlement of manufacturing workers earn comfortable six-figure salaries. Senior writers and editors at network news shows or at *The New York Times* and *The Washington Post* feel entitled to their pay because they feel they have the education and skills to be successful in a rapidly changing global economy.

---

4   For those worried about brain drain from developing countries, there is an easy fix. Economists like to talk about taxing the winners, in this case developing country professionals and rich country consumers, to compensate the losers, which would be the home countries of the migrating professionals. We could tax a portion of the professionals' pay to allow their home countries to train two or three professionals for every one that came to the United States. This is a classic win-win from trade.

5   The loss of manufacturing jobs also reduced the wages of less-educated workers (those without college degrees) more generally. The displaced manufacturing workers crowded into retail and other service sectors, putting downward pressure on wages there.

These are the sort of people who consider it a sacrifice to work at a high-level government job for $150,000 to $200,000 a year. For example, Timothy Geithner, President Obama's first Treasury Secretary, often boasts about his choice to work for various government agencies rather than earn big bucks in the private sector. His sacrifice included a stint as president of the Federal Reserve Bank of New York that paid $415,000 a year.[6] This level of pay put Geithner well into the top 1 percent of wage earners.

Geithner's comments about his sacrifices in public service did not elicit any outcry from the media at the time because his perspective was widely shared. The implicit assumption is that the sort of person who is working at a high level government job could easily be earning a paycheck that is many times higher if they were employed elsewhere. In fact, this is often true. When he left his job as Treasury Secretary, Geithner took a position with a private equity company where his salary is likely several million dollars a year.

Not everyone who was complaining about entitled manufacturing workers was earning as much as Timothy Geithner, but it is a safe bet that the average critic was earning far more than the average manufacturing worker — and certainly far more than the average displaced manufacturing worker.

Turning the debate right-side up: Markets are structured

The perverse nature of the debate over a trade policy that would have the audacity to benefit workers in rich countries is a great example of how we accept as givens not just markets themselves but also the policies that structure markets. If we accept it as a fact of nature that poor countries cannot borrow from rich countries to finance their development, and that they can only export manufactured goods, then

---

6   As a technical matter, the Federal Reserve Bank of New York is a private bank. It is owned by the banks that are members of the Federal Reserve System in the New York District.

their growth will depend on displacing manufacturing workers in the United States and other rich countries.

It is absurd to narrow the policy choices in this way, yet the centrists and conservatives who support the upward redistribution of the last four decades have been extremely successful in doing just that, and progressives have largely let them set the terms of the debate.

Markets are never just given. Neither God nor nature hands us a worked-out set of rules determining the way property relations are defined, contracts are enforced, or macroeconomic policy is implemented. These matters are determined by policy choices. The elites have written these rules to redistribute income upward. Needless to say, they are not eager to have the rules rewritten — which means they also have no interest in even having them discussed.

But for progressive change to succeed, these rules must be addressed. While modest tweaks to tax and transfer policies can ameliorate the harm done by a regressive market structure, their effect will be limited. The complaint of conservatives — that tampering with market outcomes leads to inefficiencies and unintended outcomes — is largely correct, even if they may exaggerate the size of the distortions from policy interventions. Rather than tinker with badly designed rules, it is far more important to rewrite the rules so that markets lead to progressive and productive outcomes in which the benefits of economic growth and improving technology are broadly shared.

This book examines five broad areas where the rules now in place tend to redistribute income upward and where alternative rules can lead to more equitable outcomes and a more efficient market:

1) Macroeconomic policies determining levels of employment and output.

2) Financial regulation and the structure of financial markets.

3) Patent and copyright monopolies and alternative mechanisms for financing innovation and creative work.

4) Pay of chief executive officers (CEOs) and corporate governance structures.

5) Protections for highly paid professionals, such as doctors and lawyers.

In each of these areas, it is possible to identify policy choices that have engineered the upward redistribution of the last four decades.

In the case of macroeconomic policy, the United States and other wealthy countries have explicitly adopted policies that focus on maintaining low rates of inflation. Central banks are quick to raise interest rates at the first sign of rising inflation and sometimes even before. Higher interest rates slow inflation by reducing demand, thereby reducing job growth, and reduced job growth weakens workers' bargaining power and puts downward pressure on wages. In other words, the commitment to an anti-inflation policy is a commitment by the government, acting through central banks, to keep wages down. It should not be surprising that this policy has the effect of redistributing income upward.

The changing structure of financial regulation and financial markets has also been an important factor in redistributing income upward. This is a case where an industry has undergone very rapid change as a result of technological innovation. Information technology has hugely reduced the cost of financial transactions and allowed for the development of an array of derivative instruments that would have been unimaginable four decades ago. Rather than modernizing regulation to ensure that these technologies allow the financial sector to better serve the productive economy, the United States and other countries have largely structured regulations to allow a tiny group of bankers and hedge fund and private equity fund managers to become incredibly rich.

This changed structure of regulation over the last four decades was not "deregulation," as is often claimed. Almost no proponent of deregulation argued against the bailouts that saved Wall Street in the financial crisis or against the elimination of government deposit insurance that is an essential part of a stable banking system. Rather, they advocated a system in which the rules restricting their ability to profit were eliminated, while the insurance provided by the Federal Reserve Board, the Federal Deposit Insurance Corporation, and other arms of the government were left in place. The position of "deregulators" effectively amounted to arguing that they should not have to pay for the insurance they were receiving.

The third area in which the rules have been written to ensure an upward redistribution is patent and copyright protection. Over the last four decades these protections have been made stronger and longer. In the case of both patent and copyright, the duration of the monopoly period has been extended. In addition, these monopolies have been applied to new areas. Patents can now be applied to life forms, business methods, and software. Copyrights have been extended to cover digitally produced material as well as the Internet. Penalties for infringement have been increased and the United States has vigorously pursued their application in other countries through trade agreements and diplomatic pressure.

Government-granted monopolies are not facts of nature, and there are alternative mechanisms for financing innovation and creative work. Direct government funding, as opposed to government granted monopolies, is one obvious alternative. For example, the government spends more than $30 billion a year on biomedical research through the National Institutes of Health — money that all parties agree is very well spent. There are also other possible mechanisms. It is likely that these alternatives are more efficient than the current patent and copyright system, in large part because they would be more market-oriented. And, they would likely lead to less upward redistribution than the current system.

The CEOs who are paid tens of millions a year would like the public to think that the market is simply compensating them for their extraordinary skills. A more realistic story is that a broken corporate governance process gives corporate boards of directors — the people who largely determine CEO pay — little incentive to hold down pay. Directors are more closely tied to top management than to the shareholders they are supposed to represent, and their positions are lucrative, usually paying six figures for very part-time work. Directors are almost never voted out by shareholders for their lack of attention to the job or for incompetence.

The market discipline that holds down the pay of ordinary workers does not apply to CEOs, since their friends determine their pay. And a director has little incentive to pick a fight with fellow directors or top management by asking a simple question like, "Can we get a CEO just as good for half the pay?" This privilege matters not just for CEOs; it has the spillover effect of raising the pay of other top managers in the corporate sector and putting upward pressure on the salaries of top management in universities, hospitals, private charities, and other nonprofits.

Reformed corporate governance structures could empower shareholders to contain the pay of their top-level employees. Suppose directors could count on boosts in their own pay if they cut the pay of top management without hurting profitability. With this sort of policy change, CEOs and top management might start to experience some of the downward wage pressure that existing policies have made routine for typical workers.

This is very much not a story of the natural workings of the market. Corporations are a legal entity created by the government, which also sets the rules of corporate governance. Current law includes a lengthy set of restrictions on corporate governance practices. It is easy to envision rules that would make it less likely for CEOs to earn such outlandish paychecks by making it easier for shareholders to curb excessive pay.

Finally, government policies strongly promote the upward redistribution of income for highly paid professionals by protecting them from competition. To protect physicians and specialists, we restrict the ability of nurse practitioners or physician assistants to perform tasks for which they are entirely competent. We require lawyers for work that paralegals are capable of completing. While trade agreements go far to remove any obstacle that might protect an autoworker in the United States from competition with a low-paid factory worker in Mexico or China, they do little or nothing to reduce the barriers that protect doctors, dentists, and lawyers from the same sort of competition. To practice medicine in the United States, it is still necessary to complete a residency program here, as though there were no other way for a person to become a competent doctor.

We also have done little to foster medical travel. This could lead to enormous benefits to patients and the economy, since many high-cost medical procedures can be performed at a fifth or even one-tenth the U.S. price in top quality medical facilities elsewhere in the world. In this context, it is not surprising that the median pay of physicians is over $250,000 a year and some areas of specialization earn close to twice this amount. In the case of physicians alone if pay were reduced to Western European-levels, the savings would be close to $100 billion a year (@ 0.6 percent of GDP).

Changing the rules in these five areas could reduce much and possibly all of the upward redistribution of the last four decades. But changing the rules does not mean using government intervention to curb the market. It means restructuring the market to produce different outcomes. The purpose of this book is to show how.

Chapter 2

The Landscape of Inequality

Before getting into the specifics of these five areas it is worth
reviewing some the basic facts about recent trends in inequality and also
some simple economics. As **Figure 2-1** shows, the share of income
(without capital gains) going to the top 1 percent of tax filers was
relatively stable between 1950 and 1980, starting out at 11.4 percent and
bottoming out at 7.7 percent in 1973. It then turns around and begins to
climb — 8.2 percent in 1980, 13.0 percent in 1990, 16.5 percent in
2000, and 18.3 percent in 2007, just before the downturn. It has
remained more or less at this plateau since 2008.[7]

This means that the share of the 1 percent has more than doubled
from its level during most of the period of the 1950s to 1980. Measured as
a share of total income, this increase is roughly 10.0 percentage points.
This would be sufficient to increase the income of everyone in the bottom

---

7   The modest jump to 18.9 percent in 2012 is due to the tax increase put in place in
     2013. Many high-income earners arranged to have income show up in 2012 rather
     than 2013 so that they would pay a lower tax rate on it. This shifting also explains
     the drop in the 1 percent's share in 2013, since some income from that year showed
     up in 2012.

90 percent of the income distribution by more than 20 percent. It would be almost enough to double the income of the bottom 40 percent. In short, this upward redistribution has had a substantial impact on the living standards of the rest of the population.

FIGURE 2-1
Income share of the top 1 percent

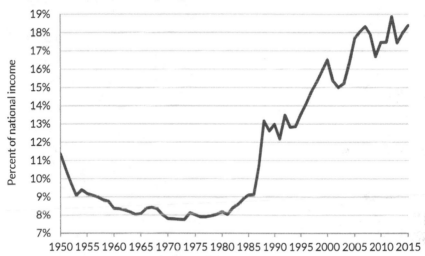

Source and notes: Piketty and Saez (2016).

The story is high-end wages, not profits

There is a basic misconception about the pattern of rising inequality of the last four decades that is important to correct. The rise we have seen in the United States over this period is almost entirely a story of growing wage inequality. No shift from wage income to profits or other forms of capital income occurred until the Great Recession, and, while there have been substantial cyclical fluctuations, there has been no clear upward trend in the share of profits in corporate income from the mid-1970s, as shown in **Figure 2-2**. The capital share does increase in the years of the housing bubble, but this rise was largely driven by an extraordinary increase in profit in the financial sector, much of which disappeared in the crash, when the mortgages issued lost much of their value. In any case, the vast majority of the rise in the income share of the top 1 percent preceded this rise in the profit share, so it cannot be the explanation. The fact that the capital share of income, which disproportionately flows to the 1 percent, has stood at an unusually high level in the years since the crash while the income share of the top 1 percent has remained stable raises the possibility that part of the upward redistribution in wage income had been reversed. But at this point it is too early to know. In any case, a shift in the profit share back to pre-recession levels as a result of tighter labor markets would certainly be good news for ordinary workers.

FIGURE 2-2
Capital share of corporate income

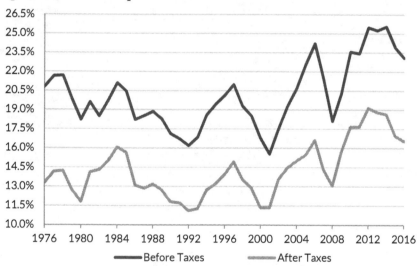

Source and notes: BEA (2016).

A likely reason for the misconception that the upward distribution of income is the result of a growing profit share is the news about relatively new companies, like Google (now Alphabet) and Facebook, becoming hugely profitable in a short period. However, the profits of these companies have primarily come at the expense of older, more established companies, not from workers' wages.

The public debate has also likely been skewed by Thomas Piketty's important and influential book, *Capital in the Twenty-First Century*. While there is a vast amount of useful data in this work, its explanation for inequality is not applicable to the United States, where rising income inequality is not associated with a greater capital share in national income.[8] To find the origins of rising inequality in the United States, we have to look to the factors that led to huge paychecks for CEOs, Wall Street traders, and other high-end earners, and it is not a story of corporate profits rising at the expense of wages.

There is a second important issue that comes directly out of this point about the profit share not rising at the expense of wages. It implies that the conditions of competition have not changed in any fundamental way over this period. Due to competition, the reductions in pay seen by middle and lower income workers were for the most part passed on in lower prices, not pocketed by companies as higher profits. This means that if the pay of high-end earners is reduced, the cost savings will be passed on in lower prices in 2016, in pretty much the same way as would have been the case in 1976. It also means that real wages will rise for those workers at the middle and bottom of the income ladder who do not see their pay cut since the items they buy will cost less.

Their money is our money

The defenders of the status quo benefit enormously by the selective use of standard economics. For example, it is standard economics that generates the classic gains from trade story in which countries benefit

---

8   The situation is somewhat different in Western Europe, which has seen more of a shift from labor income to capital income. Piketty intended his work to be a general theory of capitalist development, so the different experience of European countries is important for his thesis. Nonetheless, a theory that explains rising inequality through increasing shares of income going to capital is not appropriate as an explanation of trends in the United States over the last four decades. The one exception, which does not especially help Piketty's case, is that there has been a notable rise in rental income as a share of national income throughout this period. This is primarily owners' equivalent rent, the imputed value of rent for owner-occupied housing.

on average from reducing trade barriers. Such a story may not be immediately obvious, since it is not apparent that the United States benefits when it loses large numbers of jobs to imports, but economic theory can be used to show that the country will benefit from removing trade barriers. Economists and columnists who are happy to cite economic theory when they push the benefits of trade deals tend to ignore the fact that the assumed benefits depend on full employment, and that all groups do not necessarily benefit.

Standard economics is less likely to be invoked when the implications point in the opposite direction. For example, we almost never hear any discussion of the costs of patent and copyright monopolies, although these costs are almost definitional. If a drug would sell for $20 per prescription in a free market but instead sells for $200 because of patent protection, there are costs associated with that protection.

A basic point of economic theory that economists don't like to talk about is that reducing the rents going to a high-income person is a gain for the rest of us. This is a crucial point, since it is necessary to recognize that policies designed to reduce the incomes of high-end earners are not just a matter of being gratuitously nasty to those who were lucky enough to be successful. Whether or not these policies are nasty, it is important to recognize that the money enjoyed by these high-end earners comes from somewhere; it is not manna from heaven. And where it comes from is the pockets of the rest of us.

Imagine a person who has a huge annual income without doing any productive work. He is an extremely successful counterfeiter, supporting himself by printing $1 billion a year in high-quality counterfeit bills. No one recognizes the bills are counterfeit, and so he can spend this money in the same way as anyone else. At first glance, we might be inclined to think this counterfeiter is an asset to the economy. After all, he spends his money employing people to build and maintain his house and grounds. He provides jobs when he buys cars, boats, and other consumption goods or eats lavish meals at expensive restaurants. Perhaps he even starts a foundation that helps to finance children's health care or other useful ventures. This counterfeiter looks like a great job creator and a socially minded person who gives poor children a chance.

If this story made sense then the best economic policy would be to train people to become effective counterfeiters. But it doesn't make sense; there is a big problem in this picture.[9] With his money, the counterfeiter is diverting resources that would have otherwise been available to the rest of us. The classic story would be that the counterfeiter is bidding up wages and the prices of various goods and services that are in short supply. This would lead to inflation. The Federal Reserve Board would then respond to this inflation by raising interest rates. Higher interest rates would reduce demand for housing and discourage investment and consumption. If we take the classic story strictly, the increased spending by our counterfeiter would be fully offset by reductions in other spending elsewhere in the economy. Our counterfeiter has effectively found a way to tax the rest of us with his fake bills.

Keep the counterfeiter in mind when assessing any argument about the rents earned by CEOs, Wall Street traders, and other high-end earners. If these people actually contribute an amount of output equal to their earnings, then they are not pulling resources from the rest of us. In other words, if individual CEOs or Wall Street traders actually add $30 million to the economy with their work, then we have additional output that corresponds to their $30 million annual income. They may even add more than $30 million to the economy, effectively making the rest of us wealthier. However, if they add less than $30 million, then their income comes to some extent at the expense of the rest of us. In the extreme case, where the highly paid CEO or Wall Street trader adds nothing to the economy's output, they are in an identical situation to the counterfeiter. Their income is a pure drain on the economy, which must come out of the pockets of the rest of us.

---

9   Actually, there is an important exception. When the economy is below full employment then our counterfeiter would be doing a public service. In that situation, we need increased demand in the economy. Ideally, the government would take responsibility for boosting demand and would increase spending in areas like infrastructure and education that provide benefits to the country as a whole. But if the government was unwilling to take steps to boost demand, then the counterfeiter would be providing a public service. His personal spending patterns may not be the best way to boost demand and create jobs, but it does have this positive effect.

As a practical matter, most high-end earners are probably not like the counterfeiter who does nothing productive, but insofar as they are paid more than is necessary for their services, their excess pay does come at the expense of the rest of us. This means that if a CEO is paid $30 million, but someone else would do as good a job for one half or one third of the pay, then the rest of us are effectively subsidizing this person's pay. The channels through which the money goes from the rest of us to the high-end earners may not always be clear, but their good fortune nonetheless imposes a cost on the rest of us.

The route through which the wealthy see the benefits from this redistribution is crystal clear, and, perversely, that clarity aids their argument. A company that presses its workers for lower wages knows that it will see benefits in higher profits and more money for its higher-end employees. A drug or entertainment company pushing for stronger and longer patent and copyright protection will receive higher profits. Doctors and dentists who insist on protectionist measures that limit competition will receive higher pay. It is generally less clear to ordinary workers that they stand to gain by measures that limit the incomes of those at the top. They may see such efforts as vindictive, rather than as an essential part of a policy to reduce inequality.

If the high-end earners have enough market power to protect their income, then direct efforts to boost the incomes of those at the middle and bottom will ultimately prove largely futile by exactly the logic described above. Suppose that the CEOs, Wall Street traders, highly paid medical specialists and the rest are able to fully protect their income against any increase in prices. (In other words, their pay increases by enough to fully offset any additional expenses they must pay to sustain their standard of living.) Imagine in this case that unions are able to successfully add another 10 percent of the workforce to their ranks and then push up wages for this big chunk of the workforce. Other things equal, this will lead to higher prices and therefore higher inflation. If the Fed is committed to an anti-inflation policy, it will raise interest rates sharply. This will push people out of work and put downward pressure on the wages of a large segment of the workforce.

It is possible that newly unionized workers end up better off in this story, but that will not be the case for low- and middle-income workers generally. Insofar as the unionized workers benefit, it will be at the expense of other comparably situated workers. That is, unless there is an actual cut in the income of those at the top. For this reason, pushing down the incomes of the rich is not a question of vindictiveness; it is a necessary condition for creating the possibility of broadly based wage growth.

If doctors, lawyers, CEOs, and Wall Street-types are paid less, then we should see lower prices for a wide range of goods and services. And this means higher real wages. It is every bit as good for a worker if the prices of the goods and services they buy each month fall by 10 percent as if they got a 10 percent boost in the size of their monthly paycheck. While the benefits from reducing the rents going to the rich are unlikely to be this dramatic (at least over any short period of time), if the annual pay of high-end earners is reduced by several hundred billion dollars, this will translate into several hundred billion dollars in the pockets of ordinary workers, whether it comes in the form of higher wages or lower prices.

Really big numbers and the food stamp metric

One way in which the news media complicate economic debates is by using large numbers without providing context. This issue comes up in most policy areas but likely has the greatest relevance in budget debates. The United States is a huge country with more than 320 million people, and as a result its government has a huge budget, at least in terms of the amount of money that ordinary people see in their daily lives. This means that when we hear that the federal government is spending, say, $17 billion a year on Temporary Assistance for Needy Families (TANF), the core government welfare program, we are likely to think it's a great deal of money.[10] After all, none of us will see $17 billion in our lifetime or anything remotely close to this sum.

---

10   Data on recent trends in TANF spending can be found in CBO (2015a).

This could lead people to believe that TANF is a large portion of the federal budget. This belief would lead people to think that spending on TANF beneficiaries was a major part of their tax burden. It might also lead them to think that beneficiaries were receiving large amounts of money. These mistaken views could cause people to both resent the program as a source of strain on their own pocketbooks and to resent TANF recipients as being the beneficiaries of an overly generous program.

In fact, the $17 billion spent on TANF each year is less than 0.4 percent of the federal budget. Ending the program entirely would have only a trivial impact on the overall budget situation. It certainly would not provide enough savings to finance any substantial reduction in taxes. Furthermore, the average benefit of less than $500 a month would not likely fit anyone's definition of generous.

But few news listeners are aware of these facts. Polls consistently show that the public grossly overestimates the amount of money that goes to TANF and other programs that benefit the poor both in the United States and around the world. For example, a 2013 poll found that on average respondents thought that 28 percent of the budget went to foreign aid (Kaiser Family Foundation 2013). The actual figure is closer to 1.0 percent.

The media's pattern of reporting is likely a major factor behind this misunderstanding, and it could be easily countered if reporters made it a standard practice to put huge numbers in a context that is understandable to their audience. The most obvious way would be to report the number as a share of the budget. In the case of TANF, if people continually heard it reported as 0.4 percent of the federal budget it is unlikely they would believe the program was a major factor in their tax bill. It could also be reported as a per person number ($80 per taxpayer per year) or as a share of the economy (0.1 percent of GDP).[11] There are

---

11 Probably some of the exaggerations on the size of the budget devoted to TANF or other programs helping poor people stem from a racist desire to blame the poor, who are disproportionately minorities, for the country's problems. However, the percentage of people in polls who seriously overestimate the relative importance of these programs is far larger than the percentage that could plausibly be directly

many other ways in which this spending level could be expressed, but the point would be to put it in a context that is meaningful to readers. There is no one who will try to contend that $17 billion is a meaningful number to even the relatively well-educated readers of *The New York Times* or *The Wall Street Journal*. Yet reporters and editors continue to do budget reporting as though they were carrying through a fraternity ritual instead of trying to inform their audience.[12]

The goal of this book is to provide information, and to advance this cause we will on occasion make reference to the Supplemental Nutrition Assistance Program (SNAP) metric. SNAP, more commonly known as food stamps, is the federal government's largest anti-poverty program.[13] Roughly 45 million people received benefits in 2015, and the average benefit per person is $127 per month or just over $1,500 per year. The government is projected to spend $75 billion on SNAP in 2016, or 1.9 percent of the budget (CBO 2016). Expressed as a share of GDP, the SNAP budget is roughly 0.4 percent.

SNAP is a well-run and important program. The vast majority of the beneficiaries are children, seniors, or disabled people. It provides a modest but important supplement to family income that has helped tens of millions of people through difficult times. Since the program has been in the news frequently in recent years (often as a target of conservative budget cutters), it can provide a useful point of comparison for the sums mentioned in subsequent chapters. Comparisons to the size of the whole economy provide some context, but may still not be useful in informing readers how important the savings are from eliminating waste in the

---

driven by racist views. In fact, given the overall support for these programs, many of the people who have exaggerated views of their size must nonetheless support them.

12   Margaret Sullivan, the former public editor of *The New York Times*, took the paper to task for reporting large numbers without any context. She convinced David Leonhardt, then the Washington editor, that reporting numbers in context should be standard practice at the *Times* (Sullivan 2013). Unfortunately, it seems that little has changed. It is still possible to read articles on the budget and other topics in which numbers are expressed in a way that will be meaningless to the vast majority of *Times* readers.

13   These data come from Center on Budget and Policy Priorities (2016), which offers a fuller description of the program.

financial sector or from selling prescription drugs in a free market. Using spending on food stamps as a point of reference will allow readers to see how large prospective savings are relative to an important program that is often in the news.

Chapter 3

The Macroeconomics of Upward Redistribution

Many economists like to think that the distribution of income within society is independent of macroeconomic phenomena like unemployment and recessions. Part of the rationale for this view is that economists generally think of the economy as being near its full-employment level of output most of the time. While economists recognize that the economy experiences recessions, these are usually thought to be relatively mild and followed by a quick bounce back to its full-employment level of output.

Another reason why economists like to think of distribution of income as independent of the level of output is that this view works out nicely with the morality stories people like to tell. The standard story is that the market has a certain naturalness through which people get paid based on their marginal product. If the market distributes income based on how productive people are, then we have a basis for distributing income that is independent of political decisions or moral judgments. We may choose to alter this distribution, for example, because we think the poor have too little and the rich have too much, but the market distribution provides the initial point of reference.

However, if the market distribution is indeed dependent on macroeconomic factors, like how close the economy is to its full-employment level of output, then we lose this independent point of reference. The distribution of income is then dependent on macroeconomic policies that determine the nearness to full employment. The market distribution is then inherently a function of policy decisions — there is no independent point of reference. For someone steeped in traditional economics, this is equivalent to a true believer discovering there is no God.

Full employment and income distribution: there is a connection

There is a great deal of evidence that employment levels make a huge difference for income distribution. At the most basic level we know that minorities and those at the bottom of the income distribution suffer disproportionately from periods of high unemployment. By implication, they benefit disproportionately from periods of low unemployment.

For example, the unemployment rate for blacks is consistently twice the unemployment rate for whites. In the first six months of 2016, when the unemployment for whites averaged 4.3 percent, the unemployment rate for blacks averaged 8.7 percent. In 2000, when the white unemployment rate averaged 3.5 percent, the black unemployment rate averaged 7.6 percent. Given this 2-to-1 relationship, if we can lower the unemployment rate for white workers by 1 percentage point we can count on lowering the unemployment rate for black workers by 2 percentage points (**Figure 3-1**).

The relationship between the white unemployment rate and the unemployment rate for black teens is even more striking. This ratio tends to be in the range of 6-to-1, although it moves around. Back in 2010, in the immediate aftermath of the Great Recession, when the white unemployment rate was peaking at 9.2 percent, the unemployment rate for black teens was almost 49.0 percent. In the first six months of 2016 the rate for black teens averaged 26.3 percent. Though still a horrible unemployment rate, it is a huge improvement from six years prior. To make this point more clearly, the employment rate for black teens — the percentage of black teens who have jobs — was just 14.5 percent in 2010 but was 21.5 percent in the first six months of 2016. This means that black teens were almost 50 percent more likely to have jobs in the first half of 2016 than they were in 2010. As a practical matter it is difficult to envision a social program that would have the same effect on the career and life prospects of young blacks as increasing their probability of getting a job by 50 percent.

FIGURE 3-1
Black and white unemployment rates, 1972–2016

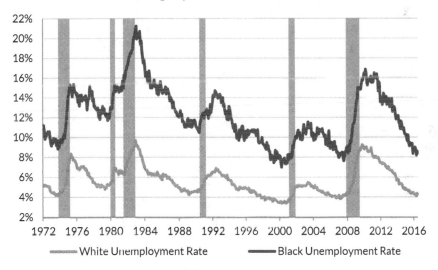

Source and notes: BLS (2016a). Shaded areas represent recessions.

The story is similar for other disadvantaged groups. The unemployment rate for workers without high school degrees was 14.9 percent in 2010. For workers with just high school degrees it was 10.3 percent. In the first half of 2016, the unemployment rate for workers without high school degrees had fallen to 7.4 percent, a drop of 7.5 percentage points. For workers with just high school degrees it was 5.3 percent, decline of 5.0 percentage points.

The logic of this relationship is pretty simple. When times are slow, employers tend to lay off manufacturing workers, retail workers, and custodians; they are slow to lay off senior management. Similarly, many professionals, like doctors and lawyers, are largely insulated from the effects of the business cycle. And the higher unemployment rates experienced by more disadvantaged groups in cyclical downturns are associated with a weak labor market more generally. This means that these workers are less well positioned to receive pay increases in periods of high unemployment.

The only time in the last four decades in which workers at the middle and bottom of the wage distribution saw consistent gains in real wages was the period of low unemployment in the 1990s boom (**Figure 3-2**).

FIGURE 3-2
Percent change in real hourly wages

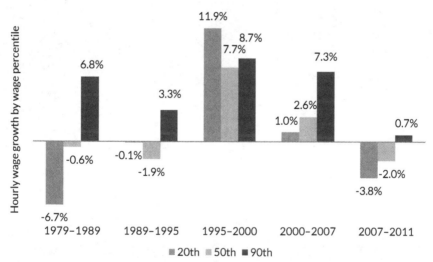

Source and notes: Economic Policy Institute (2012).

Unemployment and public policy: Nothing natural here

The fact that a weak economy has a disproportionate impact on the labor market prospects of minorities, less-educated workers, and people who are otherwise disadvantaged is difficult to deny, as is the implication that a stronger economy will disproportionately benefit those who are less well off. However, it is necessary to carry this argument a step further in order to destroy the illusions of those who want to believe that we are arguing about whether the government should intervene in the economy or simply let the market do its work.

The problem with this framing is that the second option does not exist. There is no scenario in which the market works alone. Government policies will affect the level of output in the economy. The only question is whether we want to design these policies explicitly to meet certain goals or if we want to pretend we don't notice the impact of the policies we have put in place. Regardless of what we might decide about how fiscal and monetary policy can boost or slow the economy, government policy is playing an enormous role in determining the economy's level of demand.

We can start by looking at simple patterns of consumption in the marketplace, how they are affected by redistribution. We know that middle- and low-income people tend to spend a higher share of their income than high-income people. So if income is redistributed upward, other things equal, we will see less consumption in the economy. A paper from the IMF noted the upward redistribution of the last four decades and, based on differences in propensities to consume, calculated that annual consumption is now 3.5 percent lower as a result of the upward redistribution of income over the last four decades (Alichi et al. 2016).

Since consumption is 70 percent of GDP, if taken at face value the paper's findings mean that consumption demand has fallen by roughly 2.5 percentage points of GDP due to the upward redistribution of income. This drop has the same negative effect on demand as a stimulus package equal to 2.5 percent of GDP ($460 billion a year in the 2016 economy) would have in boosting demand. It is a serious drag on the economy.

Before the 2008 crash, economists generally believed that reduced consumption would quickly translate into increased investment and/or increased net exports. Fewer economists hold this view today. Instead, reduced consumption is likely to mean reduced demand, output, and employment, barring some offsetting factor. (One potential offsetting factor would be an asset bubble, such as the stock bubble in the 1990s or the housing bubble in the 2000s. But asset bubbles are not a recipe for stable growth; see Baker (2008).)

The implication of these consumption patterns is that the U.S. economy is likely to face a persistent shortfall in demand because of the upward redistribution of the last four decades. Furthermore, since the distribution of income itself depends in part on how close the economy is to full employment, there is a risk that the economy could face a downward spiral. Weak demand leads to higher unemployment and therefore more upward redistribution, which in turn weakens demand further.

This upward redistribution had a variety of causes in deliberate policy; it was not a random outcome of market processes. In addition to the factors discussed in this book, a variety of other policy measures have contributed to the upward redistribution.

Policies to weaken unions

Perhaps the most deliberate policy on the list, since it affected almost everything else, was the weakening of labor unions. The National Labor Relations Board (NLRB) was established in 1935 to ensure that workers' right to organize was protected and to maintain a balance between labor and management. The protections provided by the NLRB, along with massive organizing efforts, allowed for an enormous expansion of union membership in the 1930s and 1940s. Union membership peaked in the mid-1950s at more than 28 percent of the total workforce and 35 percent of non-agricultural employment (Mayer 2004). It declined slowly for the next quarter century and then experienced a much sharper decline in the years after 1980, falling from just over 20 percent of total employment to just over 11 percent in 2015.

There were many factors behind this decline, not all of which were directly related to policy. For example, the share of employment in manufacturing and mining, two of the most heavily unionized sectors in the economy in earlier decades, dropped. But policy decisions were key. The ability of the NLRB to check abuses by management were always limited, and beginning in the late 1970s corporations adopted more aggressive anti-union tactics to prevent unions from organizing at workplaces that did not have unions and to undermine unions in workplaces that did.[14]

Challenging this more aggressive posture from management would have required more aggressive enforcement measures by the NLRB. Instead, under President Reagan the NLRB went in the opposite direction. In addition to being far friendlier toward management in its decisions, it also became woefully understaffed, leading to long backlogs for cases to be heard. This backlog mattered for organizing drives because one of the main powers of the NLRB is its ability to reinstate workers who are illegally fired for union organizing. If an employer is able to fire all the key workers in an organizing drive and it takes two years for them to have their cases heard, the drive is likely to be over by the time the workers are reinstated.

Another big factor undermining the strength of unions has been the use of replacement workers as substitutes for strikers, thereby costing the strikers their jobs. While hiring replacement workers to replace striking workers was always legal, a set of norms had developed around labor-management relations in the three decades following World War II in which this was rarely done. The standard practice was that companies either shut down entirely during a strike or maintained some operations with skeletal staff of management personnel. This practice changed completely in the 1980s after President Reagan fired striking air traffic controllers and replaced them with controllers from the military. While Reagan had the legal authority to fire the controllers — federal law prohibited strikes by federal employees — up until that time strikes by public employees at both the federal and state levels had generally been resolved without mass dismissals. But soon many private employers took their cue from President Reagan. In the years immediately following the air traffic controllers' strike, several major corporations, such as Eastern Airlines and the Greyhound Bus Company, hired replacements for striking workers.

---

14 For examples of some of these tactics see Levitt (1993).

With the threat of termination heightened, the strike became a less effective weapon for unions. Going on strike meant not only that workers might miss a few days or weeks of pay, it meant that they could permanently lose their jobs. As a result, unions were far more hesitant to strike, which meant they had less ability to press their demands against management. This not only directly hurt workers who were already unionized, it made unions appear much weaker to non-members. The benefits of joining a union became much less apparent in a context where unions were repeatedly forced to make concessions in contracts.

While unions have declined in importance in all wealthy countries, most have not seen as sharp a decline as in the United States. Canada provides a counter-example to the inevitability of union decline. Canada is similar to the United States in its economy and culture, yet its unionization rate has dropped only a few percentage points since the 1970s (Warner 2012) and sits at about 30 percent. The different path is explained by the fact that policy in Canada remained union-friendly over the last four decades, making it easier for unorganized workers to join unions and for unions to secure contracts.

The weakening of unions has an impact beyond just their ability to secure gains in compensation and working conditions for their members. Union contracts often set standards for an entire sector, as non-union firms feel the need to offer comparable terms to their workers both to attract and retain good workers and discourage organizing efforts. In addition, unions have played a central role in securing a wide range of government benefits and worker supports that affect the larger working population. For example, unions played a huge role in pushing through the Affordable Care Act, even though the vast majority of union members already had health insurance. Unions have been central in efforts to raise the minimum wage, both nationally and in states and cities across the country. And unions have pushed for a variety of measures that make workplaces more family friendly, such as paid family leave and paid sick days, and for a recent change in overtime rules that extends coverage to tens of millions of previously uncovered workers.

For these reasons, the sharp reduction since the late 1970s in the percentage of the workforce that is unionized has meant that workers are far less well situated to secure their share of the gains from productivity growth and keep them from rising up to people like CEOs and hedge fund partners. It is worth noting that, while there was some upward redistribution of income in Canada over the last four decades, the size of the redistribution was not nearly as large as in the United States.

Other institutional factors affecting worker power

The extent to which weak demand in the economy translates into higher unemployment and a weaker bargaining position for workers is very dependent on the institutional structure. Compared to the United States, almost all wealthy countries have more generous unemployment insurance systems, providing higher benefits for longer periods of time (OECD 2016). As a result, unemployment imposes a much greater hardship on workers and their families in the United States. Workers here are more desperate to take a new job after being laid off, even if the new job pays substantially less than the prior job and/or does not require the full use of the skills the worker has developed. If workers are more desperate for employment, the downward pressure on wages intensifies.

There is not necessarily a link between a drop in output and a decline in employment. In the Great Recession, Germany experienced a steeper drop in output than did the United States — 6.9 percent from the first quarter of 2008 to the second quarter of 2009 for Germany compared to 3.6 percent in the United States. But while unemployment rose in the United States, from 4.7 percent in November 2007 to 10.0 percent in October 2009, in Germany it *fell,* from 8.2 percent to 7.7 percent (**Figure 3-3**).

The reason for the sharp divergence in labor market experiences is that Germany encouraged its employers to reduce work time rather than lay off workers in response to a reduction in demand. While there were difference across firms, the basic story was that if a company cut back workers' hours by 20 percent, the government would make up 40 percent of the loss in pay (8 percent of total pay), the company would make up 40 percent (8 percent of total pay), and the worker would accept a 4 percent pay cut. The basic logic behind this system was that, if the government is willing make up lost pay of workers when they are completely unemployed, why not pay workers when they are partially unemployed as a result of a reduction in work hours?[15]

FIGURE 3-3
Changes in output vs. unemployment, Germany and U.S., 2007/8–2009 (percentage points)

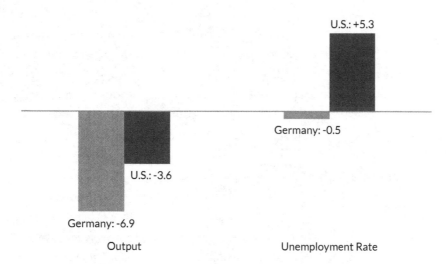

U.S.: +5.3

Germany: -0.5

U.S.: -3.6

Germany: -6.9

Output   Unemployment Rate

Source and notes: OECD (2016). GDP from first quarter 2008 to second quarter of 2009; unemployment rate from November 2007 to October 2009.

This system of work sharing enjoys strong support in Germany across the political spectrum. (The government that originally implemented it was a coalition government of the Christian Democrats and the Social Democrats.) Businesses generally support it, since it allows them to keep skilled workers on staff and therefore available to work

---

15 Twenty-six states now have work-sharing programs as part of their unemployment insurance systems, including several large states like California and New York. However, the take-up rate on these programs has been low. Most employers are not even aware that support for work sharing exists as an alternative to layoffs. In addition, the programs tend to be overly bureaucratic and in many cases have not been modernized since they were first put in place at the end of the 1970s or early 1980s.

longer hours when demand picks up. German firms also have used other mechanisms to absorb a reduction in demand without laying off workers.

In addition to having an unemployment insurance system that is both ungenerous and encourages layoffs, as a longer run matter we have an institutional structure in place that tends to encourage longer hours for workers. As a result, insofar as workers get benefits from productivity growth, they take them in the form of higher pay rather than more leisure. Specifically, because health care insurance is mostly an employment-based benefit, rather than universally provided through the government, employers typically see it as a fixed cost per worker. So rather than hiring additional workers and paying for their health insurance, employers would generally prefer their existing workforce to work more hours. The preference for longer hours is even greater in cases where employers provide defined benefit pensions in addition to health insurance.[16]

Of course, the pattern of providing health insurance and pensions as employer-provided benefits was the result of government tax and regulatory policy that favored employer-based benefits. The result was a pattern of employment in which better-paying jobs are more restricted in number than would have otherwise been the case. Consider this basic arithmetic: if we produced the same number of cars but the average work year in the auto industry had 20 percent fewer hours, we would have 25 percent more people working in the auto industry. The reality will always be more complicated, but the basic point is straightforward: for the same levels of output, shorter hours mean more workers.

In other wealthy countries, the average number of work hours in a year has fallen sharply over the last four decades. Most countries in Western Europe mandate five to six weeks a year of paid vacation. Between six months and one year of paid parental leave is standard, as is some amount of paid leave for other family reasons. In some countries, the standard work week is less than 40 hours. By contrast, in the United States

---

16   There is less of an issue of fixed costs in cases where the employers' contribution for health insurance is pro-rated based on the number of hours a worker puts in or based on annual pay. While pro-rating benefits is becoming increasingly common, this is a relatively new development. Through most of the post-World War II era, pro-rating benefits was rare.

the number of hours in the average work year has changed little over the last four decades, due almost certainly in large part to the benefit structure that creates substantial per-worker overhead costs.

As a result of our different histories, workers in the United States average considerably more hours each year than workers in Europe. According to data from the OECD, the average work year in the United States is 1,790 hours, compared to 1,419 hours in the Netherlands, 1,482 in France, and 1,371 in Germany. If the average work year in the United States were comparable to those in Western Europe, more workers would be employed at relatively well-paying jobs in sectors like manufacturing, construction, and communications instead of being forced to accept lower-paying jobs in sectors like retail and restaurants. By reducing the supply of workers in the lower-paying sectors, the reduction in average hours would lead to higher wages in low-paying sectors for the workers who were left behind. In short, it is reasonable to believe that the longer average work year in the United States has been a factor contributing to inequality.

The role of fiscal policy

These institutional factors, along with other major decisions that will be discussed in detail in the next four chapters, show ways in which policy has played an important role in determining the distribution of income. If in turn the distribution of income plays a major role in determining consumption levels, then the upward redistribution of the last four decades has been an important factor in weakening aggregate demand in the economy. In this context, the idea that the government should not intervene in the economy to increase output, but rather leave things to the market, makes no sense.

We live in an interventionist economy, an economy where the government has intervened in a variety of ways that have had the effect of shifting income upward. If this intervention in turn lowers consumption, and therefore output and employment, a policy of "not intervening" is in fact a choice to let the earlier interventions go unchallenged. The beneficiaries of the upward redistribution may like the outcome, but it is not because they prefer leaving matters to the market. Rather, they prefer government interventions that have the effect of giving them more money.

As a practical matter, it is not even clear what someone can possibly mean when they argue that the government should not try to affect the economy and instead let the market work itself out. There is a large demand for government services, like Social Security, Medicare, education, national defense, and infrastructure construction and maintenance, which the government must in turn pay for. There is no magic process that tells the government how much it should tax to pay for the services the public wants. The only reasonable way to set tax (or deficit) levels is by reference to the overall state of the economy.

It is possible to argue that the government should follow some arbitrary rule, like maintaining a balanced budget or constant debt-to-GDP ratio. But picking a rule for fiscal policy is not the same as a policy of non-intervention. It just means that the fiscal policy would be determined by something other than the immediate needs of the economy.

It is also worth noting that it is a relatively simple matter to evade whatever fiscal rules are put in place. There are many ways to hide expenditures, or at least to adjust their timing, in order to comply with a fiscal rule.[17] Also, assets can be sold to generate revenue in the year in which they are sold even if the outcome may be a loss of revenue in future years. For example, in 2008, the City of Chicago sold off the right to revenue from its parking meters for 75 years. This sale, which earned the city $1.2 billion, was booked as revenue for the year. This allowed the city to balance its budget in 2008 even though it was at the cost of losing a flow of revenue for more than seven decades. There is an infinite variety of

---

17   One frequently used method is to adjust payments on multiyear projects, like a highway or airport, in order to meet a fiscal target. Another mechanism that can be used to circumvent fiscal rules is deferred compensation payments, like defined benefit pensions. These liabilities are generally treated as payments in the years they are actually made rather than for the years in which the liability was accrued. If a pension is properly funded, the annual payments into the pension fund will be sufficient to cover the eventual liability, but there have been a number of state and local governments that have not made sufficient payments, effectively adding to the state's debt even while it could be reporting a balanced budget.

other mechanisms through which governments can sell off assets or revenue streams in order to reduce a current year deficit.

The government can also turn to non-tax mechanisms for funding public purposes, which impose tax-like burdens in the future. Grants of patents and copyrights are an obvious example. These government-granted monopolies are mechanisms through which the government provides incentives to innovate and do creative work, and in this sense can be thought of as alternatives to direct government payments for these purposes. The government could pay people and corporations to research new drugs, software, or other items, and to do creative work. In fact, it already does, paying over $30 billion a year to finance research at the National Institutes of Health and funding (modestly) creative work through the National Endowments for the Arts and Humanities and the Corporation for Public Broadcasting.

This direct funding appears as an expenditure in the government's budget and contributes to the deficit. However, if the government pays for this work with a patent or copyright monopoly, then the cost never appears on the government's books. In effect, the government is committing the public to paying a higher price for the protected item for the duration of the patent or copyright. This is a form of taxation that need never show up in the government's accounts.

A push to limit government spending can lead to longer and stronger patent and copyright protections as alternatives to direct spending, even if these monopolies are less-efficient mechanisms for financing innovation and creative work. As shown in Chapter 5, these government-granted monopolies can impose substantial costs on the public. In the case of prescription drugs alone the cost is in the neighborhood of $380 billion a year (equal to 2.0 percent of GDP). Washington is filled with politicians and organizations that hyperventilate about government debt and the burden it imposes on our children, but they ignore the burdens imposed by patent and copyright monopolies granted by the government.

The scenarios graphed in **Figure 3-4** illustrate this story by focusing on prescription drugs. Suppose that we were spending another $50 billion a year on medical research in order to replace patent-supported research, and all the findings were placed in the public domain so that all drugs were sold as generics. The annual deficit would be $50 billion higher due to the additional spending on research, but we would save $380 billion a year on drugs due to generic pricing. In Washington policy circles, the high-drug-price scenario would be the path of fiscal prudence and caring about our children. It might pull far more money out of their pockets, but money going to drug companies doesn't bother Washington-policy-types anywhere near as much as money going to the government.

FIGURE 3-4
Scenario 1: $400 billion deficit and $440 billion in prescription drug spending

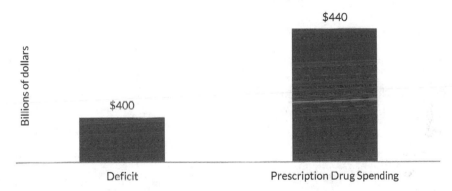

Scenario 2: $450 billion deficit and $60 billion in prescription drug spending

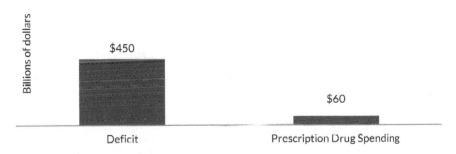

Source and notes: Author's calculations, see text.

In sum, there is no natural or neutral fiscal policy in which the government does not affect the level of output in the economy. We can try to structure accounting rules so that the public and possibly even the people making policy are unaware of the ways in which the government's actions are having an impact, but that doesn't mean it's not happening. Banning the study and dissemination of information on human-caused global warming would not change the fact that human activity is leading to global warming. That is the effect of various types of budget rules. They are not imposing some principle of neutrality or non-intervention, they are just making it more difficult to understand the government's role in the economy.

Monetary policy

Just as there is no fiscal policy that is simple and neutral in its effect on levels of output, neither is there a simple and neutral monetary policy. In principle we can pick a rule and take away from the central bank the decision on how stimulative monetary policy will be. We could tie the issuance of money to gold, or let it rise at a fixed rate, as was long advocated by Milton Friedman, the famous conservative economist. However, both approaches are arbitrary, and still require that the central bank and other regulators make some judgments.

This is clearest in the case of the monetary rule. The Federal Reserve Board and other central banks briefly experimented with targeting money supply growth in the early 1980s. However, the problem they encountered was that it wasn't clear which measure of the money supply they should target. As the Fed restricted the growth of the M2 measure of money, the banking system developed new systems of payments that were not counted in M2.[18] As a result, the Fed could meet its targets for M2 but not accomplish its goal of restricting the effective supply of money.

---

18 M2 is a relatively narrow definition of the money supply that counts money in savings and checking accounts and physical bills in existence. At the time, it was the preferred target for most supporters of a money supply rule.

This problem leaves the Fed with the peculiar task of constantly redefining money, a task that runs directly against Friedman's idea of placing the money supply on autopilot and taking away discretion from central bankers. In choosing a new definition of money, the central bank can opt for one that allows for more or less expansionary policy. Friedman's ghost might hope that such considerations are never a factor in determining how the money supply is defined, but that is not the way central bankers or anyone else functions.

There would be a similar challenge in applying a gold standard. We can legislate that the Fed tie its issuance of money to the amount of gold in its possession, a mandate that has the obvious problem of making the growth of the money supply subject to the randomness of discoveries of deposits as well the development of technology in the mining industry. The result can be a period of prolonged deflation, as the United States and other industrialized countries experienced in the decades from 1870 to 1890 (Bordo and Filardo 2005), or, if there are new gold finds, of inflation, as happened in the 1890s. If the point of the gold standard is to ensure price stability, it is not up to the task.

Furthermore, the gold standard does not remove the regulatory issues with which central banks must inevitably contend. Banks, or bank-like financial institutions, will always try to increase their volume of loans relative to their capital and reserves; it's how they maximize profits. Central banks can choose to ignore the excessive growth of credit, but then they will have no control over the rate of inflation and the price level. Such a system is also a virtual guarantee of the sort of boom-and-bust cycles and bank runs that characterized the decades before the creation of the Federal Reserve Board and deposit insurance.

It may be appealing to believe that we can just leave monetary policy to run its own course, without central bankers making conscious choices about the level of output and employment, but this is an illusion. The decisions by central banks and other financial regulators influence the levels of employment and output, and there is no way around this fact.

Fiscal and monetary policy without the illusion of non-intervention

If we move beyond the illusion of non-intervention — the idea that there is some natural fiscal and/or monetary policy that doesn't involve policy choices — then we realize that we decide, as a matter of policy, whether to have an economy with high or low levels of unemployment. The decision in the United States and most other wealthy countries over the last four decades has been to maintain relatively high levels of unemployment.

This policy has been seen most directly in the explicit decision by the Federal Reserve Board and other central banks to focus mainly, or even exclusively, on keeping inflation low. This is a sharp shift from prior decades, when central banks saw one of their main functions as promoting high levels of employment.

A simple way of measuring the policy shift in the United States is comparing the actual levels of unemployment to the estimated NAIRU, or non-accelerating inflation rate of unemployment. The NAIRU is supposed to be the level of unemployment where there is no tendency for the inflation rate to either decrease or increase. In principle, this is the lowest level of unemployment that the economy can have without the inflation rate continually accelerating. If, for example, the NAIRU is 5.0 percent but we keep the unemployment rate at 4.5 percent, then the inflation rate will keep rising and we will experience hyperinflation.

Many theoretical and empirical questions have been raised about the concept of the NAIRU; nonetheless the estimates of the NAIRU can provide a quick measure of the extent to which economic policy has focused on maintaining full employment. **Figure 3-5** shows the average gap between the actual unemployment rate and the Congressional Budget Office's (CBO) estimate of the NAIRU from 1949 to the present. As can be seen, the unemployment rate was on average 0.5 percentage points below the estimate of NAIRU from 1949 to 1980. But in the years since 1980, the unemployment rate averaged 1.0 percentage point above the estimates of NAIRU, even if we take out the years since the beginning of the Great Recession. This pattern suggests a much greater commitment to fighting inflation, even at the expense of higher unemployment, in the years since 1980.

FIGURE 3-5
Gap between actual unemployment rate and estimates of the NAIRU, 1949–present

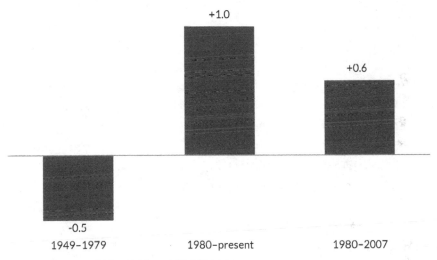

Source and notes: CBO (2016) and BLS (2016a).

As bad as the Fed has been in its quest to keep inflation low at the expense of unemployment, it actually remains more committed to high employment policies than some other central banks. The European Central Bank stands out in this respect. At the time of his retirement in October 2011, Jean Claude Trichet, who served as president of the bank through the bubble years and the subsequent crash, was proud of the fact that he kept the euro zone's inflation rate under the bank's 2.0 percent target, even though unemployment rates in the euro zone were in double digits and several countries were on the edge of defaulting on their debt (*The Telegraph* 2011).

Currency policy

An issue that is related to monetary policy is the U.S. policy towards the value of the dollar. This is related to monetary policy because, other things equal, raising and lowering interest rates sends the value of the dollar in the same direction. In other words, if the Federal Reserve Board decides to raise interest rates, it generally will also lead to a rise in the value of the dollar. Foreign investors will be more interested in holding dollar denominated assets if they can get a higher rate of interest in the United States than elsewhere. The opposite is true if the Fed lowers interest rates. In general, this means that foreign and domestic investors will look to pull their money out of dollars and instead put it in countries where they can get a higher rate of interest.

Many factors complicate this simple story, but the most obvious one is a deliberate attempt by a country to target the value of its currency at a level that is substantially above or below its market level. This has been an important issue in the last two decades as many developing countries, most importantly China, have acted to keep down the value of their currencies relative to the dollar by buying up massive amounts of dollars.

As noted in Chapter 1, developing countries as a whole have been running large trade surpluses since the East Asian financial crisis, reversing the textbook pattern where capital is supposed to flow from rich countries to poor countries. We would expect the value of their currencies to rise relative to the currencies of countries with trade deficits, like the United States, and we would expect these countries to sell the dollars they have accumulated from their trade surpluses in international currency markets, pushing down the value of the dollar.

However, these countries have chosen not to sell their dollars but are instead holding them, leading to extraordinary accumulations of reserves. In early 2014, China's reserves peaked at almost $4 trillion, equivalent to more than 40 percent of its GDP. (A standard rule of thumb is that reserves should be equal to three to six months of imports, which would have been $500 billion to $1 trillion in China's case.) Its reserves fell somewhat over the next year and a half, but were still more than $3.2

trillion in the summer of 2016, with another $1.5 trillion held in the form of sovereign wealth funds. This money could also be tapped if China were in need of foreign exchange for some reason.

The issue of currency matters because it is the main factor keeping the U.S. trade deficit high. The U.S. trade deficit had been just over 1.0 percent of GDP before the East Asia financial crisis, and while it is down from its peak of 6.0 percent in 2005, in 2016 it was still close to 2.8 percent of GDP. The trade deficit corresponds to spending that is creating demand elsewhere rather than in the United States. A $500 billion trade deficit (its level in 2016) means that there is a gap in demand of $500 billion that must be filled by other sources if the economy is going to operate near full employment.

This deficit is the result of policy, not just the natural workings of the market. When government officials sit down with their counterparts from China and other countries, they can negotiate over the currency policies that these countries are pursuing. If negotiators opt to make currency a priority, they can likely get these countries to agree to increase the value of their currencies relative to the dollar.[19] There will be a trade-off for focusing on currency values, meaning that other items will be given lower priority. For example, the United States has pressed China for increased access for the financial industry, the telecommunications industry, and retailers, and it has pressed China and other developing countries to devote more resources toward enforcing U.S. patents and copyrights. In order to get more concessions on currency values, the United States might accept fewer concessions in these areas, or agree to more demands that China makes on it.

---

19   It is often claimed by Obama administration officials that China refuses to make any concessions on the value of its currency. This is difficult to believe. Currency values don't raise issues of fundamental sovereignty, like China's claim to Taiwan. Furthermore, China has indicated its intention to further raise the value of its currency and shift to a more domestically oriented growth path. It already has done this to a substantial extent, reducing its trade surplus from 10.0 percent in 2007 to 2.7 percent in 2015 (IMF 2016). In effect, the demand from the United States would be that China pursue this route somewhat more quickly than it may have planned.

But powerful interests directly benefit from an over-valued dollar. Many major U.S. manufacturers have set up operations in China and other developing countries for the purpose of exporting back to the United States. They aren't eager to see the cost of the items produced in these countries rise by 20 to 30 percent if the dollar falls by that amount. Similarly, major retailers like Walmart have established low-cost supply chains in the developing world, and they would prefer not to see the prices of the goods they import rise along with the value of developing country currencies.

Thus, there are substantial political obstacles working against major efforts from the U.S. government to force down the value of the dollar and bring the trade deficit closer to balance. For this reason, we can see the large trade deficit as a policy choice, not just a natural outcome of the workings of the market. The outcome of this policy is a large shortfall in demand, making it harder to get to full employment. The trade deficit also takes a heavy toll on manufacturing workers, since it is overwhelmingly manufacturing jobs that are lost as a result of it. As noted in Chapter 1, the loss of manufacturing jobs puts downward pressure on the wages of workers without college degrees, as displaced manufacturing workers crowd into other sectors in search of employment.

Fiscal policy in an economy pushed toward secular stagnation

We have argued in the prior sections that the United States has pursued a variety of policies that have the effect of reducing demand in the economy. In the case of trade policy the impact is quite direct. We have supported policies that lead to large trade deficits, which create a gap in aggregate demand from other sources. However, we have also pursued a variety of policies that have the effect of redistributing income upward. As research from the IMF and elsewhere indicate, this upward redistribution leads to lower consumption, other things equal, since the wealthy spend a smaller share of their income than do the poor and middle class. Without deliberate government policy to boost demand, the result is a shortfall in demand.

In this context, a "fiscally prudent" policy that insists on balanced budgets or low deficits is a policy designed to keep unemployment high. Given the distributional impact of high unemployment, it is also a policy that has the effect of disproportionately hurting minorities and less-educated workers, both by denying them employment and by putting downward pressure on the wages of those who have jobs.

Figure 3-6 shows the path for GDP that was projected by the CBO in 2008, before the economy collapsed, compared with the actual growth path (in 2016 dollars). By 2015 the gap was $2.3 trillion. Much of this output is now permanently lost. We can't make up for the investments that were not made or the education and experience that workers did not receive, but we can still move the economy closer to its projected path by increasing demand.

FIGURE 3-6

Real gross domestic product, 2007–2015, actual and CBO's 2008 projection

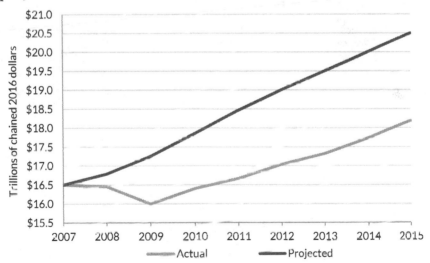

Source and notes: CBO (2016).

Figure 3-7 shows the gap between projected and actual output in 2015 measured in units of annual spending on SNAP, along with a bar showing half of the gap being closed through more stimulative fiscal and/or exchange-rate policy. The full gap is equal to 30 times annual spending on SNAP, while filling half of the gap, which may still be a reasonable target with aggressive expansionary policy, would imply a boost to incomes equal to 15 times annual spending on SNAP. In other words, getting the economy back to full employment is a really big deal.

FIGURE 3-7
Income foregone in 2016 as result of Great Recession, in units of SNAP spending

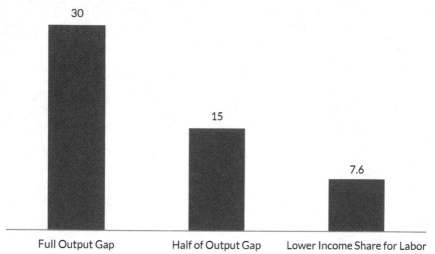

Source and notes: Author's calculations, see text.

Furthermore, as noted at the start of this chapter, the benefits of moving to full employment will go disproportionately to those at the middle and bottom of the income ladder. They will benefit from having increased employment, having the opportunity to work more hours (many are now working part time but would like full-time employment), and also having higher pay on the job. High unemployment is an important policy to redistribute wage income from those at the middle and bottom to those at the top. In addition, a policy of sustained high employment would likely reverse the shift from wage income to profits that took place in the downturn, amounting to an aggregate increase in labor compensation of more than 6.0 percent, in addition to the impact of the increase in the level of output and employment.

Conclusion: The level of employment is a policy choice

In policy debates, the idea of boosting demand to increase employment is often viewed as intervention, and the option of allowing a high rate of unemployment to persist is viewed as non-intervention. This is a convenient framing for those who are content with continuing an unnecessarily high rate of unemployment, but it does not correspond to reality. There is a long list of government interventions going on right now that directly or indirectly affect the level of demand in the economy (see **Box 3-1**).

BOX 3-1
Ways in which policy affects employment
   1) Distributional policies that affect consumption
       a) Union policy
       b) Minimum wage
       c) Regulatory policy
       d) Structure of unemployment benefit system
   2) Incentives for longer or shorter work-years
   3) Fiscal policy (more or less expansionary)
   4) Monetary policy (more or less expansionary)
   5) Currency policy (affects trade deficit or surplus)

It is hypocritical to bless the policies that have the effect of reducing demand as non-intervention and condemn the policies designed to counteract these effects as intervention. We can choose government policies that will be more or less stimulative of growth and employment, but we can't escape the fact that government policies are affecting employment. The presence of large numbers of people who are unable to find work as a result of inadequate demand is the result of policies we have chosen that keep these people from working. This is not *laissez faire* or the free market; this is operating the government to benefit a select group.

Chapter 4

The Financial Sector: Ground Zero for High Incomes and High Waste

There is a great deal of confusion about the nature of the financial sector in a modern economy. The financial industry plays an essential function in processing payments, providing insurance, allowing families to save for the future, and allocating capital to those who want to invest or borrow. However, the services it provides are almost entirely intermediate goods in that they *facilitate* economic activity; they are not end products that provide benefits in and of themselves, like housing, health care, or education.

In this regard the financial sector is like the trucking industry. Trucking, like finance, is essential to the economy. We need it for moving raw material to factories and finished products to stores. But an efficient trucking industry is a small trucking industry: we want to have as few resources as possible devoted to getting goods from point A to point B. This means that we don't want to see a huge expansion in employment in the trucking industry or an explosion in the number of trucks and warehouses just to move the same quantity of goods.

The same story applies to the financial industry. We should want to see as few resources as possible committed to it, or the minimum needed to enable it to support the productive economy. Instead, we have seen a massive expansion of the financial sector, from 4.5 percent of GDP in 1970 to 7.4 percent in 2015.[20] The more narrow securities and commodities trading sector increased from 0.49 percent of GDP in 1970 to 2.03 percent in 2015,[21] corresponding to $290 billion a year in additional spending in the 2016 economy.

Reversing this expansion in the size of the financial sector without damaging its ability to serve the productive economy would be a pure gain to the economy, just as eliminating waste in the trucking industry would be a gain. We don't benefit from having more types of financial instruments and derivatives unless these instruments make it easier to accomplish one of the sector's functions. Similarly, we don't benefit from more frequent trading of stocks, bonds, or other assets unless the additional trading somehow leads to better allocation of capital or makes our savings more secure.

These simple points are often left out of discussions of financial regulation and policy. Opponents of efforts to restructure the industry tend to point to the prospect of job loss — not in the productive economy, but within the industry itself — as though it is a compelling reason to leave the status quo in place. In effect, they are arguing that we want waste in the financial sector.

---

20 This figure includes both employee compensation and proprietors' income in finance, insurance, and real estate as well as corporate profits in finance and insurance. The number would be slightly higher if we were to include corporate profits from real estate.

21 The size of the sector was calculated from BEA (2016) by taking the lines for compensation in the securities and commodities trading industry and also investment funds and trusts (Table 6.2D, lines 59 and 61 for 2015 and Table 6.2B, lines 55 and 59 for 1970). The calculation attributes income in the financial sector from proprietorships (Table 6.12D, line 14 for 2015 and Table 6.12B, line 14 for 1970) and corporate profits (Table 6.16D, line 12 for 2015 and 6.16B, line 12 for 1970) in proportion to the narrower trading sector's share of employee compensation to employee compensation in the financial industry as a whole.

Finance is different from trucking, however, in that waste in the financial sector provides income for some of the highest earners in the economy. Bakija et al. (2012) found that 18.4 percent of primary taxpayers in the top 0.1 percent of the income distribution were employed in finance. When we downsize the industry, we are likely to reduce the number of very high earners within it, as well as the amount of money they take home.

The financial sector earns rents at the expense of the rest of the economy in five main areas:

1) As the cost of trading stocks, bonds, and other financial assets has declined over the last four decades with the development of computers and the Internet, trading volume has exploded and a variety of complex financial instruments have been created. Despite the sharp decline in costs, the amount of money spent on trading has nearly quintupled relative to the size of the economy. The increased volume and complexity of trading have not in any obvious way improved the allocation of capital or made financial markets more stable. They have, however, made many hedge fund partners and traders at large banks extremely wealthy.

2) Since lenders assume the government will act to support large financial institutions if they get into trouble, large banks enjoy the benefits of implicit too-big-to-fail insurance, which enables them to borrow at lower interest rates than would be justified by their financial situations. The IMF recently valued the implicit subsidy at $25 billion to $50 billion annually (IMF 2014).

3) Often, tasks that could be performed more efficiently by the government or by a monopoly private provider are instead parceled out to the financial sector. If the privately run defined contribution pension system were run as efficiently as the Thrift Savings Plan for federal employers, perhaps $50 billion a year in rent — a low-range estimate — could be put to productive uses.

4) The financial industry is able to take advantage of consumers through complex and deceptive contracts. At one time many debit card issuers charged large overdraft fees without telling customers they faced these charges. Though this practice has since been banned by the Federal Reserve Board (customers must now opt for overdraft coverage, knowing the fees they face), there are many other areas where the industry imposes terms that most consumers would likely not agree to if they understood them.

5) Tax shelters have long been a mechanism for corporations and wealthy individuals to escape tax liability. But often overlooked is the tax shelter industry itself, where the individuals and corporations that engineer the tax shelters receive large rents. This is a major source of profits for the private equity industry, which has great expertise in gaming the tax code.

Before getting into more detail on these sources of rent and possible remedies, it is worth pointing out that many of the people who have gotten extremely rich in the last four decades have been in the financial sector. If their fortunes corresponded to great benefits they provided to the economy there would be little grounds for complaint, but for most of the very rich people in finance, this does not seem to be the case.

Speed trading and financial transactions taxes

Unlike most other sectors, finance is generally exempt from sales taxes (IMF 2010). Excessive trading is the greatest source of rents in the financial sector, and subjecting it to a financial transactions tax (FTT) would go a long way toward bringing taxation in the financial sector in line with the rest of the economy.

As mentioned earlier, as trading costs plummeted over the last four decades due to computerization, trading volume exploded and the amount of money spent on trading nearly quintupled relative to the size of the economy. The additional money spent on trading is all income for the industry.

There is no doubt that a non-trivial FTT will substantially reduce the size of the financial sector. The key question in assessing the merits of the tax is whether this downsizing results primarily from eliminating wasteful transactions that don't affect the ability of the financial sector to serve the productive economy. This would be comparable to finding a way to monitor truckers to ensure that they only take the most direct routes to get to their destination. Alternatively, if the downsizing seriously impedes the financial sector's ability to effectively allocate capital or ensure the security of household savings, then the FTT would be imposing a substantial cost.

It is worth contrasting the impact for consumers and producers of a tax on the financial sector and a tax on normal consumption goods. **Figure 4-1** shows how a tax on new cars that raises $100 billion a year in annual revenue would affect the car market and how the tax burden might be distributed between car buyers and car manufacturers.

The top horizontal line shows the effective price to consumers once the tax has been imposed. Consumers will pay more per car, but they will buy fewer. As a result, car sellers will receive less money both because they are selling fewer cars, but also because the reduction in demand as a result of the tax will lead to a situation where they get less money per car. So the reduction in revenue to the auto industry will be the combined effect of selling fewer cars and getting less money for each car they sell.

The extent to which the before-tax price falls and the quantity is reduced depends on the relative shape of the supply and demand curves. (These curves are drawn in an arbitrary manner for purely illustrative purposes.) In this case, the tax of $5,000 per car is assumed to be evenly shared between consumers and producers. The average price paid by a consumer rises from $25,000 without the tax to $27,500 with it, and the average price received by auto manufacturers falls from $25,000 to $22,500. The gap of $5,000 per car is the tax revenue raised by the government.

FIGURE 4-1

Changes in supply and demand for cars with the addition of a tax

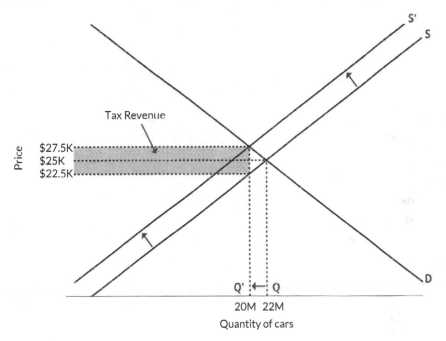

Source and notes: Author's calculations.

The tax is associated with a drop in sales from 22 million to 20 million, and the loss in revenue to manufacturers comes to $100 billion a year, the difference between selling 22 million cars at $25,000 each, or $550 billion, and selling 20 million cars at $22,500 each, or $450 billion. Consumers are paying $2,500 more per car but buying 2 million fewer, so their total spending on cars is unchanged at $550 billion.

In terms of assessing winners and losers, consumers are worse off to the extent that they had valued the 2 million cars they end up not purchasing. Also, the consumers who do buy cars will have less money to spend on other items as a result of having to pay $2,500 more for the cars they buy.

Car manufacturers, now producing fewer cars, will employ fewer workers and need a smaller amount of parts, materials, and capital equipment. Fewer people will be employed both directly in the auto industry and indirectly in the various industries that produce inputs. The manufacturers are also likely to see a reduction in profits due to the decline in prices and sales.

The extent of the negative impact on the displaced workers will depend on their ability to get other jobs at comparable pay. If the pay at auto manufacturers and their suppliers is comparable to the pay in other sectors where these workers can find jobs, then the decline in car sales will have little impact on their standard of living once the adjustment process is complete. However, if the auto industry is a source of relatively high-paying jobs, then the decline in sales would imply a reduction in their standard of living when they are forced to accept lower-paying jobs in other sectors.

The same story would apply to any other industry producing consumer goods or services, but the situation is fundamentally different in an industry like finance that is primarily producing intermediate goods. **Figure 4-2** shows the impact of a tax of $100 billion a year in the financial sector. (Again, these lines are drawn arbitrarily for illustrative purposes.)

Figure 4-2 shows a decline in trading volume that is the same as the decline in car volume, with the increase in the after-tax cost per trade equal to the increase in the after-tax cost of a car. (To be more realistic, perhaps think of these as blocks of 1 million trades.) This leaves all the dollar sums the same as in Figure 4-1; however the meaning on the consumer side is qualitatively different in a very important way.

In Figure 4-1, consumers saw a cost from the tax both because they paid more per car as a result of the tax, and also because they bought fewer cars. Cars are a consumption good, so the expectation is that if consumers end up buying fewer cars as a result of the tax, they are in some way worse off. By contrast, trading is not a good that directly provides value for consumers. They are not made worse off by engaging in fewer trades.[22]

---

22   There is a possibility that some people view trading as a form of recreation like casino gambling. This discussion assumes that the bulk of trading is not done for recreational purposes.

FIGURE 4-2
Changes in supply and demand for financial trades with the addition of a tax

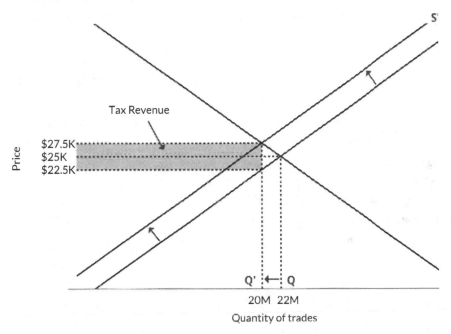

Source and notes: Author's calculations.

In Figure 4-2 the decline in trading volume fully offsets the impact of the tax in raising the cost per trade. This means that consumers spend no more on trading, including the tax, than they did before the tax was put into place; in other words, the consumer feels no direct impact of the tax. For cars, the impact of the tax depends on the extent to which the price to consumers rises due to the tax. For trading, there is no reason to care about the price per trade, because all we care about is the total amount spent on trading. If that doesn't increase, as assumed in Figure 4-2, consumers will see an impact from the tax only if a lower volume of trading reduces the ability of the financial sector to serve the productive economy.

This point is important. If the higher volume of trading was not leading to greater efficiency of the productive economy, then consumers on aggregate were not gaining from the extra trades. There will be winners and losers on any individual trade, but in aggregate this will net out to zero, and so many of the trades currently being undertaken by the people managing our 401(k)s, our IRAs, and our pension funds are wasteful. The people in the financial industry who undertake these trades earn money off of them, but, on average, investors do not. In this case, if we can reduce the volume of trading, as would be the case with an FTT, we are saving investors money and reducing the amount of resources wasted in the financial sector.

The impact of the tax from the standpoint of producers is unambiguous. It leads to both a reduction in trading volume and less money on each trade, implying that fewer people will be employed in the industry and that those who remain employed are likely to receive lower incomes. Like for the displaced autoworkers, the impact on the workers displaced from the financial sector will depend on the difference between pay in the industry and pay in other sectors. Since the financial sector pays considerably more on average than other industries, displacement is likely to mean a substantial loss of income, at least for higher-paid workers. (Displaced custodians and office assistants might not see much of a reduction in pay.)

The key point is that a tax on the financial sector is generally not borne directly by consumers. The immediate impact will be on suppliers of financial services; consumers will be affected only if the downsizing of the industry reduces its ability to serve the productive economy. If a smaller financial sector can serve the productive economy as well as a larger one, then the burden of the tax will be felt mostly or entirely by the industry.

Is a large financial sector a burden on the economy?

The idea that a large financial sector might be a drag on growth has been supported by recent research from the Bank of International Settlements and the IMF. Cecchetti and Kharroubi (2012) and Sahay et al. (2015) find an inverted U-shaped relationship between the size of the financial sector and the rate of productivity growth. For countries with underdeveloped financial sectors, they find that a bigger financial sector is associated with more rapid growth. However, once the financial sector reaches a certain level, further expansion relative to the size of the economy is associated with slower growth. This is consistent with the idea that large financial sectors pull resources away from productive uses.

These analyses imply that people who could be employed productively in other sectors of the economy are doing tasks that provide little or no value in the financial sector. Excessive trading, which is the immediate focus of an FTT, is one example of how resources could be wasted. However, the proliferation of complex financial instruments would be another aspect of the same problem. An FTT will make some types of financial instruments more costly and possibly eliminate the market for them altogether. If these instruments provide little benefit to the productive economy, then the tax would be making the financial sector more efficient.

If an FTT were to impose costs on the *productive* economy, it would be because higher transaction costs make it more difficult to raise capital. The most immediate way in which higher transaction costs could affect the economy is through higher interest rates. The tax will reduce effective returns on assets, with the impact dependent on the volume of turnover. To take a simple case, if the before-tax return on an asset is 5.0 percent annually (net of other turnover costs) and the holding time is on average six months, a tax of 0.1 percent will reduce the return (holding turnover constant) by 4.0 percent.[23] (Since the asset turns over twice in a year, the tax is equal to 0.2 percent of the price.) If the holding time increased more than proportionately in response to the tax (as implied by the assumption of a trading elasticity greater than 1), then the effect of the tax on returns would actually be positive. As noted above, the total amount spent on trading is actually less as a result of the tax, which means, other things equal, total returns would increase.

However, investors might be willing to forego a substantial portion of their returns in exchange for increased liquidity. This possibility would imply that interest rates are lower in 2016 than would otherwise be

---

23   Burman et al. (2016) includes a useful table (Table 3) showing the impact of tax rates on the rate of return for different holding periods.

the case precisely because investors have the option to trade frequently at low cost.

The impact of trading costs on returns could be substantial. For example, if there has been a reduction in average trading costs in the stock market of 0.5 percentage points over the last four decades (probably a low estimate of the actual reduction) and shares are traded on average twice a year, then the reduction in trading costs would be equivalent to 20 percent of annual returns, using an assumption of 5.0 percent real returns. (Two times 0.5 percentage points equals 1 percentage point, which is 20 percent of the 5.0 percent real annual return.) Comparable reductions in trading costs for bonds and other instruments would imply a similar impact on returns.

While this sort of impact cannot be ruled out *a priori*, few if any economic models of interest rate determination include transaction costs as a major factor. If trading costs did have a substantial impact on interest rates, we would expect real interest rates in the 1950s, 1960s, and 1970s to be far higher, other things equal, than they are today. But there has been no obvious downward path for real interest rates in the United States and other countries as transaction costs have fallen.

One reason that there may not be a return premium corresponding to the fall in average trading costs is that the typical investor is not an active trader. If most investors traded little, while a small minority traded a lot, then average trading costs would have little relevance for most investors. In that case, a rise in transaction costs matters a great deal to the active trader but little to a more typical investor.

In addition to the question of liquidity, there is also the question of whether the rise in transaction costs resulting from the tax would impair the ability of financial markets to allocate capital to its best uses. Could higher transaction costs cause the market price of assets and their "true" price based on economic fundamentals to diverge, and could this divergence have measurable consequences for the allocation of capital? The answer to the first question is possibly yes, but the extent of the consequences is more questionable.

The answer to the first question depends on the impact of trading costs on volatility. There has been some research on this topic, and a fair reading of the literature would probably support the view that lower trading costs are associated with reduced volatility.[24] However, most of the research on the relationship between trading costs and volatility is focused on short-term movements in asset prices, such as the average change in the price of a share of stock over the course of a day. But examining short-term fluctuations is really providing more information on the liquidity of markets rather than the ability of markets to direct capital to its best uses. Larger intra-day fluctuations in the price of stock or other assets may increase the risk that the investor buys the asset at a temporarily inflated price or sells it at a temporarily depressed price (these deviations should average out, so on net the typical investor is neither helped nor hurt). But it is difficult to believe that these risks would have a measurable impact on the effective allocation of capital. For instance, would a company undertake an investment it would not otherwise make or pass on an investment that would have been profitable just because its stock price was a half of a percentage point above or below its fundamental value (assuming that the market tends toward the fundamental value) for an hour or two? The same question would apply to other assets like oil or corn. If the price of a barrel of oil is 0.5 percent higher than the fundamentals would imply for a few hours, is the capital committed to drilling fundamentally less profitable?

It is worth noting that, even with a sharp reduction in trading volume, there is still likely to be far more liquidity in the market than existed just two decades ago. **Figure 4-3** shows a measure of market depth, the average value of shares available to be bought or sold, since 2003. It shows that depth has more than tripled for the most highly traded stocks, and if it fell back by two-thirds it would still be higher than it was in 2003. In other words, even with an FTT we are likely to see more market depth in 2017 than we saw in the 2003 market without an FTT.

---

24   Matheson (2011) has a good summary of the research on the relationship between trading costs and volatility.

FIGURE 4-3

Displayed market depth (bid+ask volume), largest stocks (95th percentile)

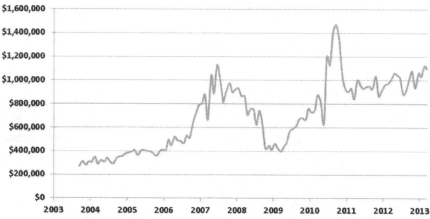

Source and notes: From Angel et al. (2013), Figure 2.7.

While longer-term and larger divergences between prices and fundamentals can affect the allocation of capital, the evidence in this area is uncertain. On several occasions in the last three decades sharp movements in price bore no obvious relationship to the fundamentals in the economy. The most obvious was the "flash crash" in 2010, which was due to a misreported price that triggered a sell-off by programmed trading. The main market indexes plunged by close to 10 percent over the course of 30 minutes. While the drop was reversed in a matter of hours, it is difficult to envision such swings being driven by human trading.

Similarly, no one ever found an explanation in market fundamentals for the crash in October 1987, which was also driven by programmed trading. It took close to two years to completely reverse the slide, although half of the loss was recovered in most markets within a week. It's not clear that the modest increase in trading costs associated with proposed FTTs would reduce the likelihood of large price swings caused by flukes, but in any case these large swings arguably have more impact on the efficiency of markets in serving the productive economy than would the modest deviations from fundamental values that may be associated with a decline in market volume and a corresponding reduction in liquidity wrought by an FTT. In other words, it is not clear that an FTT of the size being proposed here would have a sizable impact on destabilizing speculation. However, the fact that we have seen extraordinary and unexplained swings in prices in periods of low trading costs and high volume suggests that reducing trading volume with a FTT is unlikely to destabilize financial markets.

On the issue of the relationship between transactions costs and growth, it is worth noting that modeling practices among macroeconomic forecasters generally do not assume that future growth will be faster as a result of declines in transaction costs in the financial sector. That practice may be mistaken, but modelers in the 1970s, 1980s, and 1990s did not project an acceleration in growth rates in their forecasts as a result of predictable declines in transactions costs in financial markets.

Table 4-1 shows projections of revenue and trading expenses from an FTT of 0.2 percent on stock trades, 0.05 percent per year outstanding on bond trades, and 0.01 percent on derivatives. Based on 2015 trading volumes, the tax could raise between $112 billion and $158 billion a year, equivalent to 0.6 and 0.9 percent of GDP. It could also reduce the amount of resources spent on carrying through trades by $158 billion to $188 billion annually. These are vast resources that could be used elsewhere in the economy.

Figure 4-4 compares the range of tax revenue and the resources freed up to the size of the SNAP budget. The revenue range equals 1.5 to 2.1 times the SNAP budget for 2016, and resources freed up are equivalent to 2.1 to 2.5 times the SNAP budget. In many ways, the amount of resources freed up and used in the productive economy instead of in the shuffle of stocks and other financial assets back and forth is the more important issue.

TABLE 4-1

Projected revenue gains and expense reductions from a financial transactions tax

(billions)

	Tax rate (percent)	Pre-tax trading volume	Post-tax trading volume	Revenue	Reduction in trading expenses
Elasticity = -1.0					
Stocks	0.200%	$48,000	$24,000.0	$48.0	$48.0
Bonds	0.050%	$180,000	$90,000.0	$45.0	$45.0
Derivatives	0.010%	$1,300,000	$650,000.0	$65.0	$65.0
			Total	**$158.0**	**$158.0**
Elasticity = -1.25					
Stocks	0.200%	$48,000	$20,181.5	$40.4	$55.6
Bonds	0.050%	$180,000	$75,680.7	$37.8	$52.2
Derivatives	0.010%	$1,300,000	$546,582.7	$54.7	$75.3
			Total	**$132.9**	**$183.1**
Elasticity = -1.50					
Stocks	0.200%	$48,000	$16,970.6	$33.9	$62.1
Bonds	0.050%	$180,000	$63,639.6	$31.8	$58.2
Derivatives	0.010%	$1,300,000	$459,619.4	$46.0	$67.2
			Total	**$111.7**	**$187.5**

Source and notes: Author's calculations, see text.

FIGURE 4-4

Benefits of a financial transactions tax for revenue and trading expenses, in units of SNAP spending

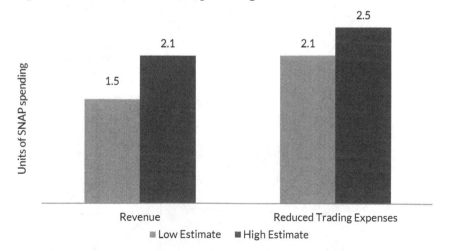

Source and notes: Author's calculations.

While it has not led to faster economic growth, the explosion in the size of the financial sector since 1970 has been associated with an explosion in industry compensation. Compensation has always been higher in the financial sector than elsewhere, but in 1970 the average compensation for a full-time financial sector employee was less than 50 percent higher than the average for the economy as a whole, while in 2014 it was almost 270 percent higher (**Figure 4-5**).[25] As noted earlier, Bakija et al. (2012) found that 18.4 percent of primary taxpayers in the top 0.1 percent of the income distribution were employed in finance.

FIGURE 4-5
Annual compensation in financial sector per full-time equivalent employee

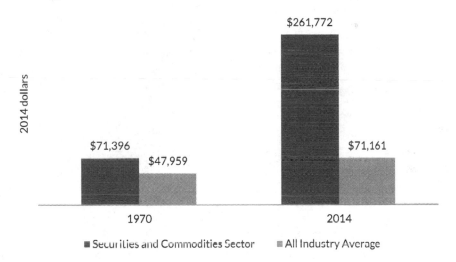

Source and notes: BEA (2016), see text.

It is likely that the downsizing of the industry that would be associated with a moderately sized FTT would lead to a substantial reduction in pay for many of its high earners. Many would undoubtedly

25 These figures are obtained from BEA (2016) by dividing total employee compensation (Table 6.2B, lines 55 and 59, and Table 6.2D, lines 59 and 61) by the number of full-time equivalent workers in the sector (Table 6.5B, lines 55 and 59, and Table 6.5D, lines 59 and 61).

move to other sectors, where their skills may still command a high wage, though likely less than they are currently earning in finance. The workers who remained in the sector may still earn more than the average for workers in other sectors, but the gap would likely be less than before the tax. In effect, to maintain their share of a shrinking market the workers in the financial sector will be forced to forego a substantial portion of their compensation.

Finally, reducing the volume of trading in financial markets will reduce the value of some of the services sold to financial markets. Michael Bloomberg, the former mayor of New York and one of the richest people in the world, made his fortune selling subscriptions to his Bloomberg Terminals,[26] highly valued because they are one of the fastest information sources available for news like crop forecasts or disruptions in oil fields. Getting this information as quickly as possible is essential to anyone who hopes to profit from trading in these markets, yet it matters little for the overall functioning of the economy. A large decrease in trading volume could reduce the income for Bloomberg LP and other companies that provide similar services.

Too-big-to-fail insurance

After the collapse of the investment bank Lehman Brothers in 2008, the Treasury Department and the Federal Reserve Board stepped in to ensure that none of the other major banks would fail. In his autobiography, Timothy Geithner, Treasury Secretary during President Obama's first term, repeatedly stated the administration's commitment that there would be "no more Lehmans," meaning that the administration was committed to doing what was necessary to ensure that another major bank did not fail. This was about as explicit a statement of "too big to fail" (TBTF) insurance as one could imagine. In other words, it was not just a rumor circulating in financial circles that the Treasury would not allow a bank to fail; it was the Obama administration's policy.

---

26   In 2013, a one-year terminal subscription sold for $24,000 (Seward 2016).

The Dodd-Frank financial reform law was supposed to both create better oversight so that the large banks did not expose themselves to excessive risk and put in place mechanisms so that even the largest banks, if troubled, could be put through a resolution process without causing major harm to the economy. In principle, these changes would put an end to TBTF insurance, since lenders would now understand that they faced some risk of losses when making loans to major banks.

It is not clear that the reforms have succeeded in their goal. Though a Government Accountability Office (GAO) analysis in 2014 found that the risk-adjusted gap in interest rates between TBTF banks and smaller banks had largely disappeared (GAO 2014), the evidence was less compelling than it seemed on its face. Since the recovery from the downturn was weak, interest rates remained extraordinarily low, and the persistence of these low rates in a relatively stable economy led to a collapse in the size of spreads for more risky bonds, i.e., the difference between interest rates for very risk bonds and government bonds or other bonds considered extremely safe. In this context, it would be difficult to pick up the impact of a belief in TBTF even if most investors continued to believe that the government would not let a major bank collapse. And the GAO study actually provided direct evidence on this issue. By most of the methodologies it used there was also no TBTF premium in 2006, another period of relative financial stability, suggesting that the benefits of TBTF insurance are difficult to measure in more stable times but may nonetheless exist. Since only one major bank was allowed to fail, the government clearly had a TBTF policy in effect during the financial crisis; therefore, investors would not have been wrong to anticipate that the government would act to save major banks. (Using a somewhat different methodology, the IMF (2014) put the size of the TBTF premium in the United States at $25 billion to $50 billion a year).

No doubt many investors will be prepared to make the same bet going forward. While regulators are being more cautious now, it is far from clear they have the ability or the will to rein in the major banks. For example, in 2012 JP Morgan concealed from regulators several billion dollars of trading losses connected with the "London Whale" incident (Hurtado 2016). Its losses were not large enough to jeopardize its financial health, but it's perhaps possible that the bank could have concealed them even if they had been large enough to make it insolvent. And this was two years after the passage of Dodd-Frank.

There is also the question of whether regulators are and will be able to accurately assess risk. In the financial crisis an asset that regulators assumed to be safe — residential mortgages — turned out to be highly risky. Regulators relied on historical default and recovery rates in assessing risks from bad mortgages and didn't imagine a situation in which plunging house prices could send default rates soaring and radically reduce the portion of the mortgage that could be recovered post-default. They also could not envision a nationwide fall in house prices, since in the past price declines had been restricted to specific markets.[27] Since regulators missed all the signs of the housing bubble, which was the basis for the collapse of house prices and the subsequent surge in mortgage delinquencies and defaults, is there reason to believe that they will be much better in recognizing the next pattern of growth that poses a threat to the economy and the financial system?

The surest way to end TBTF insurance is to break up the big banks, a proposal that is not very far-fetched considering that today's huge banks are a relatively new phenomenon. Interstate banking was seriously limited until 1994, the year the Riegle-Neal Interstate Banking Act opened the door to an enormous wave of bank consolidation. This resulted in much greater concentration in the banking industry than existed in prior decades. The concentration became even greater as a result of the financial crisis, as the Fed and Treasury actively encouraged mergers that would have raised serious antitrust concerns at other times.

To end TBTF, the largest banks need to be downsized to the levels of the 1990s or even the 1980s. There is considerable research showing that these banks were already big enough by then to enjoy all the economies of scale available to large banks today (see, e.g., Davies and Tracey 2014 and Mitchell and Onvural 1996). Certainly, it would be hard

---

27 The potential for a nationwide drop in house prices stemmed from an unprecedented run-up in prices, which was easy to see from publicly available data. See, for example, Baker (2002).

to argue that companies in the 1990s or even the 1980s were seriously hampered by their inability to get access to bank loans.

The argument most often advanced by opponents of breaking up the banks is that our banks would be disadvantaged relative to large banks in other countries. In effect, this is an argument that other countries are providing TBTF insurance and that we should do the same in order to keep up.

But that would be bad economics. Suppose other countries subsidize their car industries. The standard economics argument is not that we should also subsidize ours, but rather that we should take advantage of the cheap cars that are being made available to our consumers and focus on producing different goods and services. If we were being consistent, we would have the same attitude toward the banking industry. Of course, bankers have considerably more political power than autoworkers.

Power aside, it would be good economics to break up the large banks and restore market discipline to finance. Contrary to what is often claimed, breaking up the banks would not be a complex administrative task. The government should not be micromanaging the project; the banks could do it themselves. The banks know their business and have an incentive to break themselves up in a way that maximizes shareholder value. The government need only set size caps and a timeline, as well as penalties for not meeting the timeline. The banks can figure out how best to downsize themselves.

Waste by privatization

The financial industry draws rents when tasks that could be performed more efficiently by the government or by a monopoly private provider are instead parceled out to financial firms. Social Security is an obvious example, since the economics of privatization there have been examined extensively. A large body of literature shows that the administrative costs of running a decentralized privatized system are far greater than the costs of the current Social Security system due to the economies of scale in a single large system; the costs that inevitably accompany competition, such as marketing; the cost of government oversight; the higher pay that top management earns in the financial sector; and the profits earned by the industry (see, e.g., Orszag and Stiglitz 2001; National Academy for Social Insurance 1998).

The same findings about Social Security would apply to many sectors that are privatized now, like the privately run system of defined contribution pensions. Its average cost of 0.95 percent of assets under management (Munnell et al. 2011) compares quite unfavorably to costs of the Thrift Savings Plan (TSP) for federal employers — just 0.29 percent of assets (TSP 2015). Even if one allowed for a doubling of the TSP baseline to account for the greater costs associated with contributions from a diverse set of employers, the rents accruing to the financial sector would still be 0.37 percentage points of the $13.62 trillion in assets of defined contribution plans, equivalent to $50 billion a year.[28]

Defined benefit pension plans are in a similar situation. They often pay excessive fees to managers who provide no better returns than could be obtained from investments in index funds. Some pension funds are efficiently managed, of course, but many are avenues for cronyism, with politically connected managers able to tack on fees that far exceed market rates.[29] Reducing excessive fees by just 0.1 percent to 0.3 percent of these plans' $11.36 billion in assets[30] would free up $12 billion to $35 billion annually.

Another major source of waste is the cost associated with the private health insurance industry. Administrative costs in this sector are equal to 13.7 percent of benefits paid out compared to less than 2.0 percent in a government-run system like Canada's,[31] and getting to

---

28 The figure for defined contribution plan assets is from Federal Reserve Board (2015).

29 For example, Steven Rattner, an investment fund manager who later oversaw the bailout of the auto industry in the Obama administration, agreed to make a payment of $6.2 million to the Securities and Exchange Commission (Gallu et al. 2010) for allegedly making payoffs to gain control of a portion of New York State's pension funds.

30 As of end of first quarter 2015; Federal Reserve Board (2015), Flow of Funds Table L.117, line 25.

31 The calculation for the United States is taken from the Centers for Medicare and Medicaid Services, National Health Care Expenditures Historical Data for 2013

Canadian levels would save up over $100 billion annually (based on $120 billion of costs in 2014). Even if the costs were twice as high as Canada's, the savings would still have been over $80 billion in 2014. A universal Medicare-type system would also provide large administrative savings to providers who would no longer have to deal with a variety of complex insurance rules and forms, to employers who would no longer have to handle the administrative work associated with choosing plans and managing workers' benefits, as well to patients. Plausible estimates of the size of the first two sources of savings are comparable to the savings on the administrative cost in the insurance industry, implying total potential savings of $160 billion to $200 billion (Woolhander et al. 2003).

Waste by deception

Many industries, but especially finance, have profited by writing contract terms deceptively so as to extract money from customers. One of the clearest examples of this practice is the overdraft fees that banks charged to debit card holders. Until the Fed stopped the practice in 2010, people making payments with debit cards would not be told at the time of payment that they had insufficient funds and therefore would pay an overdraft fee. A $2.00 cup of coffee could cost $25 or $35 extra from the fees. The overdraft bill could get quite large if a person made repeated charges because he or she didn't realize there was no money in the account — for example, because a paycheck wasn't credited properly.

Before the Fed's rule, banks were collecting $20 billion a year in overdraft fees on debit cards (Martin 2010). While in some cases, people may have considered the service of having a payment covered worth the overdraft fee, in the vast majority of cases people would likely forego the cup of coffee. The rule simply requires that people be notified of the overdraft fee at the time of their purchase, unless they explicitly opt out of notification (Federal Reserve Board 2009).

(CMS 2014). Net insurance expenditures from private insurers are taken from Table 4; insurance payments from Table 2. The estimate for administrative costs in Canada is taken from Woolhander et al. (2003).

Note that this rule is not just a question of protecting naïve consumers from predatory banks. It involves a basic issue of economic logic. If it is possible to make large profits by finding devious ways to trick customers, then banks and other corporations will devote substantial resources to finding devious ways to trick customers. Instead of devoting resources to figuring out how to better serve customers, banks will devote resources to finding ways to put rules in contracts that allow them to profit at their customers' expense.

The "buyer beware" argument in this story means that consumers would have to spend much more time reviewing contracts and that firms would devote more resources to deceiving customers. That is hardly an economically optimal outcome.

It is not easy to get a good measure of the amount of payments that might be subject to deceptive terms like overdraft fees. Penalties associated with late payments on mortgages have this character, as would some credit cards fees and bank mortgage practices during the housing bubble.[32] Of course, some of these fees are legitimate charges for real services to customers who have been clearly notified of the costs. In any case, for purposes of further calculation, the $20 billion that banks had been receiving in 2009 as overdraft fees on debit cards will be used as a placeholder.[33]

---

32 The enormous costs associated with the collapse of the bubble can be blamed in large part on the recklessness of the financial industry. Competent regulators could have stopped the growth of the bubble. It can be argued that the power of the financial industry prevented regulators from acting, but this is at best only part of the story. Almost no economists saw the bubble and recognized the danger it presented prior to its collapse. This failure applies not only to economists who had ties to the financial industry, but to the majority who did not.

33 These sorts of deceptive practices are not restricted to financial companies. For example, Verizon charges customers without a calling plan around $3.50 per minute for calls to most European countries (Verizon 2016). Since these calls can be made for a few cents a minute on most calling cards, it is unlikely that anyone would ever spend more than two or three minutes on a call at these rates. However, Verizon does not inform customers of the cost at the time they place their call.

The tax shelter industry

Both progressives and conservatives have long supported reforms to the tax code that would eliminate loopholes. For most progressives the goal is to both raise revenue and to make the tax code fairer. But one aspect of the tax code that is underappreciated is the tax shelter industry itself, which is a major source of inequality.

This is perhaps mostly clearly visible in the case of private equity. While many private equity companies do what their promoters claim — providing capital and managerial expertise to companies that need both — much of the gains from private equity stem from the industry's ability to game the tax code (Appelbaum and Batt 2014). For example, it is standard practice for private equity companies to load up acquisitions with debt. The interest on this debt is deducted from taxable profits, as opposed to the dividends that would otherwise be paid to shareholders, which are not deductible. Private equity companies will typically also take advantage of other loopholes in the tax code. After all, they have access to accountants who are experts in gaming the tax code while the small companies they acquire generally do not.

There are ways to reduce the complexity of the corporate income tax without jeopardizing it as a revenue source. A simple route would be to have firms turn over non-voting shares to the government as a replacement for the income tax. For example, if the targeted tax rate is 30 percent, firms can be required to make a one-time transfer of stock equal to 30 percent of their outstanding shares.

Since they are non-voting, the shares would give the government no control: the goal is to secure a claim to corporate profits, not to run companies. Apart from issues of control, the government's shares would be treated just like other shares of common stock. If the company pays a dividend of $2 a share on its common stock, then it would also pay $2 a share on the stock held by the government. If it buys back 10 percent of outstanding shares at $100 per share, then it would buy back 10 percent of the shares held by the government at $100 per share. If a private equity firm buys out the company, paying $120 per share, then it would pay $120 for each share held by the government.[34]

It should be possible to design a share system like this as a replacement for the corporate income tax and thereby hugely reduce the complexity of the current tax code and drastically reduce the opportunities for gaming. For this reason it would also reduce the potential profits in the tax-gaming industry.

If it is too great a lift politically to adopt a system of share issuance, it should be possible to create a share issuance alternative on a voluntary basis. In other words, businesses that opted to issue non-voting shares to the government could permanently end their tax liability. This should be a major money-saving move for companies that are not trying to game the system, since they would no longer have to pay as much to accountants for calculating their taxes. This voluntary system would also reduce enforcement costs, since enforcement should be a relatively simple matter for the firms that issue shares. (The only question for the Internal Revenue Service is whether these shares are being treated the same way as the firm's common shares.) The Internal Revenue Service (IRS) could focus its attention on the companies that are actively trying to game the system, presumably making gaming more difficult.

The private equity industry provides some measure of the potential savings from reducing the gaming of the tax system. The industry had almost $3.5 trillion in assets under management in 2013 (Prequin 2014), and at a management fee of 3.0 percent, including incentive pay, the industry's income would be $105 billion annually. If closing the tax and regulatory loopholes that it exploits eliminated one-third of its income, the savings would be $35 billion annually. Eliminating half would provide annual savings of $53 billion. This is undoubtedly a conservative estimate of the potential savings from reducing access to tax shelters, since there are many law and accounting firms that are unconnected to private

---

34 There would be issues of international coordination and coordination of state and federal income taxes. (Presumably state governments could also require some percentage of non-voting shares. Of course, these issues of coordination exist under the current system as well.)

equity that also profit from exploiting these shelters. Since many private equity partners are among the richest people in the country, reducing the ability for this sector to profit would be an effective way to reverse the upward redistribution of the last three decades.

Because the returns on private equity have fallen sharply in recent years, it is no longer clear that even with the gaming private equity is beating the relevant stock indexes (Appelbaum and Batt 2016). In this case, the fees being paid out to private equity partners are pure waste. This drag on the productive use of resources can be addressed by forcing pension funds to fully disclose fees and investment returns and by withdrawing money from investments where returns do not justify the risks.

Conclusion

Eliminating the various sources of rents in the financial sector has the potential to free up $460 billion to $636 billion in 2015, or between 2.6 and 3.5 percent of GDP (**Table 4-2**). This total does not include some potentially large sources of rents that we have not discussed. For example, in the last two decades many workers' compensation programs have been wholly or partially privatized, a change that almost certainly adds to their administrative costs. It is likely that a centralized system of auto insurance, life insurance, and annuities could be administered at lower cost than the current one.

Figure 4-6 illustrates that the potential savings from eliminating waste in the financial sector are equal to 6.2 to 8.6 years of SNAP spending.[35]

Any reductions in revenue going to the financial sector will be to a substantial extent at the expense of the wealthy. As noted before, the financial sector accounts for a grossly disproportionate share of the individuals in the top 1 percent of the income distribution, and many of

---

35 There are other estimates of waste in the financial sector that are substantially higher. For example Epstein and Montecino (2016) put the cost at almost $1 trillion a year.

the very highest earners can be found at hedge funds, private equity companies, and major Wall Street banks.

TABLE 4-2

Potential savings in 2015 from reducing rents in financial sector

(billions of 2015 dollars)

	Low estimate	High estimate
Reduced trading revenue, financial transactions tax	$158	$188
Ending TBTF subsidy	$25	$50
Centralized defined contribution pension system	$51	$91
More transparent defined benefit pension system	$11	$34
Centralized health insurance system	$160	$200
Predatory practices	$20	$20
Private equity and tax shelter industry	$35	$53
Total	**$460**	**$636**

Source and notes: Author's calculations, see text.

FIGURE 4-6

Financial sector rents, 2015, in units of SNAP spending

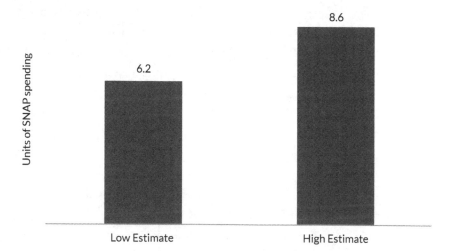

Source and notes: Author's calculations.

Chapter 5

The Old Technology and Inequality Scam: The Story of Patents and Copyrights

One of the amazing lines often repeated by people in policy debates is that, as a result of technology, we are seeing income redistributed from people who work for a living to the people who own the technology. While the redistribution part of the story may be mostly true, the problem is that the technology does not determine who "owns" the technology. The people who write the laws determine who owns the technology.

Specifically, patents and copyrights give their holders monopolies on technology or creative work for their duration. If we are concerned that money is going from ordinary workers to people who hold patents and copyrights, then one policy we may want to consider is shortening and weakening these monopolies. But policy has gone sharply in the opposite direction over the last four decades, as a wide variety of measures have been put into law that make these protections longer and stronger. Thus, the redistribution from people who work to people who own the technology should not be surprising — that was the purpose of the policy.

If stronger rules on patents and copyrights produced economic dividends in the form of more innovation and more creative output, then this upward redistribution might be justified. But the evidence doesn't indicate there has been any noticeable growth dividend associated with this upward redistribution. In fact, stronger patent protection seems to be associated with slower growth.

Before directly considering the case, it is worth thinking for a minute about what the world might look like if we had alternative mechanisms to patents and copyrights, so that the items now subject to these monopolies could be sold in a free market just like paper cups and shovels.

The biggest impact would be in prescription drugs. The breakthrough drugs for cancer, hepatitis C, and other diseases, which now sell for tens or hundreds of thousands of dollars annually, would instead sell for a few hundred dollars. No one would have to struggle to get their insurer to pay for drugs or scrape together the money from friends and family. Almost every drug would be well within an affordable price range for a middle-class family, and covering the cost for poorer families could be easily managed by governments and aid agencies.

The same would be the case with various medical tests and treatments. Doctors would not have to struggle with a decision about whether to prescribe an expensive scan, which might be the best way to detect a cancerous growth or other health issue, or to rely on cheaper but less reliable technology. In the absence of patent protection even the most cutting edge scans would be reasonably priced.

Health care is not the only area that would be transformed by a free market in technology and creative work. Imagine that all the textbooks needed by college students could be downloaded at no cost over the web and printed out for the price of the paper. Suppose that a vast amount of new books, recorded music, and movies was freely available on the web.

People or companies who create and innovate deserve to be compensated, but there is little reason to believe that the current system of patent and copyright monopolies is the best way to support their work. It's not surprising that the people who benefit from the current system are reluctant to have the efficiency of patents and copyrights become a topic for public debate, but those who are serious about inequality have no choice. These forms of property claims have been important drivers of inequality in the last four decades.

The explicit assumption behind the steps over the last four decades to increase the strength and duration of patent and copyright protection is that the higher prices resulting from increased protection will be more than offset by an increased incentive for innovation and creative work. Patent and copyright protection should be understood as being like very large tariffs. These protections can often the raise the price of protected items by several multiples of the free market price, making them comparable to tariffs of several hundred or even several thousand percent. The resulting economic distortions are comparable to what they would be if we imposed tariffs of this magnitude.

The justification for granting these monopoly protections is that the increased innovation and creative work that is produced as a result of these incentives exceeds the economic costs from patent and copyright monopolies. However, there is remarkably little evidence to support this assumption. While the cost of patent and copyright protection in higher prices is apparent, even if not well-measured, there is little evidence of a substantial payoff in the form of a more rapid pace of innovation or more and better creative work.

Stronger and longer: The path of patent and copyright protection since 1970

In recent decades, both political parties have been largely supportive of measures to increase the length of patent and copyright protection, increase the scope of these protections, increase penalties for violations of the law, and extend protections internationally through trade agreements and political pressure. As a result, protections in both areas are far stronger in 2016 than in prior decades, and a much broader set of products are subject to protection.

Prior to 1995, patents in the United States extended for 17 years after the date of issuance. In that year, Congress passed and the president signed legislation changing the length to 20 years from the date of filing to be in compliance with the TRIPS (Trade Related Aspects of Intellectual Property Rights) provisions of the Uruguay Round of the WTO (USPTO 2015). This law also included provisions allowing for the extension of the duration of patents in the event the approval process took more than three years, the average length of the process. Patents issued prior to 1995 were extended to 20 years from filling or 17 years from issuance, whichever was longer. In 2015 the duration of design patents — those that apply to the design of a product like furniture or appliances — was extended from 14 years to 15 years from the date of issuance (U.S. Government Publishing Office 2012).

Prior to 1976, copyrights lasted 28 years from the date they were secured, with the possibility of an extension for another 28 years (U.S. Copyright Office 2011). The 1976 Copyright Act increased the length of the extension to 47 years, for a total possible duration of 75 years, and the 1998 Copyright Term Extension Act increased it to 67 years, for a total possible duration of 95 years. In both cases, the extensions were applied retroactively to works whose copyright was still in effect. In 1992, Congress made renewal of copyrights automatic for works copyrighted after 1964. This is noteworthy because in the United States copyright holders do not have to formally register, a change introduced in the 1976 law. As a result, it can be difficult and time-consuming for someone seeking to make use of copyrighted material to track down the copyright holder. In fact, in many cases potential users would have no way of knowing the material was copyrighted. Legislation in the 1990s extended copyrights further to 95 years.

In addition to duration, the scope of patent and copyright protection has been expanded as well. In the 1980s, patents were extended to cover DNA sequences and life forms, and in the 1990s it became possible to patent software and business methods. The Bayh-Dole Act of 1980 allowed for universities, research institutions, private companies, and individuals operating on government contracts to gain control of patents derived from their work, thereby creating the opportunity for universities to earn large rents from patents and for researchers to form their own companies, all relying on knowledge and expertise obtained on government contracts. In 1982, Congress created a designated court to hear patent appeals cases, the U.S. Court of Appeals for the Federal Circuit, and it has been substantially more patent friendly than prior appellate court panels. In cases where a patent's validity was in question, the new court has ruled in favor of the patent holder in two-thirds of cases, compared to one-third of cases in prior appellate courts (Scherer 2009).

The scope of copyright protection has been extended to accommodate digital technology. The most important development in this area was the Digital Millennial Copyright Act of 1998 (DMCA), which applied explicit rules for digital reproduction and transmission of copyrighted work. The act allows for large fines and extensive prison sentences for willful violations (U.S. Copyright Office 1998). While it is reasonable to have rules for digital reproductions, the act was in effect a decision to preserve a form of publication rather than allow it to fall victim to changing technology (Kodak film wasn't so lucky). Even with the passage of the DMCA, the entertainment industry remains unhappy with the extent to which copyrighted material is reproduced without authorization. It has repeatedly sought measures in Congress, such as the Stop Online Piracy Act (SOPA) and the PROTECT IP Act (PIPA), and in trade agreements to strengthen copyright enforcement. These measures would require Internet intermediaries like Google, Facebook, and millions of smaller sites to proactively police postings by third parties to prevent copyright violations. These rules would shift the responsibility and cost of enforcement from the copyright holder to someone else.

As technology increases the ease of reproducing and transferring copyrighted material, copyright enforcement becomes more costly and difficult. Efforts to continue enforcement inevitably impose greater costs on society.

Administrations of both political parties have placed a high priority on extending patent and copyright protection to other countries through trade agreements and political pressure. The most important item in this area was the inclusion in the WTO of TRIPS, which required developing countries to adopt U.S.-style patent and copyright laws, albeit with a substantial phase-in period (which has been repeatedly extended) for the poorest countries. Other trade deals, like the North American Free Trade Agreement, the Central America Free Trade Agreement, and the Trans-Pacific Partnership, have included "TRIPS-plus" provisions such as data exclusivity, which prohibits generic drug manufacturers from using test data submitted by brand manufacturers to establish the safety and effectiveness of their drugs, and marketing exclusivity, which prohibits generic competitors from competing during the period of exclusivity even if they conducted their own clinical trials. These treaties have also broadened the scope of patentable items; for example, the Trans-Pacific Partnership requires patents be issued for new uses of existing compounds and for combination drugs (many widely used new drugs involve new combinations of existing molecules, rather than the development of a new chemical entity).

The United States has also pursued stronger and longer patent and copyright protections in bilateral negotiations. For example, the Obama administration has been quite public about its efforts to force the Indian government to allow patents for combination drugs. It also has sought to discourage countries from exercising their right to require compulsory licenses for drugs, as explicitly allowed under the TRIPS provisions.

Stronger patent protections in developing countries serve two purposes. The first is the obvious one of increasing the profits of drug companies. But the industry also is concerned about the large gap between the price of patent-protected brand drugs in the United States and their generic equivalents in developing countries. For example, the hepatitis C drug Sovaldi has a U.S. list price of $84,000 for a three-month course of treatment, while in India high-quality generic versions are available for $300 to $500 (Gokhale 2015). For new cancer drugs selling for over $100,000 per year, the gap with generic prices could be even larger. These enormous differences create a large incentive for patients to seek out the generic version, whether by finding a way to bring the drugs into the United States or by traveling to a country where the generic is available.[36] If the pharmaceutical industry can succeed in taking away the generic option, it will eliminate a major threat to its marketing model.

In short, we have seen considerable strengthening of intellectual property rules in the last four decades, as summarized in **Table 5-1**. The result has been a sharp increase in the size of rents for the protected items, most notably prescription drugs and medical equipment, which grew from 0.4 percent and 0.17 percent of GDP in 1975, respectively, to 2.3 percent and 0.51 percent in 2015. (In the 2016 economy, these increases would be equal to $350 billion and $63 billion, respectively.) The increase in the economic importance of patents also led to a sharp increase in patenting and in patent suits, as the growing value of these rents provided more incentive to companies and individuals to pursue and contest patents. These costs would be justified if the incentives also led to more innovation and creative work, but it is questionable that this has been the outcome.

Before examining some of the recent literature in this area, it is worth describing the nature of the possible rents in patent and copyright. With both, the government grants individuals or corporations a monopoly for a period of time as an incentive to innovate or produce creative work. The question of rents comes up in the context of whether such monopolies are the most efficient way to provide incentives and whether the system as currently structured is optimal. The rents would be the additional cost that society incurs as a result of this system being less than optimal. As the literature shows, this question does not have a simple answer because it can't be known whether alternative mechanisms will be as effective in promoting innovation and creative work. However, it is possible to get good estimates of the extent to which these monopolies compared with a competitive market raise costs. And there is some basis for assessing the

---

36 Pharmaceutical companies have sought to place extraordinary restrictions on the use of low-cost drugs in developing countries. For example, Gilead Sciences, the patent holder on Sovaldi, authorized a generic version for Egypt. However, a condition of this license is that the government carefully police the distribution of the generic. Patients are supposed to pick up the drug themselves, and open the container and take the first pill in the presence of the pharmacist selling the drug. See McNeil (2015).

efficiency of alternative funding mechanisms for innovation and creative work. These calculations can provide a basis for assessing whether alternative mechanisms are likely to be more efficient.

TABLE 5-1

Legal changes affecting patents and copyrights since 1970

Year	Change
1976	Copyright duration extended to 75 years from 58 years (applied retroactively). End of registration requirement for copyright protection.
1980	Bayh-Dole Act allows universities, research institutions, private companies, and individuals operating on government contracts to gain control of patents derived from their work.
1980	In Diamond v. Chakrabarty, Supreme Court rules that life forms are patentable.
1981	In Diamond v. Diehr, Supreme Court sets rules under which computer software can be patented, formalized by U.S. Patent and Trademark Office in 1996.
1982	Congress creates the United States Court of Appeals for the Federal Circuit to handle patent claims, a court that proves to be more patent-friendly.
1995	TRIPS provisions of the WTO require member countries to adopt U.S.-style patent law. Congress extends duration to 20 years from date of issuance, with automatic extensions in cases where approval process was delayed.
1998	Copyright duration extended to 95 years (applied retroactively).
1998	Digital Millennial Copyright Act extends copyright to digital materials. Also establishes liability for third-party intermediaries.
1998	In State Street Bank & Trust Co. v. Signature Financial Group Inc., Supreme Court rules that business methods are patentable.
2006	Central America and Dominican Republic Free Trade Agreement and Dominican Republic — includes "TRIPS Plus" provisions requiring countries to have lengthy periods of data exclusivity when a drug is approved by licensing authority. This excludes generics from the market even when no patents are applicable.

Source and notes: Various sources, see text.

Rents from patents and copyrights: What the literature shows

There is a vast literature on the benefits and the costs of patent and copyright protection. The case against such protections is best summarized in a series of works authored or co-authored by David Levine and Michele Boldrin. They note that the number of patent approvals more than quadrupled between 1983 and 2010 with no obvious benefits in terms of either expenditures on research and development (R&D) or total factor productivity growth. R&D expenditures have been near 2.5 percent of GDP since the 1970s, with no upward trend associated with the proliferation of patents. The same is the case with total factor productivity growth. It averaged 1.2 percent from 1970–1979, while falling below 1.0 percent in the decade from 2000–2009. (It has been even lower in the last six years.) Their work also includes more detailed analyses of multifactor productivity growth by sector. They find little relationship between the number of patents in a sector and the rate of productivity growth (Boldrin et al. 2011). The fit is not improved when measures like frequency of patent citations are used instead of the number of patents. In short, they find little evidence in this work of the positive benefits of patents.

These findings are consistent with a series of cross-country regressions testing whether GDP growth or productivity growth, by a variety of measures, is increased as a result of stronger patent protection (Baker 2016). The overwhelming majority of tests find no evidence of a positive relationship. In fact, in many of the specifications there is a statistically significant negative relationship, implying that stronger patent protection is associated with slower productivity growth. While these tests are far from conclusive, the implication is that the additional waste associated with stronger patent monopolies more than offsets any benefits from incentivizing innovation.

Levine and Boldrin cite a range of evidence that patents can be a major source of waste and a hindrance to productivity growth. For example, the vast majority of patents are never used, and old, established companies often stockpile them to use as competitive weapons against smaller upstarts. Examining the upsurge of patents in the semiconductor industry in the 1980s and 1990s, Hall and Ziedonas (2001) found that the main motivation was to use patents as weapons in lawsuits against competitors and as bargaining chips in the settlement of cases. Because litigation involves large costs, an established firm is much better situated to contest a patent than an upstart with few resources. As a result, a patent can be used to force the upstart to share much of the benefits of its technology, even if there is no actual dependence on the patent of the established firm.

This sort of reasoning was widely cited as the main explanation for Google's decision to buy the Mobility division of Motorola in 2011 for $12.5 billion. At the time, as a relatively new company, Google did not have a large portfolio of patents that could be used as retaliatory weapons if it were sued. The purchase of Mobility gave Google a large portfolio.

The extreme example of using patents for legal harassment is that of a patent troll, a company that exists only to push claims of patent rights against profitable companies. Boldrin and Levine (2013) note the case of NTP Inc., a patent holding company that won a patent infringement case against Research in Motion (RIM) over the Blackberry. In order to avoid having its system shut down at a point where its service was expanding rapidly, RIM agreed to pay NTP $612.5 million to license the use of the patent. On appeal, the original ruling was overturned, but RIM did not get its money back. The implication is that more than $600 million was taken from what at the time was a thriving and innovative company, due to a mistaken judicial ruling. Of course, this ruling provided an enormous incentive for other companies to follow NTP's example.

A study by Bessen and Meurer (2012), which relied on a survey of corporate executives, put the direct cost to firms of litigation with patent trolls (including settlements) at $29 billion in 2011. An earlier study involving the same authors looked at the impact on stock prices and put the cost at $80 billion a year (Bessen et al. 2012). Most of the cost in these estimates stems from payments made to the patent trolls or the need to alter a business plan in response to a patent suit. Insofar as these payments reflect compensation for legitimate innovations (a claim disputed by Bessen and Meurer), they would not constitute rents associated with the patent system; they would simply be redistributions among patent holders. But even with this generous interpretation, Bessen and Meurer still attribute more than $5 billion of their $29 billion estimate to direct litigation costs.

These litigation costs are pure waste from an economic standpoint, and the actual waste to the economy would have to be several times this size, because the patent trolls undoubtedly spent a comparable amount on litigation. In addition, this study is only looking at suits with patent trolls (formally, non-practicing entities (NPEs)), which account for roughly 60 percent of all patent suits. While suits brought by companies that actually use the technology may be more meritorious on average, the legal expenses are still a cost to the economy. Extrapolating from the $5 billion estimate of litigation costs, total litigation costs related to patents for 2011 could have easily been close to $17 billion, or 7.3 percent of total R&D spending for the year.[37] And this does not even account for the extent to which payments resulting from these suits may not be merited, as was the case with the NTP suit and which Bessen and Meurer argue is the case with most suits involving NPEs.

Boldrin and Levine (2013) also note the substantial legal costs associated with patent protection. Almost 250,000 patents were filed in 2010, at an average legal cost of more than $7,000 per patent, implying spending of $2 billion in legal fees in 2010 just to file patents. Furthermore, with the ratio of litigation to patents remaining roughly constant while the ratio of patents to R&D spending has risen considerably over the last three decades, the ratio of litigation to R&D spending has clearly increased. From the standpoint of the economy, these additional legal costs are a pure deadweight loss.

The legal issues surrounding the proliferation of patents can obstruct innovation in a variety of ways. Shapiro (2001) notes the problem of "patent thickets," situations where innovations often involve the use of a large set of patents. Patent thickets can result in large transaction costs, which may stifle innovation, and the problem can be even more serious if inadvertent infringement results in penalties. The paper notes that the problem of patent thickets has become especially serious in important sectors like semiconductors, biotechnology, computer software, and the Internet, since all have experienced a proliferation of patents in recent years. In the same vein, patents on research tools, such as transgenic animals and biological receptors, have become increasingly common in the

---

37 This calculation assumes that the patent trolls' litigation costs are equal to the defendants' ($5 billion). It then assumes that the $10 billion in litigation costs involving trolls accounts for 60 percent of total litigation costs.

last three decades. The royalty payments and transaction costs associated with these tools can make the research to develop new drugs and medical diagnostic products considerably more expensive and thereby slow the process.

Recent research has also found considerable evidence that the threat of patent litigation distorts the direction of research and is a powerful weapon of larger firms against smaller firms and start-ups. Examining the patenting behavior of biotech firms, Lerner (1995) found that firms facing higher legal costs, due to their small size, are less likely to patent in subclasses where there are many other patents. This is especially likely if the firms holding the other patents in the subclass are larger firms with substantial legal resources.

Lanjouw and Schankerman (2001a) found evidence of a strong reputation effect in which patent holders are more likely to file suits in areas where many new patents are being issued. The motivation may be that companies want to show their willingness to contest patents to intimidate competitors. Suits were also more likely if the patent had fewer backward citations. The study takes this as evidence that in new areas where the bounds of existing patents are less well established there will be a larger basis for contesting claims.

Both of these findings are troubling from the standpoint of promoting innovation. Insofar as a reputation effect is important for protecting a claim, it means that larger firms will be better situated than smaller ones that may have difficulty covering litigation costs. The finding that patent suits are more likely in new areas implies that litigation will more frequently be needed to protect patents that are opening new ground, and that patents will be of less value to smaller upstarts than to well-established firms.

Lanjouw and Schankerman (2001b) found that smaller firms and individual patent holders are far more likely to be involved in patent suits than large firms. The disproportionate negative effect on start-ups is made worse by the fact that large patent portfolios seem to provide protection from suits. Firms with large patent portfolios are less likely to be involved in patent suits even when controlling for the size of the firm itself. The conclusion of this analysis is that litigation costs are greater to smaller firms because they are less well situated to pursue litigation avoidance strategies. Patents are thus a less valuable asset to smaller firms because they are more costly on average for smaller firms to enforce.

Lanjouw and Lerner (2001) found that larger firms were 16 to 25 percent more likely to gain a preliminary injunction in a patent suit than smaller firms. This figure likely understates the bias in favor of large firms because lower litigation costs would mean that they would be more likely to pursue weak patent claims than smaller firms. The advantage indicates a substantial tilting toward large firms, because a preliminary injunction allows the patent holder to effectively maintain a monopoly in the market for the duration of the injunction and prevents the defendant from receiving a return on its investment.

There has been considerable study on the importance of patents as a subsidy for research. Most of the studies find that in most areas the subsidy provided by patents is in the range of 5 to 15 percent of expenditures on research (e.g., Jaffe 2000, Schankerman and Pakes 1986, Lanjouw 1998, and Schankerman 1998). The major exception is in pharmaceuticals, where the subsidy could be 30 percent. These studies find a tremendous skewing of patents, with a relatively small share accounting for the vast majority of the value. Also, the value of most patents seems to dissipate quickly. In several European countries in the 1970s and 1980s, patents were subject to renewal after five years; that the vast majority were not renewed suggests that companies usually did not consider the process worth the fees and associated expenses.

Cohen at al. (2000) surveyed a large number of R&D labs in the United States to gain insights into the relative importance of patents as a mechanism to support research. The study found that patents were viewed as a relatively unimportant mechanism in allowing firms to profit from their research. The respondents cited lead time advantages, secrecy, and the use of complementary manufacturing and marketing as more important than patents. The survey also found substantial differences in answers by firm size, with large firms most frequently citing patents as a major way to protect their investment in R&D.

Patents can raise the cost of R&D by making the use of research tools costly. This is a growing problem in areas like biotechnology, where many of the tests, tools, and biological materials used by researchers are themselves subject to patents. The costs stem not only from the compensation paid to patent holders, but also the transaction costs associated with all the necessary agreements. The same sort of problem comes up with the development of new drugs or software, where several patents may be involved in the finished product. The innovator must then negotiate with a number of patent holders in order to market its product. This process may prevent many products from ever being marketing. In cases where firms opt for joint licensing agreements, Lerner and Merges (1998) find that the larger firm is most likely left in control of the marketing, leaving the newer firm less likely to reap the full benefit of the innovation.

There is also evidence that the publication of patents does not serve the intended purpose of diffusing knowledge. Boldrin and Levine (2013) argue that firms deliberately write up their patents in ways that make them as unintelligible as possible precisely to avoid giving their competitors any advantage. This practice is certainly what would be predicted as profit-maximizing behavior. As a practical matter, there is no real downside for a firm to write its patent in a way that makes it difficult to understand — it's unlikely that a patent will be rejected for poor writing. In addition, competitors often deliberately avoid having their researchers review patents in order to protect themselves from infringement suits (Gallini 2002). For these reasons, the publication of patents under current intellectual property rules may do less for the diffusion of knowledge than would be hoped.

In sum, evidence suggests that patents and their enforcement impose considerable costs on the economy. There are substantial legal expenses associated with patents, as they are increasingly used as weapons in a competitive strategy. They are used more often as a tool to harass competitors than as a tool to protect innovation. The legal expenses are themselves a substantial drain on the economy, but the larger drain is the extent to which the expenses distort the innovation process, causing companies to abandon promising areas of research and instead look for segments of the market where they are less likely to confront a deep-pocketed competitor. This is likely to be an especially serious problem for smaller companies and start-ups that are less well positioned to engage in costly patent litigation.

The research shows that the effective research subsidy provided by patents in most sectors is limited, usually in the range of 5 to 15 percent of research expenditures. The major exception is with biomedical research, where the subsidy has been estimated at 30 percent. The evidence from this research raises serious questions as to whether patents are a net positive for innovation and productivity growth.

The body of work produced and compiled by Levine and Boldrin and their collaborators presents an impressive list of the problems associated with the patent system. They argue for weakening or eliminating patents in most areas. Assuming that the patent system is not eliminated in its entirety, they argue for tailoring patent length to the specifics of competition in a sector.[38] They note the need for some public mechanism for funding the R&D of pharmaceuticals, because a free market system is unlikely to support the cost of this work.

Turning now to copyright, a review by Handke (2011) of the empirical research on the cost and benefits of the copyright system begins by noting that claims by Intellectual Property Owners Association (the industry trade group) on the importance of copyright to the economy are grossly exaggerated. The industry group estimates the size of the core copyright industries at $890 billion in 2007 (6.4 percent of GDP). However, this is not a measure of the value of copyrights themselves but rather of the size of the industries, like those involving computer software or newspapers, that make substantial use of copyright protection. The group also exaggerates measures of growth by assuming a constant price on products that are in fact rapidly falling in price (e.g., software).

Handke notes that the evidence with copyrights, like the evidence with patents, is ambiguous as to whether they are a net economic positive. It cites examples of creative work, such as open-source software, that does not depend on copyright protection. It also points out that copyrights can

---

38 This suggestion goes directly counter to the thrust of recent trade agreements, which have sought to create uniformity in patent duration and enforcement across sectors.

impede creative work by raising the cost of using copyrighted material in derivative work. This can be an especially large problem in the case of copyright, because there is no official registry. It is incumbent on the user to first determine if a copyright protects material, to find the person or corporation in possession of the copyright, and then to make arrangements for non-infringing use of the material.

These transaction costs can be prohibitive in the case of limited uses of copyrighted material in books or movies, leading in many cases to a decision to simply avoid using the work in question. This issue has often been a problem for musicians doing live performances. In principle, the venue where the performance is taking place (typically a restaurant or bar) should be paying a licensing fee for use of songs to the relevant licensing organizations. However, many smaller places with only occasional performances may not want to incur this expense. To avoid potential liability on their part, they would have to ask performers not to include copyrighted material in their sets. This could be difficult for singers or musicians who typically use some amount of copyrighted material in a standard set. As a result, these musicians may find themselves excluded from some of the venues that would otherwise be available to them. Because the vast majority of performing artists will receive far more money from live performances than the sale of recorded music, copyright is more likely to be a hindrance than a support to their work.[39]

This can also be a problem for someone interested in using dated material that could still be subject to copyright protection in a book or movie. For example, a 50-year-old photograph of a not especially memorable event, would have near zero value for commercial purposes. However, it may be a useful artifact for a book on the time period. An author worried about infringing on copyright would most likely opt to forego using the picture rather than devote the resources necessary to track down the copyright holder for permission. The same would apply for a dated piece of music that almost no one has listened to for decades.

---

39   In an extreme case, ASCAP, the recording rights organization, once requested that the Girl Scouts pay fees for singing copyrighted songs at their campfires. See Bumiller (1996).

The costs of arranging permissions would dwarf the potential benefits from using it in a movie.

To get an idea of the magnitude of the expenses associated with copyright, many companies find it necessary to buy digital assessment management systems, which cost about $20,000, just to keep track of the items to which they have purchased access. [40] Legal fees from even inadvertent infringements can easily run into the tens of thousands of dollars. [41]

In the case of recorded music, the development of digital technology has had a substantial negative effect on revenue. This is arguably a positive development for the economy as a whole. Two studies (Rob and Waldfogel 2006 and Waldfogel 2010) examining the welfare effects of unauthorized copying of recorded music found net short-run welfare gains from unauthorized file sharing. While this may seem obvious, Handke cites several studies showing that the supply of recorded material actually increased following the widespread practice of file sharing. By looking at measures of "greatest hits," Waldfogel (2011) found no evidence of deterioration in quality as a result of widespread file sharing.

Another key question with copyrights is the appropriate duration. Most analysis tends to find that older works have relatively little value. Rappaport (1998) found that most copyrighted works were of little commercial value at the time of expiration, though a minority were still generating considerable revenue. Landes and Posner (2004) found that most copyright holders did not file to extend their copyright after the initial 28-year period expired. They note that in 2001 only 1.7 percent of the books published in 1930 were still in print.

Handke observes some unintended effects of copyright. For example, copyright restrictions may slow the spread of new hardware that could be complementary to recorded material. Also, copyrights may affect the mix of work that people consume in ways that favor more established

---

40   See, for example: https://www.thirdlight.com/articles/dam-cost.
41   See, for example: https://webdam.com/blog/true-costs-of-copyright-infringement/.

performers. The review cites several studies showing that less well known musicians had better sales and more attendance at live performances after file sharing became common. These studies are far from conclusive, but such an effect is plausible. In an experimental analysis, Salganik et al. (2006) found that people listened more frequently to music that they were told was popular. The implication is that marketing certain songs or musicians will increase the extent to which the public listens to them at the expense of musicians who are not favored. If copyright gives entertainment companies an incentive to promote certain performers, the public's choice in music will be skewed toward a narrower group of performers.

Copyright protection in the digital age has required increasingly punitive law enforcement measures and extraordinary efforts to inculcate respect for copyright monopolies. A Minnesota woman was fined $222,000 in 2007 for allowing 24 songs to be downloaded off of her hard drive through a peer-to-peer file-sharing system.[42] A provision of the Trans-Pacific Partnership requires that countries adopt criminal penalties for copyright infringement. In order to promote respect for copyright laws, an industry trade group even created a patch for Girl Scouts and a merit badge for Boy Scouts.[43]

These costs are in addition to the deadweight losses, which are definitionally associated with copyright monopolies, that raise the price above the marginal cost of production, and they are likely to be substantial relative to the amount paid to performers, writers, songwriters, and other creative workers. A recent analysis of the impact of the Trans-Pacific Partnership's copyright provisions in New Zealand placed the elasticity of demand for books at -1.77 and the elasticity of demand for recorded music at -1.41 (New Zealand Ministry of Business, Innovation, and Employment 2015). These estimates imply that for every dollar that copyright raises the price of books and recorded music, the effective cost to consumers in

---

42   See: http://abcnews.go.com/US/supreme-court-lets-verdict-stand-recording-
     industry-case/story?id=18765909.
43   See: http://www.ipoef.org/?page_id=30 and
     http://arstechnica.com/gadgets/2006/10/8044/.

higher prices and deadweight loss is $1.39 in the case of books and $1.22 in the case of recorded music. If creative workers gets 70 percent of the copyright margin in the case of recorded music (in other words, 70 percent of the mark-up associated with copyright goes to creative workers as opposed to promoters, marketing, and profits), this implies that the cost to consumers is $1.74 for every dollar that goes to creative workers. If the share going to creative workers is 50 percent, then the cost to consumers is almost $2.00 for every dollar going to creative workers.

Patents and copyrights are often used to protect software. Analyzing the success of open-source software, Lerner and Tirole (2000), focusing on the motivations of the individual developers, found that many of them are prepared to devote large amounts of time without any direct monetary reward. Instead, they perform the work out of intellectual curiosity or as a way to advance their reputation.

Bessen (2005) focuses on the willingness of companies to support open-source systems. The study argues that this support can be an efficient way to gain a number of programmers' insights into difficult problems that would not be addressed by standardized software. In this way, open-source software may be a useful complement to proprietary software and other services provided by a company. These insights help in assessing how technology can advance in the absence of patent or copyright protection.

In sum, there are clearly substantial costs associated with copyright protection, costs that have increased substantially as a result of digital technology. The response of the U.S. government has been to promote stronger and more punitive laws and to require third parties to share in enforcement costs.

Alternatives to the current patent system

The prior sections provide solid grounds for questioning the extent to which patent and copyright protection are efficient mechanisms for supporting innovation and creative work. While some research suggests that there is no need for any form of explicit government intervention to support innovation and creative work, it is likely that the market would undersupply both in the absence of some form of government support. This is especially likely to be the case in the areas where patents were found to provide the greatest subsidy for research: pharmaceuticals and medical equipment.[44] In these areas, survey results typically found that patents provided an effective subsidy in the range of 30 percent of the cost of research. By contrast, research on the value of patents in other sectors suggested that the subsidy provided by patents was generally in the range of 5 to 15 percent.

The higher implicit subsidy found for the pharmaceutical and medical supply industries suggests the need for different mechanisms to support research and innovation in these sectors. In these two industries, the patent is typically responsible for the bulk of the price of the product, often creating a large gap between the patent-protected price and the cost of production. The discussion below outlines a mechanism for direct public funding of research in these two industries, and then describes a modified patent system for all other sectors.

The rationale for public financing for pharmaceutical and medical equipment R&D

The importance of patents in the pharmaceutical and medical equipment industry is reflected in the large gap between patent-protected prices and the cost of production. As noted earlier, patent-protected drugs can sell at prices a hundred times higher than their generic equivalents. Medical equipment follows a similar pattern. The cost of manufacturing even the most complex scanning devices or other cutting-edge equipment will rarely be more than a few thousand dollars, yet patent protection allows these products to sell for hundreds of thousands or even millions of dollars. This cost is recouped in high prices paid by patients (or their insurers) for procedures that may have a trivial marginal cost.

---

44   Some studies have found large implicit subsidies for patents in the chemical industry, raising an argument for treating chemicals the same way as pharmaceuticals and medical equipment. However, because chemicals are mostly sold as an intermediate good, they do not raise the same set of issues as pharmaceuticals and medical equipment.

The large gap between price and marginal cost has exactly the sort of consequences that economic theory predicts. The first and most obvious is that many people are forced to get by without drugs that are actually produced at a low marginal cost.[45] Patients will also take less than the recommended dosage or skip days in order to reduce the cost of their drugs.

A simple calculation of the deadweight loss associated with patent protection of drugs indicates that patients incur substantial costs as a result of not being able to pay free market prices.[46] **Table 5-2** shows the deadweight loss based on 2016 expenditures of $450 billion, assuming alternatively that drugs would sell for 10 percent and 20 percent of their current prices if there were no patent or related protections.[47] The table applies elasticities of 15 percent, 25 percent, and 50 percent.

TABLE 5-2

Annual deadweight loss due to patent protection of drugs, based on 2016 expenditures of $450 billion

(billions of 2016 dollars)

	Elasticities		
	0.15	0.25	0.5
Free market price = 10 percent of current prices	$90.8	$171.2	$475.7
Free market price = 20 percent of current prices	$60.1	$109.0	$271.9

Source and notes: BEA (2016) and author's calculations, see text.

In the case where the elimination of patent protections reduces average drug prices by 80 percent, and elasticity is just 0.15, the deadweight loss from current protection would still be over $60 billion

---

45 Some patients don't take drugs due to their costs, resulting in adverse health outcomes. A recent study found substantial negative health effects of drug copayments in Canada among older people, even though the expected payments were relatively limited compared to what most patients would face in the United States. See Anis et al. (2005).

46 The deadweight loss represents the potential benefits that patients would have received from taking the drug, who did not do so because they had to pay the patent-protected price rather than the free market price.

47 The $450 billion is taken from BEA (2016), Table 2.4.5U, line 120. It increases the 2015 figure by 9.5 percent, the same increase as occurred between 2014 and 2015. The calculations assume a constant elasticity of substitution consumption function.

given 2016 demand and prices. In the case of a 90 percent drop the deadweight loss would be $90.8 billion at 0.15 elasticity and $171.2 billion at 0.25 elasticity.[48] These are substantial losses by any measure. The $90.8 billion loss would equal almost 0.5 percent of 2016 GDP, and the $171.2 billion loss would equal more than 0.9 percent.

In addition to the deadweight losses, patent protection also imposes substantial costs in the form of time and resources that are wasted as a result of patent protected prices. These costs take a variety of forms.

First, even where patients have insurance that covers the cost of expensive drugs, the high price often will lead the insurer to demand additional proof that the patient needs the drug in question. Insurers may require additional tests or a second opinion. The high cost of patent-protected drugs has created a whole industry of intermediaries — pharmacy benefit managers — who negotiate with drug companies on behalf of insurers, hospitals, and other institutions. There would be no need for this industry if drugs sold at free market prices.

Because the government is a big payer for drugs through Medicare, Medicaid, and other public health care programs, it can set standards that effectively determine how much private insurers pay. Thus, the pharmaceutical industry is heavily involved in lobbying, both through its own agents and through the consumer groups it mobilizes.[49] The

----

48 These calculations would understate the loss substantially insofar as the price declines are uneven. In effect, the assumption in the calculations is that the price of all drugs declines by 80 percent or 90 percent. The Food and Drug Administration (FDA) puts the reduction in the price of brand drugs in a mature generic market at more than 90 percent (FDA 2015). While many drugs are already available as generics, even these would often see large price declines in a free market. Some generics have the benefit of the six-month period of exclusivity as the first generic in the market. Also, in many cases generic manufacturers will still face licensing fees of various types, even if the main patent on a drug is no longer applicable. On the other side, the price decline for the most expensive drugs may be in excess of 99 percent. Using averages would understate the loss. Taking these differences into account would almost certainly lead to a larger measure of deadweight loss.

49 Pharmaceutical companies are often major funders of organizations established as support groups for victims of specific diseases and their families. These support groups are often encouraged to lobby insurers and the government to pay for

pharmaceutical industry ranked fifth in campaign contributions to members of Congress in 2016 (Center for Responsive Politics 2016a). The broader category of health-related industries ranked second, behind only finance, insurance, and real estate in total contributions to politicians (Center for Responsive Politics 2016b).

The efforts of drug companies to secure patent protection are not just a question of them getting more money at the expense of competitors or the general public. They may also be pursuing policies that are detrimental to public health. For example, pharmaceutical companies that produce pain relief medication have been leading the fight against medical marijuana, which has been shown to be an effective substitute for prescription pain medications (Ingraham 2016). There can be major consequences for public health as patients take stronger and more addictive medications when marijuana may be an effective treatment. Similarly, the industry uses its ties to patient advocacy groups to try to keep generic competitors from being covered by the government or insurers (Pollack 2016). This is the sort of corruption one would expect to find when there is a huge gap between the monopoly price and the cost of production.

Because so much money is at stake, pharmaceuticals are a prime target for litigation. Drug companies routinely bring suits to harass competitors, discourage generic competition, or gain a slice of the patent rents associated with a highly profitable drug. The pharmaceutical and medical equipment industries together accounted for almost a quarter of patent-related lawsuits from 1995 to 2014. The suits in the pharmaceutical sector had the highest median damage settlement, with medical equipment a close third just behind telecommunications (PricewaterhouseCoopers 2015).

In any legal battle over pharmaceuticals, where the brand drug manufacturer is defending the right to sell at a monopoly price for the duration of the patent and the potential generic entrant is looking for the right to sell in a competitive market, there is a fundamental asymmetry:

expensive drugs sold by the sponsoring pharmaceutical company. See, for example, Nuñez (2006).

the brand manufacturer stands to lose much more than the generic producer stands to gain. As a result, the brand producer has an incentive to spend much more on legal expenses, and it may be tempted to offer side payments to discourage entry by the generic competitor. Such collusion is illegal, but it is hard to detect, especially if the payment takes the form of a contract (e.g., the generic producer is paid to manufacture one of the brand manufacturer's drugs) that could have been reached without any collusion. A 2010 study by the Federal Trade Commission (FTC) estimated the annual cost to consumers of these "pay to delay" agreements at $3.5 billion (FTC 2010).[50]

Another problem with the large gap between price and marginal cost is that it provides an incentive for drug companies to conceal evidence that reflects poorly on its drugs. If they find evidence that their drug may not be as effective as claimed or possibly even harmful for some patients, the enormous gap between price and marginal cost gives them an incentive not to disclose this information. This was the allegation in the case of the arthritis drug Vioxx, where the manufacturer allegedly concealed evidence that the drug increased the risk of heart attack and stroke among patients with heart conditions. Drug companies also have an incentive to promote the use of their drug in situations where it may not be appropriate. Efforts to promote drugs for "off-label" use are a regular source of scandal in the business press.

A recent analysis that looked at five prominent instances in which it was alleged that drug companies either concealed information about their drugs or marketed them for inappropriate uses found that the cost born by patients was in the range of $27 billion annually over the years 1994–2008 (Katari and Baker 2015). While this estimate is far from precise, it suggests that the cost associated with improper drug use due to deliberate misrepresentations and mis-marketing is substantial, quite likely in the range of the amount spent by the industry on drug research. It is worth repeating that these costs, in terms of bad health outcomes, are the result of deliberate actions stemming from the perverse incentives created

---

50   The Public Interest Research Group compiled a list of 20 of the most important cases of this sort of pay for delay; see U.S. PIRG (2013).

by patent monopolies, not costs from the sort of mistakes that are an inevitable part of the research process.

Another issue with patent monopolies is that they distort the research process by encouraging drug companies to pursue patent rents rather than find drugs that meet urgent health needs. If a pharmaceutical company produces a drug for a particular condition that earns large amounts of revenue, its competitors have a strong incentive to try to produce similar drugs for the same condition, in order to capture a share of the rents.

For example, Merck and AbbVie, along with several smaller drug manufacturers, are rushing to market alternatives to Sovaldi as a treatment for hepatitis C.[51] In the context in which Gilead Sciences, the maker of Sovaldi, has a monopoly on effective treatments for hepatitis C, this sort of competition is highly desirable because it will lead to lower prices. However, if Sovaldi were being sold in a free market at $500 to $1,000 for a course of treatment, there would be little incentive to invest research dollars finding treatments for a condition for which an effective drug already exists. If drugs were sold without protection, research dollars would usually be better devoted to developing a drug for a condition where no effective treatment exists than developing duplicative drugs for a condition that can be well-treated by an existing drug.

Patent protection also is likely to slow and/or distort the research process by encouraging secrecy. Research advances most quickly when it is open. However, companies seeking profits through patent monopolies have incentive to disclose as little information as possible in order to avoid helping competitors. This pressure forces researchers to work around rather than build upon research findings. Williams (2010) found that the patenting of DNA sequences in the Human Genome Project slowed future innovation and product development by between 20 and 30 percent.

Finally, relying on patent incentives to support medical research encourages drug companies to direct research toward finding a patentable product. If, for example, evidence suggests that a condition can be most

---

51   See, for example: http://www.investopedia.com/ask/answers/052215/who-are-gilead-sciences-gild-main-competitors.asp.

effectively treated through diet, exercise, environmental factors, or even old off-patent drugs, a pharmaceutical manufacturer would have no incentive to pursue this research.[52] Ideally, the manufacturer would make this evidence publicly available so that researchers supported by the government, universities, or other nonprofit organizations could pursue it, but there is little incentive for them to go this route. In fact, if they are concerned that such research could lead to an alternative to a patentable product that they might develop or be in the process of developing, their incentive is to conceal the research.

For all of these reasons, patent-supported research is particularly ill-suited for the pharmaceutical sector, as well as for the medical equipment sector.[53] It is likely that a system of directly funded research, paid for by the government, would be considerably more efficient for the development of new drugs and medical equipment. Such a system is outlined in the next section.[54]

---

52 The United States and many other countries now allow for the patenting of a new use for an existing drug; however, there are still likely to be limits to the extent to which this might provide incentives for researching new uses of a drug. If it turned out that a common drug, like aspirin, was an effective treatment for some other condition, it would be very difficult to keep people from using the cheap generic versions for the newly discovered treatment, even if it violated the patent.

53 All the arguments made above on pharmaceuticals would also apply to research to develop medical equipment.

54 This discussion pursues the logic of directly funded research. There have been several proposals for creating a prize system for buying out patents and placing them in the public domain. While a prize system would have enormous advantages over the current system, most importantly because drugs would be available at their free market price, it shares some of the major drawbacks with the current patent system. Mainly, it would still encourage secrecy in the research process, because companies would have the same incentive as they do now to prevent their competitors from gaining the benefit of their research findings. The awarding of prizes may also prove problematic. The company that manages to patent a drug may not be the one responsible for the key scientific breakthroughs responsible for its development. In principle, prizes could be awarded for important intermediate steps, not just achieving a final endpoint, but this is likely to make the prize process complicated and contentious.

Publicly financed medical research

The basic logic of a system of publicly financed medical research would be that the government expand its current funding for biomedical research, which now goes primarily through the National Institutes of Health, by an amount roughly equal to the patent-supported research now conducted by the pharmaceutical industry. PhRMA, the industry trade group, puts this funding at roughly $50 billion a year, or 0.3 percent of GDP, a figure that is also consistent with data from the National Science Foundation. That would be a reasonable target, with the idea that public funding would eventually replace patent-supported funding.[55] Adding in research on medical equipment and tests would increase this figure by $12–15 billion (National Science Foundation 2012).

In order to minimize the risk of political interference and also the risk that excessive bureaucracy could impede innovation, the bulk of this funding should be committed to private firms under long-term contracts (e.g., 10–15 years).[56] This practice would allow for the imposition of clear rules that apply to all research directly or indirectly funded by the public sector, without a need for micro-management. The contracts would be subject to regular oversight for their duration, but the contractors would be free to set priorities for which lines of research to support. The contractors could freely subcontract, and they could use

---

55 It would be necessary to have some system of international coordination so that the United States was not funding research for the whole world. This would presumably involve some payments scaled to GDP, with richer countries paying a larger share of their income. While there would undoubtedly be some problems working through such a system, the current system of imposing patent and related protections on U.S. trading partners has been quite contentious.

56 The use of private drug companies also has a potentially valuable benefit from a political economy standpoint. There is no reason that the existing pharmaceutical companies could not bid for public research money, as long as they are prepared to abide by the conditions placed on this funding. This means that insofar as they are efficient in their conduct of research, they would be able to continue to exist and profit on this sort of system. This should reduce their political opposition to an alternative funding mechanism. But insofar as their expertise is primarily in marketing rather than developing drugs, they would run into difficulties under this alternative system.

their funds to buy research produced by other companies, just as the major pharmaceutical companies do now. As the period for a contract approached its end, the contractor could attempt to gain a new long-term contract. It would argue its case based on its track record with the prior contract.

The rules governing these contracts would dictate that all results stemming from publicly financed research be placed in the public domain, subject to "copyleft"-type restrictions. [57] Thus, any patents for drugs, research tools, or other intermediate steps developed by contractors or subcontractors would be freely available for anyone to use, subject to the condition that any subsequent patents would also be placed in the public domain. Similarly, test results used to get approval for a drug from the Food and Drug Administration would be available for any generic producer to use to gain approval for their own product.

In addition to requiring that patents be placed in the public domain, there would also be a requirement that all research findings be made available to the public as quickly as practical. This means, for example, that results from pre-clinical testing be made available as soon as they are known. This requirement should prevent duplication and allow for more rapid progress in research, and would apply to both direct contractors and any subcontractors. [58]

This disclosure requirement would not be a negative for participants in the context of this open-source contract system. Because the goal is to generate useful innovations rather than procure a patent, a contractor would be able to make an effective case for the usefulness of its work even if competitors were the ones that ultimately used the work to develop a useful drug or medical device. The incentive in this system is to

---

57 Copyleft is a type of copyright developed by the Free Software Movement, under which a copyrighted software can be freely used as long as any derivative software is also put in the public domain subject to the same condition. See: https://www.gnu.org/licenses/copyleft.en.html.

58 This is the sort of issue that would be examined in periodic reviews of contractors. Excessive delays by a contractor in posting findings on an ongoing basis would be grounds for revoking the contract. Contractors would also be held responsible for the behavior of any subcontractors, which would also be bound by the requirement to post findings in a timely manner.

disseminate any interesting findings as widely as possible in the hope that other researchers will build upon them.

The contracting system in the Defense Department offers a model for contracting in pharmaceutical research. When the Defense Department is planning a major project, such as a new fighter plane or submarine, it will typically contract with a major corporation like General Electric or Lockheed Martin that in turn subcontracts much of the project, because it is not prepared to do all the work in-house. Contractors conducting research developing pharmaceuticals or medical equipment could do the same, although the expected results will be somewhat less clearly specified. While less well-defined outcomes are a disadvantage of contracting with medical research, a major advantage is that there would be no excuse for secrecy. Military research requires secrecy to prevent access to the latest technology by potential enemies, but biomedical research will be advanced by allowing the greatest possible access. Secrecy has often been an important factor allowing military contractors to conceal waste or fraud, because only a very select group of people would have access to the specific terms of a contract and the nature of the work a company is doing. In the case of bio-medical research, there is no reason that the terms of the contract would not be fully public. And, all research findings would have to be posted in a timely manner. With such rules, it should be possible to quickly identify any contractor whose output clearly did not correspond to the money they were receiving from the government. In spite of the instances of waste and fraud in military contracting, it is important to remember that it has been effective in giving the United States the most technologically advanced military in the world.[59] In other words, direct contracting has accomplished its purpose even in a context that should be much less favorable to it than bio-medical research.

Because the system of patent protection and rules on data exclusivity are now enshrined in a large number of international agreements that would be difficult to circumvent, it is important that an

---

59   This is not a comment on the actions of the U.S. military; it is simply noting its technological capabilities.

alternative system work around this structure. As proposed here, patent protection under current rules would still be available to drug companies conducting research with their own funds. However, they would run the risk that at the point when they have a drug approved by the Food and Drug Administration (FDA), there is a new drug available at generic prices that is comparably effective. This sort of competition would likely force the company to sell its drug at a price comparable to the generic, leaving it little margin for recouping its research costs.

The risk of this sort of generic competition should make the current system of patent-financed drug development unprofitable, especially if the industry's claims about its research costs are anywhere close to being accurate. So the existing rules on patents could be left in place, even as a new system of publicly financed research comes to dominate drug development.

The cost-benefit arithmetic of an alternative system

The arithmetic summing the extra costs, deadweight losses, and wasteful rent-seeking behavior associated with patents, compared with the amount of actual research that is funded, suggests the opportunity for large gains through an alternative system. The first and most obvious advantage is that all the drugs and medical equipment developed through this process would be immediately available at free market prices. Instead of costing hundreds of thousands of dollar a year, breakthrough cancer drugs might cost $1,000 a year, or even less. The cost would be the price of safely manufacturing these drugs and with very few exceptions, that cost would be quite low. With drugs selling at prices that even middle-income families could readily afford, the whole industry of middle-men that has grown up around mediating between the drug companies and insurers, hospitals, and patients would disappear. There would be no need for it.

This would also end the horror stories that many patients must now endure as they struggle to find ways to pay for expensive drugs even as they suffer from debilitating or potentially fatal diseases. Doctors also would not be forced to compromise in prescribing a drug they consider inferior because it will be covered by a patient's insurance when the preferred drug is not. Also, doctors would likely make better informed prescribing decisions because no one would stand to profit by having them prescribe a drug that may not provide the best treatment for their patient.

A similar story would apply to the use of medical equipment. In almost all cases, the cost of manufacturing the most modern medical equipment is relatively cheap. The cost of usage is even less. For example, the most modern screening equipment only involves a small amount of electricity a limited amount of a skilled technician's time, and the time of a doctor to review the scan. Instead of a scan costing thousands of dollars, the cost would likely be no more than $200–300. Here also, the price would then be a minor factor in deciding how best to treat a patient. A doctor would naturally recommend the device that best meets the patient's needs. And in a context where no one has an incentive to mislead about the quality of the equipment, the doctor is likely to make better choices. The same would be the case with various lab tests, all of which would be available at their free market price. With few exceptions, this would be a trivial expense compared to the current system.

Table 5-3 shows the potential gains from replacing patent-supported research with direct public funding under three sets of assumptions. The most optimistic scenario, shown in column 1, assumes that 75 cents of public spending on research is roughly equivalent to $1 of spending financed by patent monopolies. The greater efficiency is based on the idea that increased openness and the elimination of unnecessary duplication will lead to more effective research. It also assumes that prescription drugs would sell for 10 percent of their current price if there were no patent or related protections.[60] In this case, the implied annual savings would be $349.5 billion. Adding in the reduction in deadweight loss from the high elasticity case shown in Table 5-2 brings the total benefits to more than $800 billion a year, equal to 4.3 percent of GDP.

---

60   With some drugs the price may be high not because the compound itself is subject to patent protection but because one of the inputs is. The implicit assumption in this discussion is that the inputs would also be in the public domain because they would have been produced with public funding.

TABLE 5-3

Gains from ending patent protection for pharmaceuticals and medical equipment

(billions of 2016 dollars)

	High savings	Middle savings	Low savings
Drugs			
Current spending	$430.0	$430.0	$430.0
Patent-free cost	$43.0	$64.5	$86.0
Additional research	$37.5	$50.0	$75.0
Net savings	**$349.5**	**$315.5**	**$269.0**
Reduction in deadweight loss	$475.7	$140.1	60.1
Total savings	$825.2	$455.6	$329.1
Medical equipment			
Current spending	$50.4	$50.4	$50.4
Patent-free cost	$15.1	$15.1	$15.1
Additional research	$11.2	14.9	$22.4
Net savings	**$24.1**	**$20.4**	**$12.9**

Source and notes: BEA (2016) and author's calculations; see text. For medical equipment, the 2016 spending level is a projection from the Centers for Medicare and Medicaid Services (CMS). The estimate for current research spending is taken from data for 2012 from the National Science Foundation and increased by 20 percent to account for growth between 2012 and 2016.

Column 2 shows an intermediate scenario in which $1 of public money for research is needed to replace $1 of patent-supported research. This case assumes that prescription drugs would cost 15 percent as much to produce as they do today if all patent and related protections were eliminated. In this case the savings would be $315.5 billion. Adding in the reduction in deadweight loss brings the total net benefit to more than $450 billion a year.

Column 3 shows a scenario in which it takes $1.50 of public money to replace $1 of patent-supported research. This ratio implies that because money is going through the government, the research process becomes hugely less efficient than is currently the case. This is in spite of the fact that the research is now fully open, so that all researchers can benefit quickly from new findings, and a main motivation for unnecessary duplicative research has been eliminated. This scenario assumes that it would cost 20 percent as much to manufacture drugs in a world without patent and related protections as is the case at present. In this scenario, the savings would still be $269 billion annually or 1.5 percent of GDP. Adding in the reduction in deadweight loss from the most inelastic scenario would put the total net benefit at $329 billion annually.

The next set of rows shows the benefits from publicly funded research for medical equipment. The assumption in all three cases is that the cost of buying and using this equipment would fall by 70 percent if it were sold in a free market. The optimistic scenario assumes that 75 cents in publicly funded research is equivalent to a dollar of patent-supported research, the middle scenario assumes they are equally effective, and the pessimistic scenario assumes that $1.50 in publicly funded research is needed to replace $1.00 in patent-supported research. In these cases, the net annual savings would range from $12.9 billion to be $24.1 billion.[61]

While publicly financed research would require the government to directly commit funding for research, additional tax revenue should not be necessary. The government already directly or indirectly pays for a large portion of prescription drug expenditures through Medicare, Medicaid, and various other health care programs. In addition, it effectively subsidizes private spending on drugs as a result of the tax deductibility of employer-provided health insurance and other expenses. **Table 5-4** shows the Centers for Medicare and Medicaid Services (CMS) projections for 2016 spending on prescription drugs and medical equipment by source (CMS 2014) as well as the assumed savings.

For Medicaid and other government programs, the assumed savings are 50 percent on both drugs and medical equipment, based on the fact that these programs typically pay substantially lower prices for drugs than do private insurers. In the case of Medicare, the savings are 70 percent on drugs and 50 percent on medical equipment, under the assumption that insurers within the program pay somewhat lower prices for drugs than do insurers not connected with Medicare. In the case of

---

61   Even these calculations don't fully capture the potential benefits from selling drugs in a free market. Centers for Medicare and Medicaid Services (CMS) projects that private insurers will pay just over $150 billion for prescription drugs and medical equipment in 2016. With insurance expenses averaging more than 20 percent of benefits paid out, a fall in these combined payments of $100 billion would imply savings of more than $20 billion in the administrative costs of insurers.

private insurers and out-of-pocket payments, it is assumed that savings to the government will equal 16 percent of current payments for drugs and 14 percent for medical equipment, based on drug prices falling 80 percent if not subject to patent protection and prices for medical equipment falling 70 percent. The calculation further assumes that 20 percent of this savings accrues to the government in the form of higher tax revenue, because taxpayers will deduct less money for health care expenditures.

TABLE 5-4

Savings to the government from publicly supported research for pharmaceuticals and medical equipment

(billions of 2016 dollars)

| | Total | Out-of-pocket payments | Health insurance | | | | | |
			Total	Private health insurance	Medicare	Medicaid	Other health insurance programs	Other third-party payers
Projected								
Spending	$342.1	$48.3	$291.8	$142.0	$105.2	$33.8	$10.8	$2.0
Savings	$126.4	$7.7		$22.7	$73.6	$16.9	$5.4	
Medical equipment								
Spending	$50.4	$24.7	$25.0	$8.9	$8.5	$7.4	$0.1	$0.6
Savings	$12.7	$3.5		$1.2	$4.3	$3.7	$0.1	
Total savings	$139.1							

Source and notes: CMS (2014) and author's calculations, see text.

Even with these relatively conservative assumptions, the savings to the government based on the 2016 projections would still be over $139 billion,[62] which substantially exceeds the amount of public funding that

---

62   These calculations are based on CMS projections of spending on prescription drugs. Data from the Bureau of Economic Analysis (BEA) show spending levels that are more than 30 percent higher. A calculation of savings based on BEA spending levels would therefore be correspondingly higher.

would be needed to replace patent-supported research in even the most pessimistic scenario described above. In other words, there would be no need for additional tax revenue even in a relatively pessimistic scenario.

It is possible that there could be some short-term need for additional funding due to the lag between research spending and the development of new drugs. At least initially, there would be no savings from publicly funded research because all the drugs being sold would still be subject to the same protections as they enjoy today. The savings would accrue over time, as new drugs were produced through the public system and were sold at free market prices. For this reason, a switch to direct public funding of research may initially increase budget deficits while leading to substantial savings soon and over a period of time.

Publicly funded clinical trials

Switching all at once to a system of publicly funded research would likely be a difficult step politically and practically, involving a radical transformation of a massive industry of a kind rarely seen in the United States or anywhere else. Fortunately, there is an intermediate step toward a system of fully funded research that would offer enormous benefits in its own right.

There is a simple and basic divide between the pre-clinical phase of drug development and the clinical phase. The pre-clinical phase involves the development of new drugs or new uses of existing drugs and preliminary tests on lab animals. The clinical phase involves testing on humans and, if results warrant, proceeding to the FDA approval process. The clinical testing phase accounts for more than 60 percent of spending on research, although this number is reduced if a return is imputed on the pre-clinical testing phase, because there is a considerably longer lag between pre-clinical expenditures and an approved drug than with clinical tests.

The clinical testing process involves standard procedures and is therefore far more routinized than the pre-clinical phase. For this reason, it could be easily adapted to a program of direct public funding. The model could be the same as discussed earlier, with the government contracting on a long-term basis with existing or new drug companies, but the contracts would specify the testing of drugs in particular areas. All results would be fully public, and all patent and related rights associated with the testing would be put in the public domain subject to copyleft-type rules. This procedure would likely mean that contracting companies might have to buy rights to a compound before initiating testing.

Separating out the clinical testing portion of drug development rather than fully replacing patent-supported research all at once has several advantages. First, particular areas of investigation could be segregated out for experimentation. For example, it should be possible to set aside a certain amount of funding for clinical trials for new cancer or heart drugs without fully replacing private support for research in these areas. Also, it should be possible to obtain dividends much more quickly in the form of new drugs being available at generic prices. The time lag between the beginning of pre-clinical research and an approved drug can be 20 years, but the clinical testing process typically takes about eight years and can be less if a drug's benefits become quickly evident in trials.

Another important early dividend from public funding of clinical trials is that the results would be posted as soon as they are available, meaning that researchers and doctors would have access not only to the summary statistics showing the success rates in the treatment group relative to the control group, but also to the data on specific individuals in the trial.[63] This access would allow them to independently analyze the data to look for differences in outcomes based on age, gender, or other factors. It would also allow for researchers to determine the extent to which interactions with other drugs affected the effectiveness of a new drug.

In addition, the public disclosure of test results may put pressure on the pharmaceutical industry to change some bad practices. The problem of misreporting or concealing results in order to promote a drug can arise during clinical testing. While misrepresented results can be a

---

63   Some information on individuals may have to be put into categories (e.g., age ranges rather than specific ages) in order to preserve the anonymity of patients. With rare diseases, these categories may have to be fairly broad, but it will still be possible to disclose more information than is currently available.

problem at any stage in the process, misrepresentations at the pre-clinical phase are unlikely to have health consequences because they will be uncovered in clinical testing. The problem of patients being prescribed drugs that are less effective than claimed or possibly harmful to certain patients due to misrepresentations occurs entirely during the clinical phase. If experiments with a limited number of publicly funded clinical trials can change the norms on disclosure of test results, they will have made an enormous contribution to public health.

Potential benefits from upfront funding and marginal cost pricing

While the savings shown in Table 5-3 are substantial, savings may not be the most important benefit from adopting a system of upfront research funding and marginal cost pricing. If drugs, scans, and tests were all sold in a free market, almost all would be relatively cheap, and all but the lowest-income households would be able to afford the drugs and tests considered beneficial to their health. The elimination of this potential financial burden would be an enormous benefit.

In addition, there are good reasons to believe that a switch to a system of marginal cost pricing with fully open research will lead to better health outcomes. First, the current system of patent monopolies provides drug companies, manufacturers of medical equipment, and proprietary testing companies with an enormous incentive to misrepresent the benefits of their products and conceal potential negatives. If all of these items were sold in a free market where competition had pushed profits down to normal levels, there would be little incentive to misrepresent the safety and/or effectiveness of a product in order to boost sales. The additional profit from increased sales in a competitive market does not provide the same sort of incentive for corruption as the opportunity to sell more of a product at monopoly prices.

The other reason why an alternative system of open research should lead to better outcomes is that the evidence for effectiveness of a drug or procedure would be directly available to doctors and researchers rather than held in secret by a drug company or medical equipment manufacturer. Doctors will be able to make decisions that focus on the specific situation of their patients. If more than one drug is available for treating a condition, a doctor will have access to evidence about relative effectiveness for men versus women, or for overweight people, or people with other health conditions, allowing the doctor to make more-informed decisions for treating patients.

Also, it is possible that better drugs and equipment will be available if openness allows research to advance more quickly. If open research turns out to advance more quickly, as some studies have indicated, the move away from patent-supported research may hasten the invention of treatments and cures for a wide variety of conditions.

In addition to the benefits to patients and savings for government, a system of marginal cost pricing will yield substantial savings to the economy. The massive marketing industry that has developed to promote sales of drugs would disappear, freeing up resources for productive uses. Lawyers specializing in intellectual property tend to be among the most highly paid members of the profession, and with marginal cost pricing the number of lawyers and lobbyists required for court contests and K Street negotiations would plummet. If the demand for lawyers to press or defend patent suits in prescription drugs declined it would free up a substantial share of these lawyers to pursue other lines of work.

Marginal cost pricing also would reduce the amount of money flowing through the health care insurance industry. On average, insurers take over 24 percent of the money paid to providers to cover administrative costs and provide their profit. [64] Reducing spending on drugs and medical equipment by $100 billion annually would imply savings on administrative expenses of more than $20 billion a year.

---

64   This calculation comes from taking the $194.6 billion estimate for the net cost of administering health insurance in 2014 from CMS (2014), national health expenditures data for 2014 (Table 2), and dividing it by $796.4 billion, the CMS estimate for 2014 payments by insurance companies after subtracting administrative expenses (Table 3).

Non-patent-supported research outside of the health care sector

While the abuses and inefficiencies of the patent system have the greatest consequence in the prescription drug industry and other health sectors, similar problems arise elsewhere. In most other sectors, patents are less important for supporting research and innovation because factors such as a first-mover advantage and complementary services tend to be more important in giving companies an edge. In this context, it might be desirable to preserve the patent system but reduce its importance.

As noted earlier, a number of trade agreements commit the United States to a set of rules, including 20-year patent duration, which would preclude simply altering the basic structure of the patent system. However, the government can incentivize firms to accept weaker patent rules. Because some of the worst abuses stem from patent trolls who make dubious legal claims based on older patents, a major reform would be a reduction in the period of patent duration (Love 2013). A patent length of three to five years would allow firms to protect their use of new technologies for a limited period while giving patent trolls little opportunity to dredge up old patents to extort successful innovators.

What kinds of incentives would convince firms to accept a shorter patent duration? One possibility is an expanded R&D tax credit.[65] The current credit is constructed as a marginal credit of 14–20 percent of R&D expenditures in excess of spending over a prior base period; as currently structured it costs $18 billion annually, as of 2016, or 0.1 percent of GDP.[66] This general credit could be eliminated and replaced with a credit of 10–15 percent of all R&D expenditures, allowed on the condition that all patents claimed by the company are open to the public under the copyleft rules after three to five years. After that, any company could make use of the patent, provided it also agreed to the shorter duration. Such rules would still allow corporations to have the full 20-year patent

---

65 Dechezlepretre et al. (2016) provide evidence on the effectiveness of the R&D tax credit as currently structured in promoting research spending.

66 The structure of the tax as well as the estimate of the cost can be found in CBO (2015b).

term required under trade agreements, but they would have to forego the R&D tax credit and free access to material subject to copyleft patents.

This set of incentives should provide a mix that is roughly comparable to that provided by the current patent system and tax credit. **Table 5-5** shows the National Science Foundation's estimates of R&D spending by sector for 2012, the most recent year available. Total spending was about 1.9 percent of GDP; removing spending by pharmaceuticals and other health related industries reduces this share to 1.45 percent.[67] A tax credit of 10–15 percent would cost between 0.15 percent and 0.22 percent of GDP if the take-up rate were 100 percent, but this assumption is clearly too high. More likely, 60–80 percent of spending would be covered by this system, implying a cost between 0.09 percent and 0.18 percent of GDP, or between $16 billion and $29 billion in the 2016 economy. At the low end, this is about the cost of the current R&D tax credit, at the high end it is about 50 percent more. If this system led to a comparable amount of research, the benefits to the economy should exceed the additional expense.

TABLE 5-5

Medical and non-medical R& D expenditures

(billions of 2012 dollars)

	2012	GDP shares	Tax credit 10%	15%
GDP	$16,155.3			
Total	**$302.3**	**1.87%**	**30.2**	**45.3**
Pharmaceuticals and medicines	$48.1	0.30%	4.8	7.2
Navigational, measuring, electromedical, and control instruments (50%)	$8.0	0.05%	0.8	1.2
Electromedical, electrotherapeutic, and other irradiation apparatus	$4.4	0.03%	0.4	0.6
Biotechnology	$7.4	0.05%	0.7	1.1
All other	$234.425	1.45%	0.15%	0.22%

Source and notes: National Science Foundation (2012).

---

67   This calculation counts 50 percent of the spending in the category "navigational, measuring, electromedical, and control instruments" as being health related.

Figure 5-1 compares the spending implied from this alternative tax credit to the expenses from the current patent system. The expenses shown are the annual costs of patent applications, the litigation costs of defending patent suits, and the annual cost of settlements as estimated by Bessen and Meurer.[68] (All numbers are scaled to 2016 GDP.)

FIGURE 5-1

Expenses associated with patents versus the cost of the tax credit

Source and notes: Bessen and Meurer (2012), Boldrin and Levine (2013), and author's calculations; see text.

In the low-end estimate, the tax credit would imply modest savings compared to the current credit.[69] At the high end, the additional cost of the credit would be $11 billion in the 2016 economy. Working off of the Levine and Boldrin calculation, companies would spend more than one-fifth of this amount just on the filing of patents. While firms would still have motivation to apply for patents under this alternative system, the incentive would be diminished, so the number of patent applications

---

68 The $5 billion estimate of defendants' litigation costs in suits initiated by NPEs is multiplied by four to include the plaintiffs' expenses and to account for the cost of lawsuits that do not stem from NPEs.

69 This is not entirely accurate, because a portion of the current credit goes to firms in the health care sector.

would likely fall sharply. The cost of litigation derived from Bessen and Meurer (2012) in the 2016 economy is $20.3 billion — almost twice as much as the high-end net cost of the tax credit. The cost of settlements with patent trolls is $28.6 billion, two-and-a-half times as much as the high-end cost of the credit.

These calculations suggest that the economy would be substantially better off with a system that relied more on tax credits and less on patent protection to support research. Of course, the costs from patent litigation would not fall to zero even in a scenario where tax-credit support became the dominant mode for financing research. There would still be some litigation even associated with the shorter patents and the government would have to be prepared to protect its patents for the duration of the copyleft period. In addition, some firms will opt to remain outside the tax-credit system.

But the increased competition from having fewer items subject to patent protection is likely to mean lower prices in a range of areas. And having more research freely available to innovators is likely to hasten the pace of innovation, particularly by smaller firms and start-ups for whom patent rights, and the negotiation of them, is a major expense. If small firms could count on supporting more of their own research through a tax credit, they could innovate in the areas dominated now by large firms and have less fear that a competitor might expose them to costly litigation.

This dual-track public and private system will require provisions to prevent gaming. Companies might exploit the free access to technology and the R&D tax credit to secure for themselves a full 20-year patent. It would be all but impossible, for instance, to police the separation whereby some parts of a firm are getting the tax credit and access but other parts are ostensibly fully funding their own research and are thereby entitled to long patents. To prevent this, the receipt of the tax credit and free access to copyleft material by any subsidiary of a firm would preclude 20-year patent protection for the whole firm. Similarly, the rules on short patents would have to apply to companies and patents purchased by a firm that was within the tax-credit/copyleft system.

If the incentives are structured properly, though, few large firms would find it advantageous to stay outside the system. The access to the tax credit and the free use of copyleft material should far exceed the potential benefits of additional years of patent protection. As a result, it would be difficult to envision a company like Google or General Electric remaining outside the system. Also, the ability of larger companies to benefit from the network effect of having their technology widely adopted would provide a further incentive to go with the tax-credit/copyleft system.

Wide adoption of the tax-credit/copyleft system would drastically reduce the number of patent suits and narrow the space of operation for patent trolls, simply in terms of the odds. If the short patent associated with the tax-credit system were five years, and everyone was in the system, then the number of patents in force at a point in time would drop by 75 percent.[70] If the patent were three years, then the drop would be 85 percent, even before taking into account the likely collapse in the number of patents in pharmaceuticals and medical equipment when direct public funding largely replaces patent monopolies in these sectors.

In fact, the actual decline in the number of patents in effect is likely to be even larger. Because the life of the patent will have been shortened, patents will be of less value. Therefore many companies may opt not to patent inventions that they would patent under the current system. The net result of this change would be far fewer resources getting wasted in filing patents and patent suits and far less concern on the part of innovative companies and individual inventors over the risk of being sued for patent infringement.

It will be necessary for the government to be vigilant in protecting the patents subject to copyleft rules, both in the case of patents that grew out of research supported by the tax credit and also patents that resulted from direct public funding in the health care sector. Enforcement of these patents would be a great activity to be contracted out to private law firms paid largely on commission. This would minimize the risk that corporations could use their power to stay outside of the public funding

---

70 This calculation assumes that the number of patents issued each year is constant.

and tax-credit system and still gain free access to the technology developed through these systems. [71]

While the shortening of patent durations in most sectors is not likely to lead to the same collapse of prices that the ending of patent monopolies would cause in the health care sector, it should result in more competition and innovation, along with some drop in prices. There would be more pressure on larger established companies to constantly innovate and improve their products, because they could not count on a lengthy period of patent monopolies to protect them from competitors. In addition, the free access to a vast amount of technology on a copyleft basis to both large firms and smaller start-ups should accelerate the process of innovation.

This system is likely to disproportionately benefit smaller firms because they would not need the legal resources to protect their patents nor to protect themselves against infringement suits. Also, the free access to copylefted technology is likely to be more of an asset to smaller firms that don't have the in-house capacity to negotiate contracts allowing for the use of patents held by other firms. While it may be a relatively simple matter for an Amazon or an Apple to work out a licensing arrangement to gain access to patented technology, this is likely to be a much more difficult process for a small start-up without a sophisticated legal department. For this reason, having ready access to the technology that is copylefted should be a major advantage.

An alternative to copyright monopolies

The clear path of copyright policy over the last four decades has been longer and stronger protection. Today, digital technology is posing a particular challenge. The law has been repeatedly adjusted to make it more difficult to use digital technologies and the web to reproduce material subject to copyright protection. In some cases technologies have

---

71   There is risk that law firms given the responsibility for enforcing copyleft patents could act like patent trolls. But the opportunities for public accountability and the option of non-renewal of contracts should limit this risk.

been blocked until effective locks could be developed to prevent unauthorized reproductions.[72]

Enforcement of protections for digital material has also meant imposing responsibilities on third parties. Recent laws require intermediaries to remove copyrighted material from their sites when they have been alerted by the copyright holders. A striking aspect of these laws is that intermediaries are liable if they do not promptly remove the material after being notified by the copyright holder; the intermediary is in effect forced to side with the entity making the copyright claim against its customer. The entertainment industry has also pushed measures to require intermediaries to proactively search their sites for unauthorized versions of copyrighted material.

This strengthening of copyright law and altering its structure to adjust to digital technology and the Internet is interesting not only because of the costs involved for the larger economy but also because it highlights alternative ways in which society adapts to technological change. Technological change has destroyed many sectors of the economy. The spread of digital cameras essentially destroyed the traditional film industry, causing the collapse of two major U.S. corporations, Kodak and Polaroid, and leading to the loss of tens of thousands of jobs. While the collapse of these companies and the job losses were unfortunate, no one would have considered it a reasonable strategy to block the spread of digital cameras.

On the other hand, when the development of digital technologies and the Internet threatened the business model of the entertainment industry, the response was to pass laws to contain these technologies to preserve the sector's mode of doing business. This is a great example of how it is not technology itself that is determining the distribution of income, but rather how various interest groups are able to write the laws governing the use of technology.

---

72 There was a major debate in the 1990s around the introduction of digital audio recorders. In response to lawsuits, the major manufacturers agreed to include locks to prevent duplication of copyrighted material. See, for example: https://partners.nytimes.com/library/tech/98/10/cyber/cyberlaw/16law.html.

Like patents, copyright terms are protected by international agreements. However, it is possible to develop a comparable system or alternative funding to work around the copyright system. It is important that the system respect individuals' choices in supporting music, books, movies, and other types of creative work rather than having a government agency decide which work should be supported. For this purpose, an individual tax credit would be appropriate.

The model for a tax credit to support creative work could be the tax deduction for charitable giving. It allows individuals to make tax-deductible contributions to religious, educational, social assistance, and cultural organizations with minimum interference from the government. In effect, the government is subsidizing the contribution at the taxpayer's marginal tax rate, which is 39.6 percent for the highest-income taxpayers. Because the deduction is not capped, it is limited only by the size of the taxpayer's tax liability (i.e. it is not refundable).

To qualify for tax-deductible contributions, an organization need only file with the IRS and indicate the sort of tax-deductible activity in which it is engaged. The IRS does not attempt to determine whether an organization is "good" as a religious organization or as a provider of food to the poor; that determination is left to the taxpayer. The only concern for the IRS is that the organization is in fact engaged in the activity that provides the basis for its tax-deductible status and that it is not engaged in prohibited activities such as political campaigning or profit making ventures.

Eligibility to receive funds through a creative work tax credit would work much the same way. Individuals or organizations would register to be eligible to receive funds by indicating the type of creative work in which they engaged as individuals or supported as organizations. This means that individuals would indicate that they are writers, musicians, video producers or engaged in some other type of creative work. The only issue from the standpoint of the IRS (or any other enforcement agency) would be whether the person is in fact engaged in the activity and whether the organization used its funding to support the type of creative work it claimed to support. In other words, if an organization claimed to support the writing of mystery novels or jazz music, then the concern would be whether they had actually used their funds for this purpose.

Because this system is intended to be an alternative to the copyright system, the condition for getting funding for both individuals and organizations is that they not would be eligible for copyright protection. In effect, creative workers would be given the option of relying on one or the other system of support. They could choose to rely on copyrights to support their work or they could opt to join the tax-credit system, but they could not do both. In order to ensure that the tax-credit system did not become a copyright farm system, in which people established their reputations in the tax-credit system and then cashed in with the copyright system, there should be a substantial gap (e.g., five years) between the last time creative workers received funding through the tax-credit system and when they could first receive copyright protection.

A convenient feature of this system is that it would be largely self-enforcing. A person who attempted to secure copyright protection on material for which he or she was not eligible would have the burden of suing the alleged infringer. Because there would be a registry of everyone in the tax-credit system, it would be a simple matter to show that the creative worker had been in the system too recently to qualify for copyright protection. In this case, there is no need for the government to do anything — it protects the integrity of the tax-credit system by doing nothing; the person does not have an enforceable copyright.

From the standpoint of individual taxpayers, the tax-credit system would specify a limited sum (e.g., $100) that they could give to individuals or organizations registered as eligible recipients. This means they could give their tax credit directly to a writer, singer, musician, or other creative worker that is in the system or they could contribute to organizations that are within the system and are committed to supporting particular types of creative work. Individual taxpayers would have the option to give the tax credit to a single individual or organization or divide it up among as many individuals as they choose. One major difference with the tax deduction for charitable contributions is that the tax credit would be refundable, meaning that every person would have the option to support creative work of their choosing, even if they had no tax liability.

There would be some risk of fraud, just as there is with the charitable deduction. However, the risks are likely to be considerably smaller with the tax credit than with the charitable deduction because the sums involved per person would be much smaller. If a high-income person contributes $1 million to a bogus charity, he or she receives an effective tax subsidy of $396,000 that the charity and the individual could, in principle, split between them. A $100 tax credit would require 40,000 people to scam the government by the same amount.

A mechanism for preventing simple frauds would be to require a modest minimum level of funding for a person or organization to be eligible to receive any funds. Requiring that an individual has a floor of at least $3,000 and an organization of $10,000 would largely prevent simple trade-off arrangements whereby people agree to give each other their credits. Coordinated tax credit swapping might still be possible, but it would require a considerable amount of coordination, and therefore risk for a relatively small payout.

A credit of $100 opted for by 90 percent of the adult population (a high percentage, but this is free money) would generate more than $22 billion a year to support books, movies, music, and other creative work. This amount would vastly exceed the amount currently going to creative workers through the copyright system, although it would total far less than the current subsidy for charitable contributions, which is likely in the neighborhood of at least $54 billion in 2016.[73]

---

73   The CBO estimated the size of this subsidy at $40.9 billion for 2006 (CBO 2011). Adjusting for the growth of the economy would put it at $54 billion in 2016. This is likely an understatement, since the tax rate for high-income taxpayers rose from 35 percent to 39.6 percent in 2013. As a result, a contribution of the same dollar amount would imply a substantially larger tax subsidy in 2016 than it did prior to 2013.

An issue that would naturally arise with this system is its scope. For example, should journalism be included as a type of creative work? [74] How about video games or software?

The logic of the system would suggest that the boundaries be drawn broadly, for two reasons. First, it would be difficult if not impossible to police the boundaries. If a person were being supported for writing non-fiction books but also posted weekly or daily pieces on the web on political events, would he or she be violating the rules if the system was not intended to support journalism? There would be a similar story with video games. At what point would interactive art become a video game? Do we want the IRS making this assessment?

The second point in favor of broad boundaries is that they would minimize the need for copyright protection. The goal of the creative work tax credit is to make a large amount of material available to the public that can be transferred at zero cost. Putting more material in the public domain in different areas is a positive benefit, as long as people value this work. The ultimate check on the boundaries of the system is what people are prepared to support with their tax credits. If few people opted to support journalism or video games, then these industries would remain largely dependent on copyright protection.

The special case of textbooks

Textbooks are an enormous expense for college students: households are on a path to spend more than $10.5 billion on them in

---

74 The Bureau of Labor Statistics (BLS) estimated the number of people employed as reporters in 2015 in print, broadcast, and Internet journalism at 44,360. The average annual pay was $50,700; the median was $37,700 (BLS 2016b). Fully supporting their pay through the creative work tax credit would require roughly $2.2 billion of revenue from the credit. Of course, newspaper and broadcast outlets require other support personnel as well. However, even in the absence of copyright protection it would still be possible to charge for print versions of newspapers or other publications and for advertising, even if the fees would be lower for material that could be duplicated.

2016,[75] or about $500 per student. The figure is even higher for full-time students. A single textbook can cost several hundred dollars, and renting one can cost $50–100 per semester. As with prescription drugs, most of this cost is attributable to a copyright monopoly.

Public funding could produce a large number of textbooks free from copyright restrictions. The arithmetic here is striking. An appropriation of $500 million a year (0.01 percent of federal spending) to finance textbook writing and production would cover 500 books a year, assuming an annual cost of $1 million per textbook. After 10 years, 5,000 textbooks would be available in the public domain to be downloaded at zero cost, or printed out in hard copy for the cost of the paper.[76]

In addition to offering enormous cost savings to students, this system would offer more flexibility to professors, who could combine chapters from different textbooks without the need for time-consuming and costly permission requests. Updating a textbook would be much simpler because there would no need to have a complete new edition to add one or two additional topics.

This is an area where long-term contracts with private publishers could work quite well. The contracts in this case, unlike prescription drugs, could be well defined. Publishers could specify how many books they intended to produce and the timeline on which they expected to produce them. Their ability to get subsequent contracts would depend on the quality of the work and the timeliness of the production. Because all information — the contract, the publication dates, and the books themselves — would be fully public, the problem of political favoritism should be minimized.

Furthermore, anyone could still produce textbooks under the copyright system. If the publicly financed texts proved to be inferior, few professors would use them. This competition would provide a clear market test of the quality of the publicly financed work.

---

75   BEA (2016), Table 2.4.5U, line 67. This spending does not correspond exactly to college textbooks because it refers to "educational books," a category that can include some other books that are not college texts.

76   Because the funding might also be used to finance updates of existing texts, the number of discrete books published through this system might be somewhat lower.

Conclusion: Savings from alternatives to patents and copyrights

The prior sections suggested alternative mechanisms to patents and copyrights for supporting innovation and creative work in a variety of areas. While prescription drugs and medical equipment are almost certainly the most important area for alternatives to the existing system, there are many other areas in which the current patent and copyright system is likely posing a drag on economic growth. Switching to a system that relies on alternative mechanisms for supporting patents and copyrights could lead to substantial savings for households and businesses.

Table 5-6 shows projected 2016 spending and potential savings in areas where the costs of current monopolies are likely to be largest. Savings for recorded music and video material as well as recreational books are pegged here at 50 percent, under the assumption that the tax-credit system will make available a vast amount of free writing, music, and video material. Savings on educational books are pegged at 70 percent, under the assumption that the bulk of textbooks will be produced through the publicly funded system. The savings for prescription drugs are based on the calculation in Table 5-3. Savings in newspapers and periodicals, motion pictures, and cable TV are pegged at 20 percent. (With cable, many people may opt to rely on the Internet and cancel cable subscriptions.) The figure for medical equipment is loosely derived from the earlier calculation in Table 5-3; it is larger here because this figure reflects spending to purchase the equipment rather than the fees charged to patients. The total potential savings are $435 billion, or 2.4 percent of GDP.

The calculations shown in Table 5-6 are speculative, of course, because there is no way to determine in advance the effectiveness of an alternative funding mechanism to replace patents and copyrights. There are good reasons for believing that an alternative would be at least as effective, especially in the case of patents. The prospect of having fully open research, where the incentive is for dissemination rather than secrecy, would almost certainly lead to more rapid progress than the current patent system.

TABLE 5-6

Total savings from patent/copyright alternatives

(billions of 2016 dollars)

	Current spending	Potential savings
Recorded music and video material (line 42)	$30.8	$15.4
Educational books (line 67)	$10.5	$7.4
Recreational books (part of 90)	$30.2	$15.1
Prescription drugs (line 131)	$430.0	$315.5
Newspapers and periodicals (line 141)	$61.2	$12.2
Motion pictures (line 210)	$15.0	$3.0
Cable and satellite television and radio services (line 215)	$95.0	$19.0
Medical equipment and instruments (Line 6)	$94.0	$47.0
Total		**$434.6**

Source and notes: BEA (2016), Tables 2.4.5U and 5.5.5U, and author's calculations; see text.

More importantly, bringing prices in line with production costs would offer enormous gains, especially in the case of drugs and medical equipment. It is difficult to understand the logic of paying for innovation at the point where a patient needs a drug or access to medical equipment. Monopoly pricing imposes an enormous burden on people at precisely the time when they are least able to bear it. A payment system should be structured to let patients and their families focus on getting well, not paying for their health care. No one would propose determining payments for firefighters when they show up at a burning house, but this is effectively what we are doing with patent monopolies in the medical sector. The absurdity is heightened by the fact that the ultimate payment is almost always a political decision, not a matter of consumer choice, so proponents of the patent system can't use the classic justification for market outcomes.

Weakening or eliminating patent and copyright support for innovation and creative work would radically reduce waste. In a market system, the best way to make profits should be to produce better products, not to run to court. But the patent system increasingly supports this second path to profits.

Economists have been successful in raising awareness about marginal cost pricing. The idea that consumers and the economy benefit from eliminating tariffs and other trade barriers is widely recognized even if not universally accepted. However, the public is less aware of the much greater gap between prices and the cost of production as a result of patent and copyright monopolies. Economic theory tells us that the costs associated with this gap are enormously larger than the costs associated with the traditional trade barriers that remain. There is little reason to believe that the gain from the innovation and creative work that is induced by these forms of protection is remotely comparable to the costs, especially when considering the potential benefits of alternative mechanisms for providing incentives.

Chapter 6

Out of Control at the Top: CEO Pay in the Private and Public Sectors

There is an old joke that conservatives told about left-wing agitators at the start of the 20th century. The story goes that the speaker jumps up on the soap box and yells out: "If I had two million dollars, I would give you one." He then says, "And if I had two houses I would give you one." He continues, "If I had two pigs." The radical then pauses and says quietly, "wait, I have two pigs."

This perspective seems to describe many of those working against inequality at our leading nonprofit foundations. While many foundations now list combating inequality as major part of their agenda, their top executives often draw paychecks in the high hundreds of thousands of dollars. For example, the average pay package for the highest paid non-financial position at the country's 10 largest foundations in 2014 was $820,000.[77] This comes to more than 20 times the annual earnings of the median worker (BLS 2016c).

77　Calculation is based on data from 990 Forms filed with IRS.

While the rise in pay at nonprofits is following the pattern of soaring CEO pay in the corporate sector, it would be interesting to ask what would happen if some of the major nonprofits committed themselves to a more modest ceiling on pay, say $400,000: the annual salary of the President of the United States. This would force down the pay of not only the president, but also of many of the other top officers at places like the Gates Foundation and the Ford Foundation. Would they still be able to find competent, hardworking people if these positions paid just 10 times the earnings of a typical worker?

Suppose that the foundations took this issue a step further and said that they would not give grants to institutions in which people were paid more than the President of the United States? That could create an interesting dynamic. If several major foundations took this step, then it would provide a substantial incentive for college and universities to comply so that their faculty was not excluded from a major potential funding source. Smaller colleges might move quickly, since in many cases the only people over this cap would the president and perhaps a few other top managers, and even for these people the pay cuts need not be too large.

If the top paid people at some schools took cuts to meet this standard, there would be pressure on others to follow suit. After all, it would be difficult for a college to recruit new faculty if prospects knew that they would be cut off from foundation funding by taking a job at that college, but not at its equally prestigious competitor. As more colleges went this path, the pressure would grow for many universities to also cut high-end pay.[78] It is certainly plausible that a dynamic would develop leading to a permanent lowering of pay for those at the top throughout the college and university system. This would mean lower tuition payments for students and more money available for less-well paid employees.

There is also a policy argument for some sort of limit, since taxpayers are subsidizing these exorbitant paychecks as a result of the tax-exempt status of foundations and universities. If we assume that the bulk of the contributions to these institutions come from people in the top

---

78   The football coach would pose a problem. This is discussed later in the chapter.

income bracket, on which the tax rate is 40 percent, the taxpayer subsidy on the $820,000 average pay for foundation CEOs would come to $328,000 a year. That's a good sized subsidy to be going from taxpayers to people who are way into the top 1 percent of wage earners.

It would be impressive if one or several of the large foundations took the president's pledge and committed itself to keeping the pay of its own staff under $400,000 a year and also imposing this ceiling on the institutions that receive grants from the foundation. But, we may not see this one anytime soon. After all, the foundations may be committed to fighting inequality, but like the radical with two pigs, there is a limit to this commitment.

Trends in CEO pay

The top executives of major corporations have always been well paid. It is a demanding job, and people generally rise to the top position only after a establishing long records as a competent managers. But the pay of top executives has exploded relative to everyone else over the last four decades. As **Figure 6-1** shows, in the 1960s a CEO could expect to earn around 20 times as much as a typical worker. The ratio rose slightly to 23-to-1 by 1973, to 32-to-1 by the end of the decade, to 58-to-1 by the end of the 1980s, to 120-to-1 in 1995, and to 376-to-1 at the peak of the stock bubble in 2000. It drifted somewhat lower in the 2000s, but stood at 276-to-1 in 2015.

We could believe that this explosion in pay is due to the fact that today's CEOs are hugely more productive than CEOs were in the 1960s. If the pay reflects productivity, then CEOs went from being 20 times as productive as the typical worker to more than 200 times as productive in recent years and almost 400 times as productive in the late 1990s. It is also worth noting that United States is an outlier in this respect. CEO pay has risen everywhere but not by as much as in the United States. So this means that our CEOs not only became hugely more productive relative to the typical worker, but they also became hugely more productive relative to the CEOs in Europe, Japan, and South Korea. Since there are plenty of large, highly profitable companies in Europe, Japan, and South Korea, this doesn't seem likely.

There also are many examples of CEOs getting exorbitant pay packages who certainly did not in any obvious way contribute to generating large amounts of shareholder value. Marissa Mayer, who took over as CEO of Yahoo in 2012, provides a recent example.

FIGURE 6-1
CEO-to-worker compensation ratio

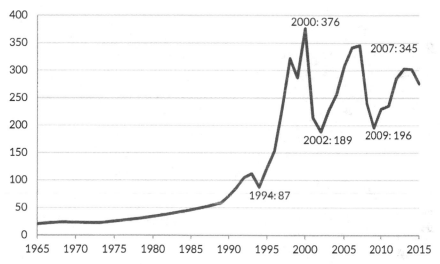

Source and notes: Mishel and Schieder (2016).

At the point where Mayer stepped in, Yahoo was in a state of disarray. It had been one of the Internet pioneers of the 1990s and still had a huge base of users. But its traffic and revenue had been falling, as competitors like Facebook were rapidly pulling away users. The company lacked clear direction and had gone through three CEOs in less than four years. Mayer was seen as the best hope for a turnaround, having established an impressive reputation as a top executive at Google.

She undertook a number of initiatives, including several large acquisitions, but none were very effective and the downward trend in revenue and earnings continued. Mayer negotiated the sale of the core company to Verizon in 2016 for $4.8 billion, by some calculations considerably less than its value when she took the helm.[79]

According to calculations by Stephen Gandel, a reporter at *Fortune* magazine, Mayer stands to walk away with more than $120 million when the deal is completed (Gandel 2016). This is quite a chunk of money for running a $4.8 billion company for four years. (This assumes the value of the company did not change during her tenure.) If Yahoo shareholders could have expected a return of 7.0 percent a year on their shares (the long-term average for stock), the money paid out to Mayer was a bit less than 10 percent of their expected earnings.

Mayer's compensation pales next to that of Robert Nardelli, who was CEO of Home Depot from 2001 to 2007. Nardelli left with $210 million in compensation even as the company's stock lost almost 40 percent of its real value. The Home Depot's poor performance can't be explained by bad things hitting the home retail sector; the stock price of its main competitor, Lowe's, nearly doubled over the same period.

How CEOs get away with ripping off their companies

The reason that CEO pay includes a large component of rent is that corporate governance is subject to serious collective action problems. It is very difficult for the shareholders to get together to do what may be in their common interest; in this case reduce CEO pay. The problems of running corporations effectively should be viewed the same way that conservatives often correctly point to problems in running government efficiently.

Conservatives point to patronage, favoritism, and outright corruption in government as arguments to restrict its domain. The logic is that it is difficult for the average citizen to do much to rein in abuses. The personal stake of a citizen in preventing wasteful government is small.

---

79   The calculation of Yahoo's value is complicated by the fact that it owns a substantial stake in Alibaba, the Chinese Internet retailer, and Yahoo Japan, which is a separate publicly traded company. Most of the value of the traded stock is derived from these assets, not the value of the company managed by Mayer.

People may end up paying higher taxes than necessary or receiving worse services than they should, but their personal gain from taking action would be dwarfed by the amount of time and money they would have to commit to an effort with an uncertain outcome. By contrast, the direct beneficiaries of the corruption — for example, contractors receiving excessive payments, have a large stake in maintaining the status quo.

The problem with corporate governance is very similar. In principle, the shareholders would hire their CEO and other top management at the market wage, paying them as much as their next best alternative and no more. [80] However, the structure of modern corporations does not typically allow for this sort of market transaction in setting CEO pay.

Stockholders are a diffuse group of individuals and institutions, most with little direct stake in the running of the company since the dividends and capital gains are a small portion of their income. Organizing among shareholders to improve corporate practices and to change top management has high transaction costs, and so it is far easier for shareholders to simply sell the stock of a company if they are unhappy with its performance. In this environment, top management will often have effective control over the running of a company.

Ostensibly, CEOs and other top management are answerable to the corporation's board of directors, but corporate boards are generally composed of people who have other demanding jobs and can at best devote a small fraction of their time to the oversight of the corporation. In fact, it's common for directors to sit on multiple boards, further reducing the time they can devote to overseeing the operations of any one company.

One of the champions in this area was Erskine Bowles, who served as Chief of Staff to President Clinton in his second term and later went on to be president of the University of North Carolina. While

---

80   This discussion works from the assumption that the duty of the corporation is maximizing returns to shareholders. This is a debatable issue, but is accepted as the standard framing in this chapter. The argument is that corporations are not currently being run in ways that best serve the shareholders.

serving in this latter position, Bowles simultaneously sat on the boards of General Motors, Morgan Stanley, and Cousins Properties. The first two companies needed bailouts from the government to stay in business, but sitting on the board of two companies that faced bankruptcy did not damage the demand for Bowles as a director. After General Motors' bankruptcy cost Bowles his directorship there, he added directorships at Norfolk Southern and Facebook to his portfolio. This is an impressive collection of moonlighting jobs given that being president of a major university is ordinarily thought of as demanding work. It seems fair to assume that not much is expected of the directors of major corporations.

Bowles attractiveness to companies as a director likely has more to do with his political stature and connections than his insights into running a large corporation. But this is not uncommon; many directors have held high-level political positions. (**Table 6-1** in the Appendix gives a list of directors from the 100 largest publicly traded companies in the United States who have previously held positions in government.) The political connections of these directors may prove useful to the companies in getting contracts or dealing with regulators, but they are unlikely to be especially useful in ensuring that a company is well managed and serves the best interests of its shareholders.

Furthermore, even if directors had the time and ability to challenge management, they typically have little incentive to do so. CEOs often play a role in selecting board members. In many companies, the CEO sits on the board, sometimes as chair. Directors are generally well compensated for their work, usually getting yearly stipends that run into the hundreds of thousands of dollars for attending a few meetings (typically six to 12 a year). They are unlikely to put their positions at risk by challenging top management than just going along with them and presumably most of the other directors.

It is almost impossible for directors to be voted out through a shareholder revolt. An analysis of director elections in 2012 by Investor Shareholder Services found that 99.6 percent of the 17,081 directors nominated by management were approved (Stewart 2013). Even among the 61 who were defeated, 55 were still on the payroll many months later at the next proxy filing. Their fellow directors were apparently willing to shelter them from the wrath of shareholders.

For these reasons, the pay of top executives is not determined in anything resembling a normal market. There is little downside to directors signing off on increasingly excessive pay packages. And it is difficult for shareholders to override the directors, either by directly forcing down CEO pay or putting in a more responsible slate of directors.

The amount of money at stake is huge. Lucian Bebchuk, one of the country's leading experts on CEO pay, calculated that total compensation paid to the top five executives at public companies amounted to $350 billion over the 10-year period from 1993 to 2003 (Bebchuk and Grinstein 2005). Furthermore, the amount going to the top five executives increased from 5 percent of after-tax profits in 1993–1995 to 10 percent in 2001–2003. If this 10 percent figure still held in 2015, then around $120 billion a year was being paid out to the top five executives. Cutting this figure in half to its mid-1990s level would imply savings of $60 billion annually, or a year of SNAP spending, as shown in **Figure 6-2**. Cutting it by 75 percent would leave the ratio of the pay of CEOs to ordinary workers at 70-to-1, more than twice its 1970s level, and save $90 billion a year, or one-and-a-half years of SNAP.

FIGURE 6-2

Impact of reducing the pay of the top five executives in the U.S., in units of SNAP spending

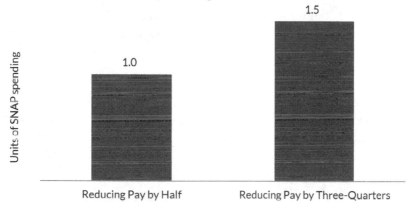

Source and notes: Author's calculations; see text.

Academic research on CEO pay

A considerable body of academic work has been devoted to the question of whether the value of their work justifies CEOs' salaries. Answers point in both directions, but there is no shortage of studies indicating that CEO pay cannot be justified by the returns to shareholders.

Bebchuk et al. (2006) compiled much of the evidence available at the time supporting the case that a large portion of CEO pay is rents. For example, the study notes research showing that superstar CEOs, those who win awards or are featured on business magazine covers, receive a large pay premium in subsequent years even though shareholders receive below-normal returns (Malmendier and Tate 2008). It also cites research showing that CEOs at companies that score highly on measures of good corporate governance receive lower pay than those at companies that score poorly (Core, Holthausen, and Larcker 1999). This finding suggests that if corporate directors actually did their jobs in representing shareholders, CEOs might make less money. Finally, the study notes research showing that CEO pay responds strongly to factors occurring by chance that affect company profits, such as a sharp rise in world oil prices affecting an oil company's profits (Bertrand and Mullainathan 2001).

A number of other anomalies cited in research indicate a lack of connection between CEO pay and returns to shareholders. One study found that the companies of CEOs who bought mansions provided lower returns to shareholders in subsequent years (Liu and Yermark 2007). The study took this finding to indicate that CEOs who feel secure enough in their position to buy large homes feel less need to perform for shareholders. Yermark (2005) found that allowing a CEO to use a corporate jet was associated with a lower subsequent return for shareholders. Another study found that CEOs of companies in states with strong antitakeover provisions received higher pay than CEOs in other states (Barnhart, Spivey, and Alexander 2000). The implication is that if CEOs feel less threatened by the risk of takeovers, then they are more comfortable pushing up their pay.

Evidence suggests that stock options to CEOs give them an incentive to manipulate earnings so that share prices will rise just before the CEO is in a position to exercise the options. One way of finding evidence of this sort of manipulation is measuring the frequency with which earnings are restated. Burns and Kedia (2003) found that larger option grants are associated with more frequent restatements of earnings. This pattern would be consistent with a situation in which top management deliberately misstated earnings to increase the value of stock options at the point of exercise. Deliberately misrepresenting earnings is illegal, of course, although executives are almost never charged with it. However, there are many ways in which CEOs can affect the timing of earnings that are totally legal. For example, they can delay writing down a bad investment or shutting down a money-losing operation if they fear these actions would depress the share price. The timing on stock options could give them this sort of incentive, even if the action is contrary to shareholders' interests.

A recent paper provided remarkable evidence on the issuance of options in the 1990s (Shue and Townsend 2016). This analysis found that corporate boards failed to recognize that the value of an option was rising hugely over the course of the decade as share prices soared. Since they did not want to appear to be cutting the pay of their CEOs, they felt the need to give them the same number or more option grants, even though this implied a substantially larger pay package than was warranted by their performance. If this finding holds up to further scrutiny, it means that corporate boards had no idea how much they were paying their CEOs. Certainly, directors cannot effectively rein in CEO pay if they do not even know how much they are paying their CEOs.

Quigley, Crossland, and Campbell (2016) looked at the impact of unexpected CEO deaths, like from an airplane or car crash, on stock prices. The reason for focusing on unexpected deaths is that it takes away the possibility that the death may have been anticipated and its impact already reflected in the stock price, as might be the case when a CEO dies after a long illness. In almost half of the cases examined since 1990 (44.3 percent), the price of the company's stock rose following the death of the CEO. If incumbent CEOs are uniquely talented individuals who cannot be easily replaced, then their loss should be unambiguously bad news for the company's shareholders. In fact, the market might be expected to overreact on the negative side to the unexpected death of a CEO, since there might be the expectation that the CEO actually was a major asset to the company even in cases where it is not true. After all, why else would they be paying them so much money?

Finally, Marshall and Lee (2016) looked at long-term (10-year) returns to shareholders relative to total CEO pay at 429 large corporations over the years 2006–2015. The study found a significant negative relationship, with high CEO compensation being associated with worse returns to shareholders. The analysis divided CEO pay by quintiles and found that the total return to shareholders of companies with pay in the bottom quintile was more than 60 percent higher than the return to shareholders with CEO pay in the top quintile. These findings are hard to reconcile with a story in which the pay of CEOs reflects their ability to increase returns to shareholders.

Some research suggests that CEOs are worth their pay. For example, Fernandes et al. (2009), which examined CEO pay in the United States and 14 other wealthy countries, argued that most of the higher CEO pay in the United States is explained by the fact that a much larger share of CEO compensation here is paid in stock options and other risky forms. The study argued further that if these payments were assigned their risk-free value, most of the differences in pay would go away. But boards generally remove much of the risk of option-based pay by offering options at lower strike prices (the price at which the option can be exercised), in case the stock underperforms. The study also found that stronger corporate governance in other countries makes a substantial difference in CEO pay, but this is consistent with the rent story.

A study that has attracted considerable attention, Cronqvist and Fahlenbrach (2012), is an analysis of CEO pay at companies that transition from public ownership to ownership by private equity. The rationale for focusing on these companies is that with private equity ownership there is no separation between ownership and control, and so if the problem of CEO pay is one of a corporate board that does not act in the interest of shareholders, then a takeover by private equity should remove this obstacle. The private equity company stands directly to gain by minimizing CEO pay, insofar as the pay is consistent with maintaining the performance of the CEO. From this perspective, if CEOs of publicly held companies are drawing rents, then they should see sharp cuts when private equity owners take over. But Cronqvist and Fahlenbrach found little reduction in non-performance-based pay, such as straight salary and benefits, and a large rise in incentive pay. This outcome is often taken as evidence against the claim that CEO pay involves a substantial rent component.

While Cronqvist and Fahlenbrach have performed an interesting analysis of the issue, their findings are far from conclusive on the question of rents in CEO pay. A major problem with using companies held by private equity as a comparison is that, almost by definition, the private equity firm is expecting the company it takes over to undergo major transitions. This is the point of the takeover. The private equity firm hopes that by restructuring the company, it can increase profitability. Its plan is to bring its takeover back on the market and resell it as a public company in three to 10 years.

Under these circumstances, it is not surprising the CEO's pay would go up. Much more is being demanded of the CEO than had been the case previously. In effect, the private equity company is looking for firms that have not been especially innovative and fast-growing and then turn them around into ones that are. The fact that a CEO of a firm undergoing this sort of transition would get higher pay than the CEO of a firm that was stuck in a rut doesn't seem to offer much insight into whether or not CEOs typically draw rents.

Like most academic debates, the one on CEO pay is not completely conclusive. Still, there is enough solidly grounded research to support the intuition that CEOs earn pay that is not proportionate to their contribution to shareholders.

There seems little dispute that luck plays a large role in CEO pay with many CEOs getting huge payouts because of factors that were completely out of their control. The risks faced by CEOs in this way are clearly not symmetric. A CEO of an oil company can earn tens of millions of dollars if the price of oil doubles or triples, but she will not have to pay tens of millions if the price of oil collapses. The CEO in that case will still get her base salary and benefits which will be in the neighborhood of 50 times the compensation of ordinary workers.

We also know that corporate boards are often ignorant of both their companies' activities (how many directors of major banks realized the bank was on the edge of collapse in the summer of 2008) and the value of the compensation packages that they are giving to their CEOs. Moreover, directors face an asymmetric incentive structure in which there is almost no downside risk associated with supporting management. It is almost impossible for directors to be voted off boards, and so if they want to keep a very part-time job that pays several hundred thousand dollars a year, the easiest path is to go along with management.

Taking all of these factors into account, it is reasonable to believe that there is a substantial component of rent in CEO pay. In other words, it should be possible to find competent people who would work hard to increase profitability and shareholder returns for considerably less pay.

It is worth noting that pay at poorly governed companies will inevitably affect the pay at well-governed companies. While it is not common for CEOs to jump companies, having overpaid CEOs at poorly governed companies in the reference group for determining CEO pay will tend to increase the pay for CEOs at even the best-run companies. If the norm is for CEOs at large companies to be paid between $10 million and $20 million a year, a well-managed company will have a tough time retaining top-quality executives for $3 million to $4 million a year, even if that pay package were more appropriate given the marginal contribution of the CEO to profitability.

The importance of bloated CEO pay for the economy

The issue of high CEO pay is not just a moral question of whether some people are getting too much money. Bloated pay for CEOs levies a substantial cost on the economy. But their pay and the pay of those immediately under them and on down through the corporation is only part of the picture. The run-up in CEO pay has the effect of raising salaries for top executives in educational institutions, hospitals, and private charities. The salaries of these executives can be expected to loosely follow CEO pay, since the top executives of these organizations can legitimately say that they could make more in the corporate sector. As a result, nonprofits have to offer competitive pay to attract people with high-level management experience.

Table 6-2 shows the pay of the presidents of the country's 10 largest charitable foundations. The highest paid is James Cuno, who got just less than $1.1 million in 2014 for serving as president and a trustee of the J. Paul Getty Trust. The average pay for this group is just over $856,500. It is interesting to compare this to the pay of the median worker. According to the Bureau of Labor Statistics (BLS), the median worker would have earned less than $40,000 in 2014 working the year-round (BLS 2016c). This means that the ratio of Mr. Cuno's pay to the median worker's pay was a bit more than 27-to-1 for the year. That is higher than the ratio of the pay of CEOs to the typical worker in the early 1970s. Taking the average for this group, the ratio is more than 20-to-1. That is roughly the same as the average ratio for the 1960s, meaning that the compensation of these foundation presidents is as high relative to the pay of an average worker as what a CEO would have received 50 years ago.[81]

Bloated pay structures also affect the top administrators at colleges or universities, although at public institutions the biggest paychecks go to athletic coaches. Table 6-3 shows the top five salaries at the University of California, Berkeley and the University of California at Los Angeles, along with the pay of the schools' chancellors. It also shows the five highest-paid employees at five schools in the California State University system.

---

81 The foundation president is generally not the highest-paid person at the foundation. In most cases the top-paid person is the chief investment or financial officer. In the case of the Getty Trust, the treasurer and chief investment officer earned $1.6 million in 2014. The high pay for investment officers reflects the extent to which pay in finance is out of line with pay in the rest of the economy.

TABLE 6-2

Pay of presidents of 10 largest charitable foundations (2013 or closest year)

(2013 dollars)

Person	Foundation	Annual salary
Sue Desmond-Hellmann	Bill & Melinda Gates Foundation	$897,868
Darren Walker	Ford Foundation	$714,200
James Cuno	J Paul Getty Trust	$1,083,310
Risa Lavizzo-Mourey	Robert Wood Johnson Foundation	$835,116
Sterling Speirn	W.K. Kellogg Foundation	$860,008
La June Montgomery Tabron	W.K. Kellogg Foundation	$434,523
Larry Kramer	William and Flora Hewlett Foundation	$634,592
Carol Larson	David and Lucile Packard Foundation	$688,399
Robert Gallucci	John D. and Catherine T. MacArthur Foundation	$666,543
Stephen McCormick	Gordon and Betty Moore Foundation	$603,750
Earl Lewis	Andrew W. Mellon Foundation	$755,189
Don Randel	Andrew W. Mellon Foundation	$392,221
	Average salary	**$856,571.90**

Source and notes: IRS 990 forms of listed institutions. Salaries for Andrew W. Mellon Foundation and W.K. Kellogg Foundation are part-year.

TABLE 6-3

Five highest-paid employees at selected California schools (including chancellor or president)

(2014 dollars)

Person/institution	Position	Annual salary
UC Berkeley		
Daniel Dykes	Head Coach	$1,805,400
Jeff Tedford	Head Coach	$1,800,000
Cuonzo Martin	Head Coach	$1,188,381
Michael Montgomery	Head Coach	$893,149
Anne Barbour	Head Coach	$634,305
Nicholas Dirks	Chancellor	$532,226
UCLA		
James Lawrence Mora	Intercol Ath Head Coach EX	$3,476,127
Stephen Todd Alford	Intercol Ath Head Coach EX	$2,745,341
Khalil Tabsh	HS Clin Prof-HComp	$2,303,327
Ronald Busuttil	Prof-HComp	$2,232,921
Abbas Ardehali	Prof-HComp	$1,556,331
Gene Block	Chancellor	$430,116

TABLE 6-3

Five highest-paid employees at selected California schools (including chancellor or president)

CSU Chico

Paul Zingg	President	$344,959
Lorraine Hoffman	Administrator IV	$219,838
Belle Wei	Administrator IV	$204,120
Drew Calandrella	Administrator IV	$202,782
Arnoldus Rethans	Instructional Faculty – 12 Month	$198,755

CSU Northridge

Dianne Harrison	President	$304,775
Reginald Theus	Administrator III	$275,808
Harold Hellenbrand	Administrator IV	$227,994
Colin Donahue	Administrator IV	$214,662
Robert Gunsalus	Administrator IV	$210,844

CSU Fullerton

Mildred Garcia	President	$335,486
Anil Puri	Administrator IV	$244,027
Jose Cruz Rivera	Administrator IV	$214,384
Gregory Saks	Administrator IV	$209,883
Dedrique Taylor	Administrator IV	$198,094

CSU Long Beach

Donald Para	President	$244,362
David Dowell	Administrator IV	$218,477
Mary Stephens	Administrator IV	$208,823
Forouzan Golshani	Administrator IV	$200,673
Jeetendra Joshee	Administrator IV	$198,148

CSU Sacramento

Alexander Gonzalez	President	$368,943
Sanjay Varshney	Instructional Faculty – Academic Year	$296,958
Ming-Tung Lee	Administrator IV	$207,054
Thomas Sperbeck	Administrator IV	$203,079
Lori Varlotta	Administrator IV	$196,370

Source and notes: Transparent California (2016). Does not include benefits.

One head coach at UCLA earned $3.5 million and another earned $2.7 million in 2014; two head coaches at Berkeley earn $1.8 million each. The other high-end earners on this list are heads of medical clinics at UCLA. The pay of the chancellors at both schools is modest in comparison: Berkeley's chancellor received $532,000, UCLA's $430,000.

The schools in the California State University system provide an interesting contrast. The highest-paid person in this group is Alexander

Gonzalez, president of California State University, Sacramento, who received $369,000 in 2014. While the California State University system is clearly a big step down in its stature in academia from Berkeley and UCLA, these are large institutions with tens of thousands of students and budgets that are well over $100 million. In other words, the top administrators have positions of considerable responsibility.

The chancellors of Berkeley and UCLA fare poorly even compared to some of their counterparts elsewhere. The top-paid university presidents earn well over $1 million a year, as shown in **Table 6-4**. Yale's Richard Levin earned $1,653,000 to come in 10th on the list. Some presidents who may have been a surprise were Anthony Catanese who earned $1,884,000 at Florida Institute of Technology, Dennis Murray who earned $2,688,000 at Marist College, and Joseph Aoun who earned $3,122,000 at Northeastern University. In fairness, many university presidents are paid largely for their ability to attract donations, and it is possible that these presidents were especially successful in attracting contributions. However, this is a skill that matters much more in an unequal society that depends on donations from the rich to support higher education. Being able to develop relationships with the wealthy is a much less valuable skill in a society where the wealthy have less money and education is supported through other channels.

TABLE 6-4

Top paid university presidents		
(2013 dollars)		
Person	Institution	Annual salary
Robert Zimmer	University of Chicago	$3,358,723
Joseph Aoun	Northeastern University	$3,121,864
Dennis Murray	Marist College	$2,688,148
Lee Bollinger	Columbia University	$2,327,344
Lawrence Bascow	Tufts University	$2,223,752
Amy Gutmann	University of Pennsylvania	$2,091,764
Anthony Catanese	Florida Institute of Technology	$1,884,008
Esther Barazzone	Chatham University	$1,812,132
Shirley Ann Jackson	Rensselaer Polytechnic University	$1,752,642
Richard Levin	Yale University	$1,652,543

Source and notes: Westerholm (2013).

Policies to combat high pay at the top

The implication of CEOs and other top executives earning large rents is that they are taking away money that would otherwise go to shareholders and perhaps to lower-paid workers. This means that shareholders have a stake in reining in CEO pay in order to increase returns. But the current corporate governance structure makes it difficult for shareholders to exert control and push CEO pay down to its market level. The solution is to find ways to increase the ability of shareholders to rein in pay.

The Dodd-Frank Act of 2010 included a modest step in this direction. The law requires that every three years companies hold a "say-on-pay" vote in which shareholders can vote up or down on the pay package provided to the company's top executives. The vote is non-binding, so it doesn't require the company to alter its pay package, but it provides at least some opportunity for shareholders to provide feedback. As a practical matter, it is difficult to rally shareholders in a say-on-pay vote, just as it is difficult to organize for an election to the Senate or for the presidency. A large number have to be contacted to have any hope of winning, and there is not much incentive to organize since, even if the measure succeeds, it's not binding.

Furthermore, the voting structure is stacked against unhappy shareholders. A large portion of corporate shares are voted by mutual funds and asset management companies. Blackrock, the world's largest asset management company with $4.6 trillion under management and control of the largest block of proxies at many of the country's largest companies, has supported management in 97 percent of say-on-pay votes. TIAA-CREF, the huge retirement fund for college and university faculty, has supported management at even higher rates (Marriage 2016). Just as directors may view corporate CEOs as their friends rather than their employees, it seems that a similar relationship exists with many of the asset managers who control the bulk of company stock. They have little reason to pick fights with the management on behalf of the people they ostensibly represent.

However, there are ways to change the incentive structure of the people in a position to act. Suppose, for example, that the rules stipulated that directors lost their stipend for the year in the event of a "no" vote on management pay. Directors would stand to lose hundreds of thousands of dollars, and the risk might cause them to think about pay packages a little more carefully.

Congress could institute such a measure just as it included the say-on-pay package in Dodd-Frank. Note that this rule would not in any way limit the pay that CEOs receive. Rather, it gives shareholders more power to contain pay. Since CEOs ostensibly work for the shareholders, this rule might even be considered a pro-business measure, and it would be reasonable to ask corporations to adopt it voluntarily. After all, given that less than 3 percent of say-on-pay packages are rejected, it hardly seems to be asking too much of directors to risk their pay on the possibility that they will be in the bottom 3 percent.

It is possible to envision going even further and constructing pay packages for directors that give them a direct incentive to limit CEO pay. Suppose that directors were given the opportunity to share half of the savings from cutting the pay of the CEO and the next four highest-paid executives, provided that the subsequent stock returns matched or exceeded those of a peer group.

This would mean that if the directors of a steel company cut the pay of their CEO by $3 million a year for a three-year period and they achieved comparable savings from the compensation packages of the next four most highly paid executives taken together, then they would be able to split a total of $9 million (half of the $18 million in savings) if the returns on the steel company's stock at least matched those of its competitors for these three years, and a subsequent five-year period. The latter is necessary to avoid incentivizing short-term behavior.

There are many ways to design contracts that would incentivize directors to restrict CEO pay. From the standpoint of shareholders, this is the way directors should be thinking. They should constantly be asking whether it is possible to get comparable performance from the CEO and other top executives while paying less, just as management tries to minimize costs by paying ordinary workers as little as possible given their levels of productivity. Remarkably few if any companies design the compensation packages for directors along these lines.

It would probably be too much micro-management for the government to mandate incentive packages that encourage directors to hold down CEO pay. However, it is certainly reasonable for shareholders such as pension funds, foundations, and universities to ask the companies in which they hold stock why directors have no incentive to limit CEO pay. This is consistent with maximizing returns to shareholders. After all, if a CEO is being paid more than necessary for a person with his or her abilities and performance, then the shareholders are throwing away their money. And in cases like Yahoo and Home Depot, the money wasted on CEOs who didn't produce amounted to a large percentage of shareholders' expected returns.

Limiting pay at nonprofits

The tax-exempt status of nonprofit organizations amounts to a substantial subsidy. Since donors can deduct their contributions from their taxable income, taxpayers effectively pick up much of the tab. A person in the top 39.6 percent income bracket saves 39.6 cents in taxes for every dollar contributed to a tax-exempt organization, money that must be made up by other taxpayers. If the contribution takes the form of a bequest in a will, the public foregoes the 40 percent estate tax that otherwise would have been collected. [82] In short, taxpayers are major contributors to these organizations.

For the top executives of foundations and universities, the amount of the taxpayer subsidy is impressive. The president of the Getty Trust received $1,083,000 in compensation in 2013. If we assume that most of the money for the foundation came from people in the 39.6 percent

---

82   The story is little changed if a foundation or university has an endowment that provides a substantial portion of the executive's income. If not for the tax exemption, the original contribution would have been substantially smaller, which would make the current year income smaller by the same percentage.

bracket, the taxpayer subsidy for that year amounts to $642,000, [83]
equivalent to more than 281 food stamp years, based on the $127 a month
average benefit (**Figure 6-3**). The subsidy for Robert Zimmer, the
University of Chicago's president, amounted to $1,330,000 in 2011, or
873 food stamp years. The subsidy for James Mora, the head football
coach at UCLA, who received a salary of $3,476,000 in 2013, was
$1,376,000, or 903 food stamp years.

FIGURE 6-3
**Taxpayer annual subsidies to high-end earners working at
nonprofits, in years of food stamp benefits**

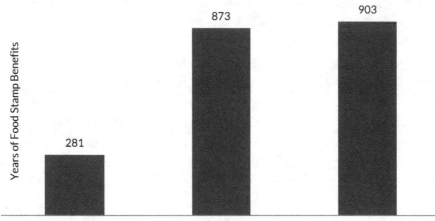

Source and notes: Author's calculations; see text.

The fact that the salaries of these executives are subsidized by
taxpayers is important because it is reasonable to then ask whether they
should be limited in some way. Note this does not mean telling the Getty
Foundation, the University of Chicago, or anyone else how much they can
pay their top executives. It simply means that if they want to get a subsidy
from taxpayers in the form of tax-exempt status, there will be a limit on
what they can pay their top executives. The restriction is attached to the

---

83   Alternatively, if the money is from an estate, the heirs saved 40 percent of this
      money on their estate tax.

subsidy, if they don't want the subsidy they can pay people whatever like, but if they want the taxpayers to foot a large part of the bill, then they have to accept limits.

The President of the United States earns $400,000 a year, and every four years many people with impressive credentials compete vigorously for this position. If a foundation, university, or private charity can't attract good help for this price, perhaps it does not deserve taxpayer support.

The case of athletic coaches raises interesting issues. The major college programs compete directly with professional teams that routinely pay millions of dollars to top coaches, and it is likely that college programs would have a problem getting and retaining good coaches without offering comparable pay. However, should these highly visible athletic teams be getting special tax treatment as a result of their ties to the university? There is a solid argument for public subsidies for higher education, but the argument for subsidizing Ohio State's football team is less clear cut.

We wouldn't expect a university to own a steel factory or a hotel chain and then claim special tax treatment for these for-profit businesses. The athletic programs at major universities are clearly business enterprises that have nothing to do with the traditional function of the university. If imposing a $400,000 cap on pay for the head coaches made it impossible for them to attract top quality talent, then the schools might make a decision to divest themselves of the affected programs. A private business could run "Ohio State football" or "University of North Carolina basketball," there is no reason for taxpayers to be footing a large share of the cost for these teams. Their fans can pay the cost without a taxpayer subsidy.

Conclusion: Letting the market work to rein in pay at the top

This chapter has argued that the explosion in CEO pay over the last four decades is largely attributable to a failure for the current system of corporate governance to impose effective checks on the pay of top corporate executives. The pay of CEOs is largely at the discretion of corporate boards of directors. These directors often owe their job to the

CEOs and in any case have little incentive to ever try to push CEO pay down. It is nearly impossible for shareholders to remove directors and almost no director ever loses their position because of a failure to hold down the pay of top executives.

In this context the incentives push directors toward going along with ever higher pay packages. The problem is not only that these lead to bloated pay for CEOs, but also for the other top executives in the corporate hierarchy. In addition, the high pay in the corporate sector spills over to high pay for top executives in private foundations, universities, and charities. Changing the rules of corporate governance to make it easier for shareholders to hold down CEO pay and to give corporate directors a direct incentive to hold down pay would be a market-friendly approach to applying discipline to CEO pay. Stockholders would never have incentive to vote for lower CEO pay if they believed that paying less to their top executive would lead to lower returns to them as shareholders. For this reason, making it easier for them to reduce CEO pay is very much a market-oriented reform.

The argument for the nonprofit sector is that these institutions are paying their top executives with public funds since they benefit from large tax subsidies. Just as the government puts all sorts of other restrictions on the activities of organizations receiving tax-exempt status, it can also make caps on pay a condition. Foundations and universities would still be free to pay their top executives whatever they wanted, but they wouldn't be able to receive a subsidy if they violated the pay ceiling.

Chapter 7

Protectionism for Highly Paid Professionals

The United States will spend more than $3.3 trillion in 2016 on health care (CMS 2015), more than $10,300 per person and roughly twice the average for other wealthy countries. But for all this extra spending it is not clear that we get better quality health care. By some measures, like life expectancy and infant mortality rates, the United States ranks low among rich countries. While treatment for some conditions is better here, we cannot say that the quality overall is better.

A big part of the difference in costs is that our doctors are paid twice as much as doctors in other wealthy countries. Average pay for doctors in the United States is over $250,000 a year, and in some highly paid areas of specialization the average is over $500,000. Paying our doctors the same as Germany, Canada, and other wealthy countries pay theirs would reduce our health care bill by close to $100 billion a year.

Doctors are able to maintain such high salaries in large part because of measures that protect them from competition. We have limits on the number of people who go to medical school and on the number of foreign medical school graduates who can enter U.S. residency programs, the completion of which is a requirement for practicing medicine in the United States. [84] State laws also limit the extent to which nurse practitioners and other health care professionals can perform tasks, such as prescribing medicine, that might limit the demand for doctors.

Protectionist barriers limit competition among other highly paid professions as well. Dentists cannot practice their field in the United States unless they graduated from an accredited dental school in the United States or, recently, Canada. State rules limit the extent to which dental hygienists can perform tasks like cleaning teeth without the supervision of a dentist. State bar exams limit the number of people who can practice law, sometimes sharply curtailing the supply of attorneys by making the exam more difficult.

It is interesting to contrast the array of barriers that protect high pay in these areas with efforts to free up trade and remove barriers in other areas. While recent trade pacts have sought to limit the basis for imposing health, safety, and environmental regulations, they have done little to facilitate freer trade in the services of highly paid professionals. Do our trade negotiators really believe that doctors cannot be competent to practice medicine unless they completed a residency program in the United States? Or do these barriers persist because doctors and other highly paid professionals have more political power than the workers whose pay has been reduced as a result of international competition?

This chapter argues that the barriers to competition and high pay exist because the professionals who benefit have far more political power than ordinary workers. No economic rule states that doctors, dentists, lawyers, and other professionals at the top of the pay ladder should be protected from the wage-depressing effects of globalization. Millions of smart and ambitious people in the developing world would be happy to train to U.S. standards and have the opportunity to work as professionals in the United States, but U.S. regulations make it difficult, if not

---

84 There are exceptions, with prominent foreign physicians generally able to get licensed to practice in the United States, but the typical doctor practicing in Europe or Canada would not have the option to practice in the United States without completing a U.S. residency program.

impossible, for them to go this route. The goal of current trade policy is cheap shoes and steel from the developing world, not low-cost doctors and lawyers.

Excessive pay for doctors and other high-end professionals, a group that makes up a large share of the top 1 percent of the wage distribution, should be thought of as a tax. The rest of the country is paying more than necessary for health care and a variety of other services. Freeing up markets for highly paid professionals can both reduce inequality and lead to more rapid economic growth.

Surveying the landscape of professionals' high pay

Comparing the compensation of highly paid professionals in the United States and other wealthy countries is not entirely straightforward due to the fact that many of these professionals have their own practices, especially in the United States. As a result, standard measures of labor income tend to be inadequate, since much of the income of these professionals, especially the higher-paid ones, will show up as income from owning a practice rather than as payments for services. [85] Nonetheless, a variety of surveys, many from professional organizations, seek to get around this problem. While the data may not be as accurate for high-paying professions as for other occupations, we can get a reasonably good idea of salaries based on the data that are available.

Physicians

Physicians are a good place to start, since they are the highest paid of these professions and there is also a large number of practicing physicians in the United States. A recent analysis of physicians' pay (Laugesen and Glied 2008) found large differences in pay for both general practitioners and orthopedic surgeons (the only area of specialization

---

85   The structure of the income tax, which taxes capital income at a lower rate than labor income, gives professionals who own their own practice an incentive to have labor income appear as capital income.

examined) between the United States and the other wealthy countries included in the comparison group (Australia, Canada, France, Germany, and the United Kingdom). Average pre-tax earnings in the United States for primary care physicians was $186,600 in 2008 dollars, compared to an (unweighted) average of $121,200 for the other five countries (the U.S. number would be over $215,000 in 2016 dollars). The average pre-tax earnings for orthopedic surgeons in the United States was $442,500, compared to an average of $215,500 in the reference countries.

An analysis by the OECD (Fujisawa and Lafortune 2008) put the average compensation for general practitioners in the United States in 2004 at $146,000, more than 40 percent higher than the average for the other countries in the analysis, even when excluding the Czech Republic as an outlier on the low side. This analysis found an even larger gap between the pay of specialists in the United States — $236,000 in 2003 (in 2003 dollars) — and most other OECD countries: $159,000 in Canada, $153,000 in the United Kingdom, $144,000 in France, and just $93,000 in Denmark. (The Netherlands, where specialists were paid more than in the United States, was the exception.) The levels and gaps would be almost 30 percent higher in 2016 dollars.

A more recent analysis suggests that doctors' pay in the United States is somewhat higher than indicated by these earlier studies. A 2012 survey by the Association of American Medical Colleges and American Medical Group Association put the *median* pay for family medicine at $208,900 (*Washington Post* 2012). The median for general surgeons was $367,300, for anesthesiologists $372,800, and for cardiologists $422,900. These figures are striking because there is much more room on the upside than the downside, the median is almost certainly well below the average.

A factor affecting physician compensation in the United States is the skewing of the mix of doctors toward specialists. In most other wealthy countries, close to two-thirds of physicians are general practitioners and one-third are specialists. In the United States the mix is in the opposite direction. This difference implies that we pay more for physicians both because we pay more for each type of physician than in other wealthy countries and because we have a much larger share of expensive specialists and relatively fewer primary care physicians. An analysis by the Commonwealth Fund (2006) found that, on a purchasing power parity basis, the United States spends almost three times as much per capita for physicians as the median for other wealthy countries.

An implication of this difference in composition is that primary care physicians in other countries perform many of the diagnoses and procedures that are reserved for specialists in the United States. If this difference is not associated with improved outcomes, then the increased use of specialists in the United States is likely due to rent-seeking by specialists. In that case, we would expect to see specialists setting and imposing medical standards that produce more demand for their specializations.

While many cases call for the expertise of a specialist, evidence shows that specialists are used in cases in which general practitioners have sufficient training (see e.g., Sharp et al. 2002).[86] And if specialists in the United States are spending much of their time performing tasks that in other countries are routinely performed by less highly trained general practitioners, then the gap in pay is likely larger than the raw data indicate. We are paying specialist wages for general practitioner work.

On the other side, the implication is that general practitioners in other countries have a higher level of skills than in the United States because they are capable of performing tasks that would be assigned to specialists in the United States. In that case, the effective gap in pay may still be larger since general practitioners in other countries have more skills and responsibilities than GPs in the United States.

The low density of doctors in the United States might also be a factor in the pay gap. The United States has 2.6 physicians per 1,000 people (OECD 2014), compared with 2.8 in the United Kingdom, 3.3 in France, and 4.0 in Germany. But the relatively low density in the United States is a matter of deliberate policy. In 1997, the Accreditation Council on Graduate Medical Education decided to limit medical school

---

86 The evidence for the impact of specialists on outcomes is mixed. A review of published work on the benefits of specialists found that, in 13 papers with 33 clear findings, 16 showed positive benefits from the use of specialists, 14 showed no effect, and three showed negative impacts.

enrollments in the United States, which had previously been growing more or less in step with population growth (Cooper 2008). More importantly, the federal government caps the number of residency slots that Medicare supports, which is an effective limit on the number of residents in the United States. That might not matter if we could fill the gap with medical school graduates from other countries. But since a U.S. residency is virtually a requirement for practicing medicine in the United States, the cap on Medicare-supported residency positions effectively limited the number of practicing physicians in the country. According to Cooper, the United States is the only country that requires practicing physicians to complete a residency within the country.

The result of these policies has been to limit physician density as demand was growing due to rising incomes and the aging of the population. The United States is an outlier in this respect, as shown in **Figure 7-1**. The deliberate constriction of supply is consistent with a story of rising rents, as non-market forces denied trained people, both domestically and internationally, the opportunity to work in the United States.

FIGURE 7-1
Physician density in select OECD countries, 1995 and 2012

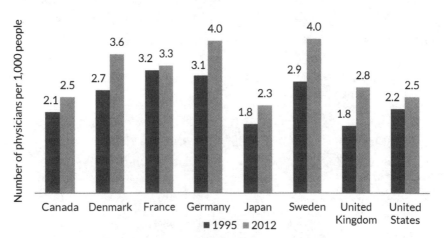

Source and notes: OECD (2014). Data for Japan for 1995 is the average of 1994 and 1996.

Limiting the number of U.S. medical school positions and the number of residency positions, together with requiring a U.S. residency for licensure, are explicit efforts to limit the supply of doctors. At the same time, limiting the extent to which less highly paid medical professionals like nurse practitioners and nurse midwives are allowed to engage in tasks such as prescribing medicine or delivering babies increases the demand for physicians' services. While there can be legitimate safety concerns associated with restrictions on the scope of practice of less highly trained professionals, the economic implications are straightforward: higher pay for doctors and higher health care costs for patients.

Dentists

The compensation of dentists in the United States, like the pay of doctors, is out of line with dentists' pay in other wealthy countries. According to World Salaries (2016), the average pay of U.S. dentists is almost 40 percent higher than in the next highest country (Japan) and more than twice as high as in the United Kingdom, Italy, or Finland, as shown in **Figure 7-2**.

FIGURE 7-2
Average net monthly income for dentists, select countries

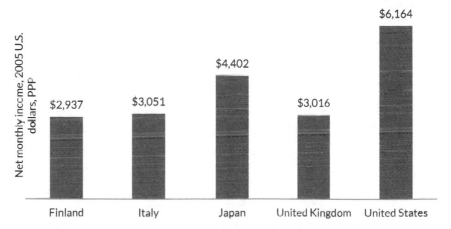

Source and notes: World Salaries (2016). Underlying data from International Labour Organization. Salary for the United Kingdom is a median.

These data, drawn from a survey of dentists who are employees, almost certainly understate the disparity. Most U.S. dentists have their own practices, and this group on average has considerably higher pay than dentist-employees. According to a survey by the American Dental Association (ADA 2015a), the average pay in 2014, net of expenses, for all general practitioner dentists who owned their own practices was $183,340, and for all general practitioners it was $174,780 (**Table 7-1**). As is the case with physicians, specialists earn much higher pay than general practitioners. The average pay for specialists who owned their own practice was $344,740, compared with $322,200 for all specialists. The average pay for all dentists was $201,920, with a median of $170,000. This median places the bulk of dentists in the top 2 percent of workers.

TABLE 7-1

Average and median net income for general practitioner dentists, specialist dentists, and all dentists

(2014 dollars)

Type of dentist	Average net income	Median net income
General practitioners		
All owners	$183,340	$160,000
All general practitioners	$174,780	$150,000
Specialists		
All owners	$344,740	$290,000
All specialists	$322,200	$250,000
All dentists		
All owners	$213,690	$180,000
All dentists	$201,920	$170,000

Source and notes: 2015 Survey of Dental Practice from the ADA (2015a).

There are also substantial differences in pay by specialty. At the top are oral surgeons, with an average annual pay in 2014 of $413,410 and a median of $348,000. The least highly paid specialty is prosthodontist, with an average pay of $221,030 and a median of $175,000 (**Table 7-2**).

TABLE 7-2

Average and median net income for dentist specialties
(2014 dollars)

Type of dentist	Average net income	Median net income
Oral and maxillofacial surgeons	$413,410	$348,000
Endodontists	$325,840	$290,000
Orthodontists and dentofacial orthopedists	$301,760	$245,000
Pediatric dentists	$347,310	$273,000
Periodontists	$257,960	$200,000
Prosthodontists	$221,030	$175,000

Source and notes: 2015 Survey of Dental Practice from the ADA (2015a).

As with doctors, dentists benefit from licensing restrictions that protect them from international and domestic competition. Here too, the licensing rules are set primarily by members of the profession. In terms of international competition, the law requires that dentists graduate from an accredited dental school in the United States (an exception for Canada began in 2011). Dentists protect themselves from domestic competition by limiting the scope of practice of dental hygienists, who often have the skills to perform many of the tasks performed by dentists. As with restrictions on the scope of practice of nurses, real public health concerns may underlie these restrictions, but their economic impact is to increase the demand for the services of dentists and presumably raise their pay.

Lawyers

The legal profession uses formal licensing requirements to restrict entry, most obviously by requiring lawyers to pass a state bar examination. Lawyers also use state governments to reserve for themselves tasks that could be performed by workers with less legal training, such as paralegals, or by clients themselves. While there is some legitimate basis for barriers to foreign lawyers practicing in the United States — not all countries have the same criminal or civil codes and penalties as the United States — standardization could allow for more foreign lawyers or legal workers to perform U.S.-based legal work. (The work could be outsourced through the Internet, eliminating the need for foreign legal workers to physically enter the United States.)

Though there are few good measures of the openness of the legal profession across countries that include the United States, there are indications that the United States has a less-open legal market than most other wealthy countries. A recent analysis by the OECD noted that in 2000, the United Kingdom issued 881 work permits to lawyers from the United States alone. By contrast, the United States issued a *total* of 775 work permits for lawyers in the same year (Hook 2007). The United States can certainly be more open to both more foreign lawyers working in the United States and more legal work being done overseas.

Consistent with the idea of law being a protected profession, a recent analysis found that the pay of lawyers rose substantially more rapidly from 1990 to 2000 (49.2 percent) than the pay of PhDs in engineering (41.0 percent), the life sciences (37.5 percent), and the natural sciences (29.7 percent) (Freeman 2006). Another study found that, after controlling for education, experience, and other standard variables, lawyers enjoyed a pay premium of 49.0 percent (Winston et al. 2011).

Apart from erecting legal barriers that prevent non-lawyers from engaging in many types of legal work, lawyers can also increase the demand for their services by ensuring that tasks are more complicated than necessary in order to force people to hire more lawyers. For example, the documents associated with closing on a mortgage are now largely standardized, and it should be possible in most cases to structure them so that it would not be necessary to have a lawyer review them and be present at closing. Many states now have standardized forms for wills that can be downloaded from the Internet. People without extensive assets or complicated family situations can typically fill out these forms without the assistance of a lawyer.[87]

---

87 Individual income tax filings is another area that provides a considerable amount of often unnecessary work for lawyers. It should be possible for the IRS to calculate the returns of most low- and moderate-income workers and send the completed forms back to the taxpayer for approval. This is the practice in several European countries.

Several big rent-seeking sectors of the economy require the services of lawyers, and typically offer very high pay. Intellectual property law requires lawyers with narrow areas of specialization, and since large sums are often involved the lawyers tend to be well paid. The National Association for Law Placement found that starting pay was higher at law firms that did intellectual property law and that median pay among senior associates was $65,000–75,000 higher at firms with lawyers performing intellectual property law than it was for the average of firms (NALP 2015). The other rent-seeking sector that requires considerable legal work is corporate and individual tax avoidance. Many corporations devote enormous resources to finding ways to minimize their tax bill (Kocieniewski 2011), and compensation can be substantial, since an effective loophole can be enormously valuable.

The United States has more lawyers per capita, 3.65 per thousand, than other wealthy countries, such as Canada (2.2) and Germany (1.3) (Magee et al. 1989). While the relatively large number of lawyers in the United States is a drain on the economy, factors unique to the United States might explain the higher ratio. Specifically, the rate of incarceration in the United States is far higher than in other wealthy countries, and so the demand for prosecutors and criminal defense lawyers is higher. In addition, the fact that the United States does not provide universal health insurance and has extraordinarily high health care costs means that people would have incentives that do not exist in other countries to pursue legal actions over physical injuries. Finally, regulation and litigation are alternative forms of protection. In countries with more extensive regulation for consumer protection and safety, there may be less need for legal action.

These qualifications are crucial, since it is important to recognize the factors that may lead the United States to devote a larger share of its resources to its legal system than other countries. However, even if these

---

Adopting this approach would radically reduce the need for tax consultants and for lawyers to challenge the work of these consultants.

factors may lead to more need for lawyers, it does not necessarily follow that they should get higher pay than in other countries.[88]

It is worth noting that in recent years there has been somewhat of a glut in lawyers, with many new law school graduates having difficulty finding jobs in the profession and others receiving salaries insufficient to allow repayment of their educational loans. But at the same time, top law firms are still offering students just out of law school salaries well over $100,000 a year, suggesting that rents in the legal profession may be getting distributed to a more narrow group of lawyers.

Cumulative pay and rents

How much would the United States save if, rather than receiving rents, physicians, dentists, and lawyers earned pay comparable to the levels paid in other wealthy countries (**Table 7-3**, Column 4) or if the gap were cut in half (Column 5)? One might argue that comparisons with other countries should be adjusted for the United States' higher per capita income of 20 percent, on average, compared with other wealthy countries, but an adjustment of this size would still leave a large gap.

For physicians' pay, we would save $80 billion a year if the gap were fully eliminated and $40 billion if the gap were cut in half. While the numbers in the table for average salaries are somewhat imprecise given the limits of the data and differences across sources, they are consistent with other findings. For example, the Commonwealth Fund (2006) calculated that the United States spent $1,362 per capita in 2004 on physicians' services, compared to a median of $482 across the OECD, $319 in Canada, and $307 in Germany. These differences imply a gap of $270 billion between physicians' payments in the United States and the OECD median and a gap of more than $320 billion between payments in the United States and payments in Canada and Germany. The Commonwealth

---

88   There is evidence that a larger number of lawyers per capita is associated with slower economic growth. Magee et al. (1989) found that more students of law (a proxy for lawyers) was associated with slower growth.

Fund's analysis includes more than just doctors' pay, but its numbers are consistent with the sort of gap shown in Table 7-3.

TABLE 7-3

Potential savings from eliminating rents for doctors, dentists, and lawyers

(2014 dollars)

	Number	Average pay	Average pay other countries	Savings with no gap	Savings with 50% gap
Doctors	800,000	$250,000	$150,000	$80 billion	$40 billion
Dentists	150,000	$202,000	$60,000	$21.2 billion	$10.6 billion
Lawyers	1,268,000	$260,000	n.a.	$108.4 billion	$54.2 billion
			Total	**$209.6 billion**	**$104.8 billion**

Source and notes: 2015 Survey of Dental Practice from the ADA (2015a); BLS (2014); World Salaries (2016); Winston et al. (2011, p. 27); ABA (2013); Author's calculations; see text.

For dentists, the savings would be $21.2 billion if the gap were eliminated and $10.6 billion if the gap were cut in half. The comparable savings for lawyers are $108.4 billion and $54.4 billion.[89]

In all, the potential savings if rents were eliminated in these three professions total $209.6 billion (about 1.2 percent of GDP). Reducing them by half would save $104.8 billion (about 0.6 percent of GDP). These calculations indicate there would be large potential savings to consumers and benefits to the economy if the pay of these professionals can be brought closer in line with their counterparts elsewhere in the world without a deterioration in the quality of the services provided. The next

---

89   Average pay for lawyers in the United States is taken from Winston et al. (2011, p. 27), where the figure of $191,000 for 2000 was adjusted upward by the CPI for 2014. This is an average for lawyers in law firms, so it is likely higher than the average for all lawyers. On the other hand, it is likely missing the earnings of many of the most highly paid lawyers who are senior partners who may report earnings as capital income. For this reason, it is not clear that the number is necessarily too high. The number of licensed lawyers is from the ABA (2013). Since the data on international comparisons is limited, the number calculated for the "savings with no gap" column is based on the 49.0 percent wage premium calculated by Winston et al. (2011).

section reviews some of the research on professional licensing to examine the evidence that unnecessarily strict requirements have raised the pay in these professions. It also presents some original analysis that explores this question in a slightly different way. The following section explores the possibility of increased openings to foreign professionals.

Licensing and rents in highly paid professions

There has been a considerable body of research in recent years looking at the role of licensing requirements in raising the wages and limiting supply of the affected occupations. While most of the work has focused on licensing in middle or lower paying occupations, there is some research that examines the impact of licensing requirements on high paying occupations. This work provides some evidence that excessive licensing requirements (meaning beyond what is necessary to ensure quality) reduce supply and raise pay for these occupations.

Kleiner and Kudrle (2000) found that states with lower pass rates for their dentistry licensing exams from 1980 to 2000 had fewer dentists and higher prices than states with higher pass rates. Using a unique dataset of dental exams for incoming army recruits (which identifies the recruits' state of origin), the study found no evidence of differences in outcomes based on the states' pass rates.

Kleiner and Park (2010) examined whether regulations allowing for more independence for dental hygienists affected their pay and the pay and demand for dentists. The analysis found that giving hygienists the opportunity to be self-employed increased their pay by 10 percent and decreased the pay of dentists by 16 percent.

Kleiner et al. (2014) found that restrictions on the ability of nurse practitioners to prescribe medicine led to an increase in the cost of a well-child exam, lower hours for nurse practitioners and increased hours for doctors. The study used eight years of data from the American Community Survey (ACS), compared the hours of nurse practitioners and doctors in states with more and less restrictive prescribing rules. Wages of nurse practitioners in states with more restrictive rules were about 14 percent lower and physician wages about 7 percent higher than in states with fewer restrictions. Annual hours of nurse practitioners were 6–14 percent lower while physicians' hours were 6–9 percent higher. The study also found that tighter restrictions increased the price of a well-child medical exam by 3–16 percent. The study found that weaker restrictions were not associated with either an increase in infant mortality rates or higher malpractice premiums.

In contrast, Stange (2013) tested for the impact of an increase in the density of nurse practitioners and physician assistants on the number of doctor visits, total medical expenditures, and other outcomes over the period 1996–2008. The study also tested whether restrictions on the ability of nurse practitioners to prescribe drugs affected outcomes. In virtually every specification, the analysis found no significant impact of the density of nurse practitioners or physician assistants on utilization or spending.

A striking finding of the research estimating the impact of flexible practice rules on the hours and wages of nurse practitioners vis-à-vis doctors is that the impact is quite large even though there are only about a quarter as many nurse practitioners as doctors. Furthermore, insofar as nurse practitioners substitute for doctors, they would be substituting for general practitioners, who are paid much less than specialists. But a simple substitution of the time of nurse practitioners for the time of general-practitioner doctors cannot explain the size of the estimates for impact on doctors' hours and pay. In effect, the results imply that for every hour reduction in the time of a nurse practitioner due to tighter regulations, a doctor works 1.7 to 6.0 hours more. This is unlikely.

A more plausible story, which the study suggests, is that nurse practitioners are less likely to recommend follow-up procedures or exams with more highly paid specialists. This suggests that increased use of nurse practitioners may lead to a type of health care more in line with that in other wealthy countries, where fewer procedures require specialists.[90]

---

90 The study did examine two outcome measures to look for evidence of quality being affected by the substitution of nurse practitioners for doctors, although neither would seem conclusive. One was infant mortality rates, which showed no change associated with the increased prescribing authority of nurse practitioners. The other

The findings on the relationship between the pay and hour of dentists and dental hygienists suggest a similar pattern. While the implied substitution of labor between the two professions is more plausible, given the much closer relationship between the size of the two occupations, the implied impact of the pay of dental hygienists on the pay of dentists cannot be explained simply by substitution. With the average pay of dental hygienists roughly one-third the pay of dentists, the estimates imply that a one dollar increase in the pay of a dental hygienist is associated with roughly a three dollar decrease in the pay of dentists. Here also, a more plausible explanation is that, in addition to substituting lower-cost labor for higher-cost labor, self-employed dental hygienists are less likely to recommend the services of more expensive specialists.

While not directly examining the impact of licensing, Hall et al. (2011) found evidence that highly skilled immigrants often work at jobs with educational requirements far lower than their skill levels. Using ACS data for the years 2006–2008, the study found this mismatch to be the case for 11.3 percent of highly skilled immigrants compared to just 6.1 percent of native-born workers. The study notes that having been educated in the United States has a large effect on employment, so the gap would likely be higher if the analysis were restricted to immigrants who earned their degrees outside the country.

This finding is consistent with the possibility that licensing requirements are preventing many qualified immigrants from working in high-paying professions. These workers presumably came to the United States knowing that they would unlikely be able to work in the professions for which they were trained, but it is also probably the case that more highly educated immigrants would come to the United States if they had

---

was malpractice premiums for doctors, which also did not rise in states with greater authority given to nurse practitioners. This finding is not necessarily compelling since the ability to win a malpractice case against a doctor depends on the responsibilities assigned doctors relative to nurse practitioners in a specific state. If an error by a nurse practitioner, operating without a doctor's supervision, leads to harm for a patient, it is presumably more difficult to win a malpractice suit against the doctor than if the nurse practitioner were operating under the doctor's oversight.

the opportunity to work in their professions. In the case of physicians and dentists, the barriers are explicit: no license if a person was not trained in a U.S. medical residency program or a U.S. dental school (except for an accredited dental school in Canada). Allowing immigrants trained as doctors or dentists in their home countries to come to and practice in the United States, perhaps after completing additional training to meet U.S. standards, would have a beneficial impact for the productive economy and public health.[91]

In sum, the evidence shows that licensing of highly paid professionals has the effect of increasing their pay,[92] and weaker licensing requirements are not associated with a deterioration in the quality of the service. The standards seem to serve more as protectionist barriers than as means of assuring quality care.

The potential impact of international competition on the earnings of highly paid professionals

Doctors, dentists, and lawyers have been largely protected from international competition over the last four decades even as trade has expanded as a share of GDP. While this privileged outcome is partly due to the nature of the services involved, it is also in part the result of a deliberate decision to leave protectionist barriers in place. For doctors the wall is completion of a U.S. residency program. This is very clear in the case of physicians and dentists. In the former case, only doctors who have completed U.S. residency programs are able to practice medicine in the United States.[93] In the case of dentists, to get a license it is necessary to

---

91   Developing countries face the risk of a brain drain if a large portion of the professionals emigrate to the United States or other wealthy countries. This could be countered by refunding a portion of the gains, for example, the income tax on the earnings of immigrant doctors, to the home country. Such a rule would allow for the training of several professionals for every one that comes to the United States.

92   Not all the research finds that licensing leads to a pay premium. Some research has found a relatively small premium for licensing that went away altogether in some specifications (e.g., Gittleman and Kleiner 2013).

93   There are exceptions, with prominent foreign physicians generally able to get licensed to practice in the United States, but the typical doctor practicing in Europe

graduate from a dental program in the United States, with the exception that Canada also now has some programs that are accredited by the United States as well.

Increased international competition might affect prices and pay in these highly paid professions through three main routes. The first is by allowing more foreign-trained professionals to practice in the United States. The second route is through medical travel, though mostly for physician services, since the difference in price for dental care might not be large enough to justify foreign travel. The third route is through the emigration of U.S. retirees. If retirees could access their Medicare benefits outside of the United States (and share in the savings from lower cost health care), they may be more inclined to move abroad, and Medicare would enjoy the savings from the lower cost of their health care.

Increased use of foreign-trained professionals

Ensuring that doctors and dentists trained in other countries have been educated to U.S. standards is a legitimate public health concern. But just as the United States was able to put in place a reciprocal accreditation process for dental schools with Canada in 2011, it should be possible to establish a process on a broader basis (ADEA 2014). In principle, doctors and dentists from countries with comparable standards to those of the United States can be tested for proficiency and then work in their profession with the same freedom as someone who was trained here. Such is already the case within the European Union, where doctors who meet a common set of standards are free to practice in any E.U. country (Kovacs et al. 2014).

Persons trained in developing countries with lower professional standards could be trained to U.S. levels. Such a practice would mirror general trade policy — the creation of uniform standards in a range of areas has been a major component of every trade pact negotiated over the last quarter century. The removal of barriers that prevent workers in

---

or Canada would not have the option to practice in the United States without completing a U.S. residency program.

highly paid professions from working in the United States could have been included too.

How many foreign-trained physicians would come to the United States if there were a standardized licensing process? Data on the number of foreign-born and foreign-trained physicians now practicing in the United States can provide a useful point of reference. These are physicians who in almost all cases completed a U.S. residency program in addition to their foreign training. According to the American Medical Association (AMA), approximately 25 percent of practicing physicians in the United States were international medical graduates (IMG), meaning they graduated from a medical school outside of the United States (AMA 2016). Roughly a fifth of them graduated from medical schools in the Caribbean and were likely U.S. citizens who went overseas for medical school. That leaves roughly 20 percent of practicing physicians who are foreign born and foreign trained.

The question is how many more IMGs would be practicing in the United States if foreign trained physicians had the opportunity to take part in a U.S. equivalent residency program in their home country, and then have the same right to practice in the United States as a U.S. citizen who had completed all of their training within the United States. Under current rules, IMGs are effectively subject to a quota system that limits the number of residency slots available to them (Desbiens and Vidaillet 2010). An open system would allow IMGs to have a larger share of the U.S. residency slots (the quota system suggests that many are rejected in favor of less-qualified U.S. graduates) and also allow them to receive equivalent training to residency in their home countries.

In addition to allowing for an increase in the overall supply of doctors, the logic of greater openness to IMGs is simple: it's cheaper to train doctors in other countries than in the United States. Given the large gap between the pay of physicians in the United States and other wealthy countries, and the even larger gap between the pay of physicians in the United States and developing countries, it is reasonable to expect a large supply response to a policy that allowed foreign-trained physicians to practice in the United States as long as they completed an equivalent residency program.

Table 7-4 shows the change in annual inflows, the cumulative change after 10 years, and the percentage increase in physicians that would result from this policy. The rows assume alternatively that the number of IMGs entering the United States each year increases by 50 percent, 100 percent, and 150 percent from 6,300, the number accepted into U.S. residency programs in 2015 (ECFMG 2015).[94] It is worth noting that the number of IMGs who applied to U.S. residency programs in 2015 was just under 12,400, almost twice the number accepted (ECFMG 2015). This might give some indication of the likely increase in foreign IMGs who would enter in a more open system.

The estimates range from a cumulative gain after 10 years of 65,000, a 7.6 percent rise in the number of physicians, assuming the increase in the flow is at the low end of 50 percent, to 195,000 at the high end, representing a 22.7 percent increase in supply. While these numbers are large relative to the projected supply of doctors, they focus on the inflow of new medical school graduates and so are likely to understate the number of foreign-trained physicians who would be practicing in the United States under a more open system. In a more open system it is likely that many practicing physicians in other countries would opt to practice in the United States. In short, a more open system of licensing of foreign-trained physicians would likely have a large impact on the supply of doctors in the United States.

TABLE 7-4

Impact after 10 years of allowing foreign-trained physicians to practice in United States		
Percent increase in flow of new residents	Cumulative increase after 10 years	Percentage increase in supply of physicians
50%	65,000	7.6%
100%	130,000	15.1%
150%	195,000	22.7%

Source and notes: ECFMG (2015), Dill and Salsberg (2008), and author's calculations; see text.

---

94 The projection for the total number of doctors practicing in the United States in 2025 (860,000) is taken from Dill and Salsberg (2008).

Medical travel

A second route through which foreign professionals can be placed in competition with their counterparts in the United States is through medical travel. There are huge gaps between the price of major medical procedures in the United States and other countries. These gaps in price are substantial when comparing the cost in other wealthy countries, but the price can be an order of magnitude when comparing prices in the United States with the prices charged in countries like Thailand and India, which have sought to cultivate their medical travel industry. In these cases, procedures are performed in modern facilities comparable to those in the United States or Western Europe.

The average price of hip replacement surgery in the United States is $40,400 compared to less than $12,000 in the United Kingdom (**Table 7-5**). (There is enormous variation around this $40,400 figure within the United States, which raises another set of issues.) The cost in Argentina is just $3,600, less than one-tenth the U.S. cost. Heart bypass surgery costs an average of $73,400 in the United States, compared to $14,100 in the United Kingdom and $8,900 in Argentina. These gaps indicate an enormous potential for savings if a substantial portion of major surgeries needed by people in the United States were performed in lower-cost countries.

TABLE 7-5

Comparative prices of medical procedures, U.S., Argentina, Spain, and U.K., 2012			
(2012 dollars)			
	United States	Argentina	Spain	United Kingdom
Hip replacement	$40,364	$3,565	$7,731	$11,889
Knee replacement	$25,637	$3,192	$7,827	$7,833
Heart bypass surgery	$73,420	$8,882	$17,437	$14,117
Angioplasty	$28,182	$2,851	$9,446	$14,366

Source and notes: International Federation of Health Plans (2012).

Table 7-6 shows the number of each of these four procedures performed in the United States in 2010. The third column estimates potential savings by assuming that total costs, including travel expenses, are $10,000 above the costs in the low-cost country, which is Argentina in each of these cases. (Argentina is an outlier among this group of developed countries. But a full list that included modern facilities meant to accommodate medical travel in countries like India and Thailand would likely show several countries with prices comparable to those in Argentina.)

TABLE 7-6

Potential savings from having medical procedures performed in other countries

(2010 dollars)

	Number (2010)	Total spending (millions)	Savings per procedure	Total savings (millions)
Hip replacement	332,000	$13,401	$21,799	$7,237
Knee replacement	719,000	$18,433	$7,445	$5,353
Heart bypass surgery	395,000	$29,001	$49,538	$19,568
Angioplasty	500,000	$14,091	$10,331	$5,166
Total		**$74,926**		**$37,323**

Source and notes: International Federation of Health Plans (2012).

The last column shows the potential savings if all the surgeries in each category in 2010 had been performed in the low-cost country with the $10,000 travel cost assumption. The savings total $7.2 billion for hip replacement surgery, $5.4 billion for knee replacements, $19.6 billion for heart bypasses, and $5.2 billion for angioplasties, and sum to $37.3 billion.

While it is unrealistic to imagine that most of these medical procedures would be performed in other countries, it is plausible to think that a substantial fraction might be if insurance companies and government health programs offered to split the savings with patients. Many people would be attracted to an offer of several months' pay in exchange for having an operation performed in a high-quality facility in another country. And since most of these procedures are performed on a non-emergency basis, patients could make plans well in advance with their families, their regular physicians, and the facilities in the host countries. If

30 percent of these procedures were performed in other countries, the savings would be over $11 billion annually, and a fuller list of procedures would likely take the potential savings to more than $15–20 billion a year.[95]

The biggest factor obstructing medical travel is the lack of an institutional structure. First, few would want to travel to another country for a major medical procedure without an assurance of the quality of the care. There are private accreditation groups, but issues have been raised about their integrity. Instead, an intergovernmental organization, relying on existing national systems in countries with a track record of maintaining high standards and on a system of inspections in other countries, could certify that facilities met quality standards. It could be financed by a tax on medical travel.

A second institutional step would be to establish a system of legal liability to ensure that patients would be compensated if a procedure were not carried through properly. The system need not replicate the U.S. malpractice system, but it should provide patients with the confidence that they will be compensated for additional medical care and lost earnings associated with a failed procedure.

The third issue is that the vast majority of these procedures are paid for by third parties, either government programs or private medical insurance. As a result, the savings would not directly accrue to patients, giving them no incentive to consider medical travel. This could be remedied by setting up a system where the patient is rebated a portion of the savings. For government programs this could be done directly. For example, Medicare could rebate half of the savings it would receive from having a procedure carried through outside of the United States. Private insurers could also adopt similar policies. Setting up these rules would likely involve some regulatory issues, since regulatory boards would have to authorize the practice. That could happen on a state-by-state basis, or alternatively the federal government could impose rules that require state regulatory boards to allow the rebates.

---

95   Issues connected with medical travel are discussed in Matoo and Rathindran (2006).

Of course, many patients might not want to travel to a foreign country for a medical procedure, given the stress that can be associated with a major operation. However, there is no obvious reason not to give people the option and to share in the savings, if they choose to go this route.

It is possible that an increased demand for a developing country's doctors from wealthy-country patients might pull doctors away from treating their own country's population. But in principle, host countries could tax medical travel and use the revenue to train additional health care professionals, thereby ensuring that the host country's population benefits as well.

Though the potential savings from medical travel are substantial, only a fraction would come at the expense of doctors. If one-third of the cost of the procedures is attributable to doctors' fees, and 10–30 percent of the $100 billion in outsourceable surgeries were performed outside the United States, then the reduction in the demand for doctors would translate to between $3 billion and $10 billion annually, based on 2014 levels of demand and prices.

Emigration of retirees

A third channel through which international competition could exert downward pressure on the pay of doctors is through increased emigration among retirees. The issue here is that retirees may often have an interest in living in other countries. By definition, they no longer are tied to the United States by their work. While many may have family ties that make them reluctant to move to other countries, many people in the United States also have family ties to people in other countries. This will be increasingly true in the decades ahead as a larger share of the retired population will be foreign-born. Even small movements of retirees abroad could make a substantial difference in the demand for health care.

Currently about 1.5 percent of the people receiving Social Security retiree, spousal, or survivor benefits live outside the country.[96]

96   From SSA (2014a) and (2015a).

This number will likely increase in the decades ahead even with no change in policy due solely to the growing share of the foreign born over-65 population, from 13.2 percent in 2014 to an estimated 18.6 percent in 2035 and to 25.8 percent in 2050 (U.S. Census Bureau 2015). While there do not appear to be projections for the number of retirees who will decide to move back to their country of birth, it is reasonable to believe that the number of older immigrants who opt to spend their retirement outside of the United States will be larger than the number of native born retirees.

But the number of retirees who choose to live outside the country could be substantially larger if the government adopted policies to encourage emigration. The simple motivation for the government is that health care is cheaper in other countries, and because the bulk of retiree health care costs are covered by Medicare and Medicaid, the government could save substantially by encouraging retirees to take advantage of the health care systems in other countries. It could reimburse other countries for the cost of caring for U.S. retirees and still have large savings.[97] Reimbursement agreements such as this are already in place between countries in the European Union (Footman et al. 2014).

Emigration by retirees would have a sizable impact on the demand for health care in the United States. According to the Centers for Medicare and Medicaid Services, the average health care expenses of a person over 65 are 260 percent of the overall average (CMS 2010).[98] As a result, in 2010 the over-65 population accounted for almost 34 percent of total spending even though they were just 13.0 percent of the population.[99] And this share is projected to rise rapidly over the next two decades, reaching 20.7 percent by 2035. Assuming no change in the distribution of health care costs by age implies that the over-65 population

---

[97] There is already an agreement for Social Security benefits under which other countries integrate their programs with the U.S. Social Security system. This way, benefits for people who worked in other countries are adjusted for the benefits they receive from the United States. This is described on page 12 of SSA (2015a).

[98] See: https://www.cms.gov/Research-Statistics-Data-and-Systems/Statistics-Trends-and-Reports/NationalHealthExpendData/Age-and-Gender.html.

[99] CMS (2010), Table 1; share of the population from SSA (2015b).

will account for more than 47 percent of health care spending in 2035
(**Table 7-7**).

TABLE 7-7

**Foreign-born shares of over-65 population and over-65 share
of health care spending**

(percent)

	2014	2035
Foreign-born share	13.2%	18.6%
Over 65 share of total population	13%	20.7%
Over 65 share of health care spending	33.9%	47.2%

Source and notes: U.S. Census Bureau (2015), CMS (2015), and SSA (2016a); see
text.

According to the OECD (2015), per capita spending on health
care in the United States in 2013 was $8,700, compared to an OECD
average of less than $3,500 (in 2013 purchasing power parity dollars).
Germany was the second-highest spender at just over $4,800 per capita,
and Canada was third at under $4,400. Per capita spending in the U.K.
was under $3,200 and several of the lower income countries in the OECD
spent less than $3,000 per person. This is shown in Column 1 of **Table 7-
8**.

The second column shows per capita spending for the over-65
population under the assumption that the ratio in each country is 260
percent of per capita spending for the population as a whole, as in the
United States. This is almost certainly an overstatement, since spending is
not as skewed toward the elderly in other countries.

Column 3 shows a projection of per capita health care spending
for the over-65 population in 2035 under the assumption that real per
capita spending increases at an annual rate of 1.5. This is somewhat more
rapid than the recent rate of growth across the OECD.

Column 4 shows the difference between projected per capita
government spending on Medicare in 2035 and the projected per capita

cost of health care in each country in 2035.[100] It is a projection of the difference between what the government will be spending on Medicare for each beneficiary in 2035 and what it would cost a beneficiary to get care in other countries. In the case of Germany this gap is more than $1,000 a year, and in some of the lower-cost countries the gap is more than $10,000 a year.

TABLE 7-8

Current expenditure on health, per capita

(US$ purchasing power parities)

	Overall 2013	Over 65 2013	Over 65 2035	Gap between Medicare cost and cost in other countries	Gap including Medicaid
OECD average	**$3,453**	**$8,977**	**$12,456**	**$5,947**	**$8,847**
Australia	$3,866	$10,051	$13,946	$4,456	$7,356
Canada	$4,351	$11,313	$15,698	$2,705	$5,605
Chile	$1,606	$4,175	$5,793	$12,610	$15,510
France	$4,124	$10,722	$14,877	$3,525	$6,425
Germany	$4,819	$12,529	$17,385	$1,018	$3,918
Greece	$2,366	$6,153	$8,538	$9,865	$12,765
Ireland	$3,663	$9,524	$13,215	$5,188	$8,088
Israel	$2,428	$6,312	$8,758	$9,644	$12,544
Italy	$3,077	$7,999	$11,099	$7,304	$10,204
Mexico	$1,048	$2,726	$3,782	$14,620	$17,520
Poland	$1,530	$3,979	$5,521	$12,882	$15,782
Portugal	$2,514	$6,538	$9,072	$9,331	$12,231
Spain	$2,898	$7,536	$10,457	$7,946	$10,846
United Kingdom	$3,235	$8,410	$11,669	$6,733	$9,633
United States	$8,713	$22,655	$31,435	n.a	n.a

Source and notes: OECD (2015).

---

100 The projection for per capita spending on Medicare in 2035 is taken from CMS (2015). These projections run through 2024. Real per capita costs were assumed to grow at the same rate after 2024 (2.1 percent annually) as they did from 2023 to 2024. The numbers were deflated to 2013 dollars using the CPI-U.

Column 5 adds a projection of per capita Medicaid spending. Medicaid spending adds almost $2,900 a year (in 2013 dollars) to average per capita spending, substantially increasing the gap between what the government is projected to spend on Medicare beneficiaries and the per person cost of health care in other OECD countries.[101] The average figure in this case is somewhat misleading, since most of the over-65 population will not receive Medicaid. But for those who will, the gap between combined Medicare and Medicaid spending would be considerably larger than the numbers shown in Column 5.

There are a few points worth noting about the size of the spending gaps shown in Columns 4 and 5. First, they are likely to understate the true gap because the calculations assume that spending on the elderly in other countries is as out of line with overall spending as in the United States. This will not be true in most or all cases. Second, a portion of the health care costs of the over-65 population are not covered by Medicare (out-of-pocket costs and the costs of private add-on insurance can be substantial), and retirees remaining in the United States and receiving Medicare would incur these expenses. Table 7-8 is comparing government spending on beneficiaries in the United States with *total* per person health care spending in other countries. The potential savings to beneficiaries from having the option to buy into other countries' health care plans would also include their savings on out-of-pocket spending and private insurance in the United States. This means that the total per person savings for a retiree buying into a health care system in other countries would be substantially larger than the amounts shown in Table 7-8. The projected gap between total per capita spending in the U.S. and spending in other countries is more than $15,000 per person in the case of high-cost countries and more than $20,000 per person in the case of the lower-cost countries.

Finally, it is important to keep in mind that these figures are for per person savings. So the potential savings would be over $5,400 annually

---

101 Per capita Medicaid costs were obtained by taking 2010 per capita spending for Medicaid beneficiaries over age 65 from CMS (2010), Table 10, and projecting the same rate of increase in real per capita costs as for Medicare.

for a retired couple moving to Canada, to Australia more than $10,000, and to Mexico more than $30,000, even before counting the savings in out-of-pocket costs. By comparison, the median income for a couple over the age of 65 in 2013 was just over $50,000, and $18,600 for an individual (SSA 2015c), implying that the potential savings from taking advantage of the health care system in another country is comparable to the income of much of the elderly population. Gaps of this magnitude would allow the federal government to pocket savings on Medicare, pay a premium to the host country, and provide a financial incentive to beneficiaries.

Allowing seniors to buy into other countries' health care systems could be complicated. The system would have to be designed to limit the risk of adverse selection on both sides. If the immigrants to a country were relatively unhealthy, a compensation system based on average costs would cause the host country to lose money. Conversely, the emigration of healthier-than-average people would hurt Medicare's finances if it reimbursed host countries based on age-group averages. There also will be issues with people who want to reverse their decision.

But these complications are not qualitatively different than the issues Medicare already faces. People who have opted for Medicare Advantage have been healthier on average than most beneficiaries, and the program has sought to adjust premiums to compensate. Complications also arise when people want to switch between insurance plans when they realize the plan they have chosen does not provide the coverage they need for a specific condition. It is not possible to find mechanisms that work perfectly and treat beneficiaries fairly in all cases, but providing an additional option to buy into another country's health care system should on net be a huge positive to retirees.

How many retirees might opt to emigrate? As noted earlier, about 1.5 percent of Social Security beneficiaries already live in other countries, and it is reasonable to believe that this number will increase as incentives are implemented, as the percentage of the foreign born among the retired rises, as the quality of health care abroad increases, and as growing communities of retirees in places like Ireland and Mexico inspire more people to relocate.

Table 7-9 shows the impact on U.S. health care spending after 20 years under the assumptions that 5 percent, 10 percent, and 20 percent of the retired population decides to emigrate if given the option to use their Medicare payment to buy into the other country's health care system. Projected spending reductions range from 2.4 percent to 9.4 percent, and it would be reasonable to assume that any of the projections would correspond with an equivalent reduction in the demand for doctors.

TABLE 7-9

Impact on health care spending in 2035 from varying rates of emigration	
(percent)	
Over 65 share of health care spending	47.2%
Percentage savings from 5 percent emigration	2.4%
Percentage savings from 10 percent emigration	4.7%
Percentage savings from 20 percent emigration	9.4%

Source and notes: Author's calculations; see text.

Cumulative effect on the doctors' compensation

This chapter has discussed on four channels — the elimination of licensing restrictions, reduction of barriers to entry for foreign-trained professionals, medical travel, and retiree emigration — through which the effective demand for domestically trained doctors and other professionals can be reduced. These channels would directly save money by encouraging the use of lower-cost services and indirectly save money by pushing down the wages for highly paid professionals.

Physicians

For doctors, the largest and clearest potential source of gains is through allowing more foreign-trained physicians to practice in the United States (**Table 7-10**). Given that roughly half of the applicants to U.S. residency programs are rejected solely on the basis of quotas, there clearly is a large potential supply of foreign-trained physicians who are already near to meeting U.S. standards. A policy to encourage foreign-trained physicians to practice in the United States would probably produce higher numbers than the ones in Table 7-10.

The next largest source of gain is from eliminating licensing restrictions that reserve tasks for physicians that other health care professionals are capable of doing. Another important dimension of these restrictions would be requiring specialists to do tasks for which general practitioners are fully qualified. The latter are less often legal requirements than norms of practice, which may be enforced by the threat of malpractice suits. Though this discussion has focused on restrictions affecting nurse practitioners, the list of professionals who would be able to substitute for physicians includes nurse midwives, nurse anesthesiologists, and radiation therapists. As diagnostic technology develops, it is likely that more of the tasks now performed by physicians can be well accomplished by workers with less medical school training.

TABLE 7-10

Impact on the demand for doctors — 2030			
(percent)			
	Low	Middle	High
Changes in licensing	3%	5%	10%
Immigrant physicians	7.6%	15.1%	22.7%
Medical travel	1.5%	3.0%	5.0%
Emigration of retirees	2.4%	4.7%	9.4%
Total	**15%**	**28%**	**47%**

Source and notes: Author's calculations; see text.

The potential gains from increased foreign medical travel and emigration of retirees are both substantial, although smaller than from the first two paths. Both practices are likely to become more common even without any policy changes, due to continuation of current trends. However there is a potential for large gains from policies that promote both trends.

In aggregate these policies would have a substantial impact on the pay of physicians in the United States. The elasticity of demand for health care is estimated to be quite low, usually around -0.2 percent (see Ringel et al. 2002). If the elasticity of demand for physicians is comparable to the elasticity for health care more generally, then even the 15 percent decline in the demand for physicians shown in the low scenario should be large enough to eliminate most or all of the differences between physicians' compensation in the United States and in other wealthy countries. Of course, there would be some supply response, with fewer students from the United States opting to become physicians and some currently practicing physicians retiring earlier. Nonetheless, it seems quite plausible that policies designed to reduce protections for physicians could substantially reduce their pay relative to other workers and provide substantial economic gains.

Dentists

As noted earlier, there are opportunities to increase competition for dentists by allowing a broader scope for practice for dental hygienists. The evidence in Kleiner and Park (2010) indicated that the cost of dental care could be reduced with no loss in quality, by substituting dental hygienists for some of the procedures now performed by dentists. As is the case with substituting nurse practitioners for doctors, the savings found in that analysis would imply that the benefits go beyond just substituting the lower-cost labor of dental hygienists for the higher-priced labor of dentists, but likely also reflects less use of specialists in cases where their services may not be necessary. In addition to the reduction in the demand for dentists that could result from greater use of dental hygienists, there is also the possibility that more foreign-trained dentists could be licensed to practice in the United States if there was a liberalized licensing regime. Unlike the situation with foreign medical graduates seeking admission to U.S. residency programs, there is not a pool of qualified or nearly qualified foreign-trained dentists actively seeking to practice in the United States. While this makes it more difficult to project the number who might apply, the projections for doctors should provide some guidance.

In the case of doctors, the number of foreign medical school graduates who applied for U.S. residency program was equal to 40 percent of the slots available. Since the disparity in pay between dentists in the

United States and other countries is comparable to the disparity in pay among doctors, it would be reasonable to expect a comparable inflow of foreign-trained dentists if the licensing restrictions were relaxed. However, since the current inflow of foreign-trained dentists is near zero, in contrast with foreign-trained physicians who make up more than 20 percent of new residents, the impact would be twice as large, effectively increasing the supply of new dentists by 40 percent annually (i.e. going from 0 to 40 percent, as opposed to going from 20 percent to 40 percent).

Table 7-11 shows the impact that expanded scope-of-practice rules and a relaxation of restrictions on foreign-trained dentists could have on the effective demand for dentists trained in the United States. The first row makes the same assumptions concerning the potential gains from expanding the scope of practice of dental hygienists as were applied to expanding the scope of practice of nurse practitioners and related occupations. The second row doubles the potential impact of relaxing restrictions as applied to doctors, since the current inflow of dentists is near zero.

TABLE 7-11

Impact on the demand for dentists — 2030

(percent)

	Low	Middle	High
Changes in licensing rules	3%	5%	10%
Immigrant dentists	15.2%	30.2%	45.4%
Total	18%	35%	55%

Source and notes: Author's calculations; see text.

The estimates for the effective reduction in demand for dentists range from 18 to 55 percent. The impact of this reduction on the price of dental care and the earnings of dentists would be less than a comparable reduction in the demand for doctors, since the demand for dental care is estimated to be somewhat more elastic — between 0.5 and 0.7 percent (Nash and Brown 2012) — than the demand for doctors. The implied reduction in the price of dental services would be between 20 and 30 percent at the low end and between 35 and 45 percent using the mid-range of assumptions. As is the case with doctors, an offsetting reduction in the supply of domestically trained dentists is likely, since some would opt for other professions and others would retire earlier. But in any case these changes in demand would be large enough to eliminate most or all of the rents in this area.

Lawyers

While much of the work performed by lawyers can be performed by workers with less legal training, the decision to use lawyers rather than paralegal workers is more attributable to norms of practice rather than legal prohibitions. Nonetheless, there is a substantial difference in the pay of lawyers and paralegals, as shown in **Table 7-12** by state.[102]

TABLE 7-12
Hourly pay of lawyers and paralegals, by state
(2014 dollars)

	Lawyers	Paralegals
United States	**$68.32**	**$26.02**
Alabama	$52.78	$19.58
Alaska	$48.10	$25.46
Arizona	$62.54	$24.68
Arkansas	$58.85	$17.64
California	$75.14	$30.05
Colorado	$66.81	$25.65
Connecticut	$84.22	$30.18
Delaware	$64.72	$24.63
D.C.	$103.33	$28.63
Florida	$62.97	$25.56
Georgia	$64.79	$26.12
Hawaii	$82.22	$21.19
Idaho	$51.15	$21.82
Illinois	$71.43	$26.77
Indiana	$54.19	$22.57
Iowa	$62.34	$21.29
Kansas	$53.64	$21.77
Kentucky	$54.83	$25.97
Louisiana	$57.11	$22.43
Maine	$53.08	$19.40

---

102 In some states the sample size is too small to provide a reliable estimate.

TABLE 7-12

Hourly pay of lawyers and paralegals, by state

State	Lawyer	Paralegal
Maryland	$73.98	$31.14
Massachusetts	$71.17	$27.34
Michigan	$56.57	$21.34
Minnesota	$64.93	$23.91
Mississippi	$57.12	$20.23
Missouri	$53.29	$22.23
Montana	$46.20	$18.14
Nebraska	$47.15	$19.54
Nevada	$67.70	$25.11
New Hampshire	$50.27	$23.45
New Jersey	$78.74	$28.88
New Mexico	$61.47	$25.05
New York	$77.52	$29.10
North Carolina	$59.08	$22.10
North Dakota	$53.62	$17.34
Ohio	$52.86	$24.11
Oklahoma	$66.29	$21.30
Oregon	$55.86	$22.69
Pennsylvania	$62.49	$24.66
Rhode Island	$54.68	$26.56
South Carolina	$57.65	$20.31
South Dakota	$40.70	$16.25
Tennessee	$72.89	$22.99
Texas	$66.04	$26.24
Utah	$57.24	$24.13
Vermont	$151.72	$20.40
Virginia	$77.18	$30.83
Washington	$63.22	$24.77
West Virginia	$46.51	$18.59
Wisconsin	$56.05	$22.83
Wyoming	$45.48	$16.90

Source and notes: CEPR analysis of American Community Survey, 2010–2014 (U.S. Census Bureau 2014).

In every state the average pay of lawyers is at least twice as high as for paralegals and in some states it is almost three times as high. This gap should provide a strong incentive to substitute paralegals for lawyers in routine tasks like drafting a will or reviewing a mortgage and transferring documents at the closing of a house sale.[103] Ideally these processes would be simple enough that in most cases no legal assistance is required. Many states have taken steps to simplify some legal processes, but more can be done.

Many of the highest-paid lawyers are involved in areas of practice that are strongly associated with rent seeking. **Table 7-13** shows the average compensation of partners in law firms by areas of specialization. Partners have the highest compensation in corporate, intellectual property, and tax and ERISA (Employee Retirement Income Security Act) law. **Table 7-14** shows the number of lawyers in each area of practice. Intellectual property law stands out as a large and growing area of law, employing almost 12 percent of all lawyers in 2014.

While it is not possible to eliminate the sorts of legal actions that create demand for lawyers in corporate law, the demand for lawyers in intellectual property law is entirely the result of patents, copyrights, and other types of intellectual property claims. The extension of these forms of property in length and scope has naturally led to increased demand for lawyers' services. One of the main benefits of intellectual property reform would be a reduction in the resources tied up in legal actions related to these claims.

TABLE 7-13

Average compensation for partners by practice area	
(2014 dollars)	
	2014
Litigation	$700,000
Corporate	$893,000
Intellectual property	$855,000
Labor and employment	$503,000
Tax/ERISA	$832,000
Real estate	$573,000
Other	$620,000

Source and notes: Major, Lindsey & Africa (2014), Partner Compensation Survey.

---

103 This is an area that seems ripe for a new business that could use trained paralegals to handle the necessary legal documents for a house closing at a fraction of the cost charged by lawyers.

TABLE 7-14

Number of lawyers by area of practice

(number of lawyers)

	2010	2012	2014
Litigation	254,259	297,398	343,865
Corporate	252,273	217,004	225,546
Intellectual property	142,359	154,744	155,294
Labor and employment	87,402	84,021	99,216
Tax/ERISA	56,281	70,118	62,857
Real estate	85,415	64,678	63,473
Other	325,108	357,241	340,168
Total	**1,203,097**	**1,245,205**	**1,290,419**

Source and notes: Major, Lindsey & Africa (2014) and ABA (2013).

There is a similar story with tax law, although the number of lawyers employed is considerably lower. The role of many of the highest-paid tax lawyers is to design creative mechanisms for corporations to minimize their tax liability. A dividend of corporate tax reform, such as the one described in Chapter 4 that would sharply reduce the number of companies paying the corporate income tax, is that fewer resources would be committed to developing tax-avoidance strategies.

Certainly insofar as it is possible, it would be desirable to standardize procedures so that more lawyers from other countries could perform legal work in the United States. But there are still likely to be substantial areas of law where the differences between the United States and other countries are large enough that a foreign-trained lawyer would need considerable training to competently practice here.

Conclusion: Highly paid professionals are highly paid because they set their own rules

Doctors, dentists, and lawyers don't face the same downward pressure on their wages as textile workers, autoworkers, and retail clerks because the government's policies are not trying to push their pay lower. We aren't designing trade agreements to expose these professions to competition with lower-paid counterparts in the developing world. Nor are politicians constantly looking for new ways to alter regulations in ways that undermine these workers' bargaining power. The workers in these professions sit near the top of the pay ladder not because of the inherent dynamics of globalization and the market economy, but because they have much more say than other workers in setting the rules.

It will become increasingly important to challenge the power of these professionals in setting the rules in the years ahead; otherwise the country is likely to pay an ever greater price in the form of the rents earned in these professions. These rents are likely to grow both because the supply of well-trained professionals excluded from the U.S. market will be expanding hugely in the decades ahead, but also because developments in technology are likely to reduce the need for the most highly skilled professionals in many areas. For example, developments in diagnostic technology may make it possible for a skilled technician to assess a patient's heart condition as well as an experienced cardiologist. As robotics develops further, we may be far better off having our surgeries performed by robots than highly skilled and highly paid surgeons. There will always be genuine quality concerns in making these decisions, but if the assessment of quality issues is left to the professionals who stand to benefit, we can expect that these professionals will be enriching themselves at the expense of the rest of us.

There is one final point worth mentioning in this discussion. Of course, many young professionals, especially doctors, have put in years of training and have incurred large debts to practice in a field that they expected to be financially rewarding. It is reasonable to have some sympathy for them and perhaps lessen the blow from market-opening measures by, for example, offering student loan forgiveness.

However, why apply a different standard to market openings for highly trained professionals than to market openings for textile workers and autoworkers? For less highly paid workers we take steps that increase efficiency and promote growth and pledge that we will help those left behind. (In most cases the help has not been especially useful.) It does not make sense to believe that the most educated workers in society somehow are in need of greater protection from the government than the millions of less-educated workers who have been displaced by trade openings and other measures. Sympathy might be appropriate, special protection is not.

Chapter 8

The Political Economy of an Anti-Rent-Seeking Equality Agenda

Progressives have long been suspicious of the market. Some see it as an aberration to be contained, if not actually overcome. In the extreme case, the goal is some form of central planning in which the government makes the bulk of decisions on allocating resources. More tempered versions have the government taking possession of key industries, with smaller firms and less-consequential sectors left in private hands. The social democratic vision dominant in Western Europe leaves the market largely in private hands. The government provides a safety net to ensure health care, education, and other basic needs, and it acts to redistribute economic gains to partly reverse inequality created by the market, at least.

However, neither vision takes into account the notion that the government structures the market in fundamental ways that determine market outcomes. Both visions largely accept the view of the market held by Friedman-esque conservatives — that it is a fact of nature. Undesirable outcomes such as poverty or extreme inequality are givens, and the issue is the extent to which we want the government to supplant the market or ameliorate its effects.

Markets are not fixed by nature; rather, they are infinitely malleable. They are and can be structured in different ways depending on the desired outcomes. The enormous upward redistribution in the United States of the last four decades was not an inevitable outcome of technology or globalization. It was the result of deliberate policies, the purpose of which was to redistribute income upward.

To sustain progressive politics in the decades ahead it is essential that progressives understand the causes of upward redistribution and get a clearer understanding of the market. The suspicion of market outcomes is a prejudice that needs to be overcome. The market is a tool, like the wheel. Many horrible acts have been done with wheels — young children have been run over by cars, sometimes even deliberately — but no one in their right mind would see this as a serious basis for not using wheels.

In the same vein, we can point to plenty of cases where the market has led to really bad outcomes. Tens of millions of people have faced unemployment. Hundreds of millions have faced poverty and hunger. But these outcomes were not necessary features of a market economy. To some extent poverty has been a result of a genuine lack of resources: actual scarcity. More frequently, poverty is the result of the way we have organized markets and structured property rules. If we had rules designed to lead to more equal outcomes, there would not be so much poverty co-existing alongside great wealth for the few.

The chapters in this book have outlined ways in which different policies can be put in place to reverse the upward redistribution of income. This chapter discusses some of the political economy issues around these policies and assesses the political coalitions that could potentially advance the economic agenda described in this book.

The full employment agenda

In principle, a full-employment agenda should be the easiest goal among the major policy areas, since the winners hugely outnumber the losers. Full-employment policy, first and foremost, is explicitly about making the pie larger, even if full employment also has important implications for distribution. We are foregoing a great deal of potential output simply because there is not enough demand in the economy. With more demand, the economy will produce more, more workers will have jobs, and in principle everyone can be better off.

The potential gains from maintaining a full-employment economy are enormous compared to almost any other policy. In 2008, before the severity of the recession was clear, the CBO projected that GDP in 2015 would be $20.5 trillion in 2016 dollars, $2.3 trillion more than it actually was in 2015. The cumulative gap between the CBO's 2008 projection and actual GDP from 2008 to 2015 is more than $13.5 trillion, which comes to $42,000 for every person in the United States. Even if we assume that the CBO hugely overstated the economy's potential back in 2008, the lost income would still be enormous.

We don't have to speculate about the benefits from a full-employment policy since we experienced it in the late 1990s. In 2000, when the unemployment rate fell to 4.0 percent as a year-round average, the economy was 11.7 percent larger than the CBO had projected it would be back in 1996. This difference is the equivalent of $2.2 trillion in the economy of 2016, or $6,800 per person.

The gains from getting to full employment will not be evenly shared. They will go disproportionately to blacks and Hispanics and to people with less education. This was the case in the boom of the late 1990s, though it's not clear that there need be losers at all. The profit share of income may drop somewhat, but if the pie is larger, businesses can still come out ahead. After all, few corporations saw 2000 as a disastrous year.

The impact of full employment will vary across sectors. Businesses that depend on low-wage labor will face difficulties as workers with better options either leave or demand higher pay to stay. A predictable result of a full-employment economy is that we will have fewer convenience stores and fast food restaurants, since some of these businesses will not be profitable if workers are paid a substantially higher wage.

Other businesses may take a hit as wages for many of their employees rise rapidly due to a tight labor market. For example, the clerical staff at a legal firm or the custodians in a software company can be expected to receive higher pay in a tight labor market, and their gains may have some modest effect in reducing profits if the costs cannot be fully passed along.

However, some businesses will benefit from an increase in demand. Traditionally, a major beneficiary of a high-employment economy has been the manufacturing sector. Auto and steel manufacturers can expect to see higher profits as increased demand pushes them closer to capacity. Their ascent may be somewhat less lofty today than it was 30 to 40 years ago as these companies are increasingly competing in a global market, but most manufacturing firms are still likely to see an increase in demand as a net positive for their bottom lines.

If there is an industry that is a plausible loser from a strong economy it would be the financial sector. Banks and other financial firms will almost always have a large volume of long-term loans on their books. While securitization has reduced the volume of loans that these firms are likely to hold on their books, they are almost certain to still be on net holders of long-term debt. They stand to lose if increased wages lead to price increases and higher inflation. Since their loans are almost always set at a fixed rate, e.g., a five-year car loan at 4.0 percent interest, the value of the repayment will decline if inflation rises.

To take the simplest case, if they offered the 4.0 percent car loan with an expectation that inflation would be 1.5 percent, the bank would have expected a real interest rate of 2.5 percent (4.0 percent minus 1.5 percent). If the inflation rate ends up being 2.5 percent then the real interest rate on this loan falls to 1.5 percent (4.0 percent minus 2.5 percent). The bank will then have taken a large loss on this loan since it will be getting substantially less money in real terms than it had anticipated due to the rise in the inflation rate.

Fear of inflation is why many financial firms are opposed to full-employment policies. They may see little gain from the prospect of more growth and lower unemployment (bankers and their families are not the ones typically hurting in a recession), while they face a big risk to their profits if full employment leads to higher inflation. But different businesses within the financial sector may have different interests. Increased growth will increase the opportunity for making loans, a clear source of profit. And a stronger economy will improve the average quality of loans, reducing the number of defaults. Since banks can take large hits on defaulted loans, a lower default rate is a big plus for the financial sector. Nonetheless, the financial sector does seem to be the place where there are the greatest concerns over inflation, and for this reason, the greatest source of pressure against full-employment policies that could lead to more inflation.

But obstacles to full-employment policies exist well beyond those sectors with a direct interest in preventing inflation and keeping workers from gaining more bargaining power. Tens of millions of ordinary workers, who would win from expansionary fiscal and monetary policies designed to lower the unemployment rate, staunchly oppose these policies.

The problem is the prevailing myths about the virtues of austerity and fears about easy money. Polls and focus groups regularly find that the story that the government budget is like a family budget has enormous appeal, but few people have a clear enough understanding of the economy to recognize that this analogy is inappropriate. Everyone understands that using credit cards to balance income and spending each month will lead to trouble. The idea that the government's finances are qualitatively different — that the government does not face the same constraints as a family — strikes most people as bizarre and fanciful.

The same attitudes apply to expansionary monetary policy. The notion that the government can print money and thereby create wealth seems crazy. Everyone has heard stories of Weimar Germany, or more recently Zimbabwe, where governments facing economic crises sought to resolve their problems by printing money. It is difficult to distinguish the idea of printing money when demand is weak and printing money when the government can't pay its bills. If these two situations look similar to people, it is understandable that they would prefer to be on the safe side and avoid the risk of hyperinflation. This preference for security probably explains the continuing appeal of the gold standard even for an economy that has been suffering from too little inflation rather than too much.[104]

---

104 It is also true that few people have any clear idea of the actual rate of inflation in the economy. Most people are not following economic statistics closely. Their

Politicians are happy to exploit this confusion even in the cases where they do not share it themselves. (Most politicians have not studied economics extensively, so there is little reason to believe that most of them have a clearer understanding of these issues than the bulk of the population.) For example, many Democrats who likely recognize the virtues of deficit spending, will tout the budget surpluses of the Clinton years as a triumph of wise policymaking. They contrast their fiscal prudence with the reckless tax cutting of Republicans.

While the purpose of Republican tax cuts may be to give more money to the wealthy, the idea that the economy will often benefit from larger deficits is accurate. Deficits driven by tax cuts for higher-income people offer less of a benefit for the economy than deficit spending on infrastructure, education, or child care because in the former case some of the money is saved, not spent, while in the latter case all of the money is spent, providing a larger short-run boost to the economy and a long-term boost to productivity from the investments. But the constant warnings about deficits make it difficult to gain political support for progressive stimulus measures.

For example, then-Senator Obama knew better back in 2006 when he said that a vote to raise the debt ceiling "is a sign of leadership failure. It is a sign that the U.S. government can't pay its own bills." He voted against raising the debt ceiling (Kessler 2013), even though he presumably knew that there was no problem with the federal government running the modest deficits of 2006 and that there was no problem with raising the debt ceiling, which simply authorizes borrowing to meet commitments already made. He was making a pitch that would resonant politically because most of his constituents did not understand the way the economy works and the difference between their own borrowing constraints and the federal government's. He chose to reinforce these misconceptions for short-term political gain.

---

perception of inflation will be determined by the prices that they happen to see. And, it is also likely that rising prices will have more of an impact on their perceptions than stable or falling prices, so a jump in the price of milk or gas will stand out, even though the prices of most other items might be stable or falling (Federal Reserve Bank of New York 2010).

There is no simple route for circumventing the large-scale confusion people have about the basics of macroeconomic policy. The public's conservatism on these issues is deeply held and believed to be common sense. Few people spend their time contemplating the dynamics of the economy or studying the history of instances of successful fiscal and monetary stimulus. Unless the public deepens its economic understanding, it will be difficult to overcome the fear of debt as a barrier to full employment. This task is not made any easier by the fact that there is a whole industry devoted to fanning these fears.[105]

If it is not possible to make progress on full employment through larger budget deficits, the obvious alternative is smaller trade deficits. In this case, the popular prejudices go in the right direction. Just as people think it is bad for the government to run a deficit, they also generally believe it is bad for the country to be running a trade deficit. And when we are below full employment, they are right.

A simple remedy for a trade deficit is to reduce the value of the dollar, because a lower-valued dollar makes U.S.-made goods and services more competitive internationally. With a lower-valued dollar, our exports become cheaper for other countries; therefore, they will buy more of them. On the other hand, imports become relatively more expensive, meaning that we will buy fewer imported goods and more goods produced here. The result is more domestic demand and more jobs, bringing us closer to full employment.

While this route may seem straightforward, powerful industries have a direct interest in blocking it. As discussed in Chapter 3, many U.S. corporations directly profit from the trade deficit. Most major manufacturing firms produce a substantial portion of their parts and/or products in other countries. They are not anxious to see the cost of the items they import rise by 15–20 percent, if the dollar falls by a comparable amount. Also, major retailers like Walmart have worked hard

---

105 The private equity billionaire Peter Peterson has devoted a substantial portion of his wealth to supporting organizations that promote fears of budget deficits. This list includes the Concord Coalition, Fix the Debt, the Committee for a Responsible Federal Budget, and others.

to establish low-cost supply chains in the developing world. They don't want to see the prices they pay rise sharply due to a drop in the dollar.

Another obstacle is the need to negotiate a lower-valued dollar with China and other major trading partners. These negotiations will involve trade-offs, and making a lower-valued dollar a top priority would mean downgrading some industry priorities, like Microsoft's enforcement of its copyrights or Pfizer's enforcement of its patents. It would also mean downgrading demands from Goldman Sachs and other banks for increased access to foreign financial markets or Verizon to telecommunications markets. These are not trivial obstacles.

One argument that should not be accepted is the claim that we should accept higher trade deficits — and by implication lower employment — because smaller trade deficits will hurt poor people in the developing world. But as pointed out in Chapter 1, this contention is just bad economics. Relatively fast-growing developing countries should be borrowing capital from rich countries like the United States, which means that they should be running trade deficits in order to build up their capital stock and infrastructure. As a practical matter, successful developing countries like China, South Korea, and Taiwan have eschewed this practice by running trade surpluses while experiencing growth. However, their experience reflects a serious failing of the international financial system, which has not supported regular flows of capital from rich countries to poor countries. So instead of pointing fingers at workers in the United States and other rich countries who just want to be employed, we should take a hard look at the actions of the IMF and U.S. Treasury Department.

Another route toward full employment is shortening average work time. As was noted in Chapter 3, Germany managed to reduce its unemployment rate in the Great Recession, even though it was experiencing a steeper falloff in output than the United States, because it encouraged firms to reduce hours rather than lay off workers. There is both a short-term cyclical aspect to this issue and a longer term institutional dimension. The short-term is simply the structure of the system of unemployment benefits. The unemployment system in the United States is primarily designed to encourage layoffs, rather than shorter hours, since workers can more easily be compensated for layoffs. In the longer term, the German experience speaks to trends in work hours. In other wealthy countries, the length of the average work year decreased dramatically over the last four decades. A benefit of shorter work weeks is that more workers have the opportunity to work at better-paying jobs.

There has been some progress in both areas in recent years in large part because these are policies that can be put in place at the state level or in some cases even the local level. In terms of unemployment benefits, 29 states and the District of Columbia now have a work-sharing (short-time compensation) program as part of their system of unemployment insurance. Take-up rates have been low because many employers are unaware of the program and because the system is highly bureaucratic and difficult for employers to use. However, this is an area where progress can, in principle, be made without too much difficulty. It should be possible to better publicize work-sharing programs so that employers at least know they have the option as an alternative to layoffs. And if the existence of work-sharing programs were more widely known, workers may pressure their employers to go the work-sharing route. As for the bureaucratic side, most of the existing programs were designed in the late 1970s or early 1980s. In many cases, they require filing forms on paper. There are also many aspects of these programs that unnecessarily make work sharing far more difficult for employers than just laying off workers. In order for take-up rates to expand significantly, the rules must be adapted so that they don't impose needless burdens.[106]

In terms of hours more generally, the incentive for companies in the United States is to have fewer workers putting in longer hours rather than to have more workers worker fewer. The issue is overhead costs per worker, but those costs are falling as employers reduce their benefits — defined benefit pensions, for example, are rapidly disappearing from the private sector — and as the Affordable Care Act (ACA) reduces the dependence of workers on employer-provided health insurance. While the

---

106 The federal government set aside money for the modernization of the program and provided subsidies to states to use work sharing (Baker and Woo 2012).

ACA does not seem to have had much impact on employer-provided insurance thus far, a larger share of the workforce is likely to procure insurance through the exchanges in the future. If pension and health care benefits are no longer a per-worker cost, then employers have less incentive to force workers to put in longer hours rather than just hiring more workers.

On the other side, progress has been made at the state and local levels to require employers to provide paid family leave and paid sick days. If workers can take time off to deal with child care or care for sick relatives, or take days off when they are sick themselves, their average hours will probably fall. The arithmetic is striking: an increase in average time off of 2.5 days a year would reduce work time by 1.0 percent. If total hours of work needed did not change, an additional 1.4 million people would be hired in the 2016 economy. Of course, how such changes play out will never be this simple. But, as a general rule, if the average worker puts in fewer hours, we will need more workers.

The main reason for promoting measures like paid family leave and paid sick leave is to accommodate people's needs. Paid vacation should also be included in this mix, and the United States is an outlier in not guaranteeing it. Most other wealthy countries guarantee workers four to six weeks a year of paid vacation (Ray, Sanes, and Schmitt 2013), but the United States inadvertently put in place a structure of benefits that pushes workers toward taking the gains from higher productivity in the form of higher income rather than time off. There is nothing natural about this, and evidence suggests that many workers would value more leisure time even at the cost of income or less rapid income growth in the future.[107] But beyond these reasons, reducing average work hours spreads good jobs around more broadly and tightens up the labor market, improving workers' bargaining positions.

---

107 There is also reason to believe that taking the benefits of productivity growth in leisure rather than income will have environmental benefits (Rosnick 2013).

The macroeconomy and everything else

Maintaining a full-employment economy is the key element in ensuring that the benefits of growth are shared equally throughout the income distribution. However, we cannot assume that governments will always opt for progressive macroeconomic policy for reasons noted above. Furthermore, progressives may be in a position to gain power at a level where they can't set macroeconomic policy, as would be the case for state governments in the United States or the national governments within the euro zone. No progressive government should ever find itself in the situation of Syriza when it took power in Greece in 2015, with little clear agenda other than hoping Germany would grant it better bailout terms than were granted to its right-wing predecessor.

And, there is more than a little truth to the concerns of fiscal conservatives about high interest rates and/or inflation. It is certainly possible for excess demand to create a serious inflationary threat in the context of a high-employment economy, even if we have seen little evidence of this problem in the wealthy countries for the last three decades. For this reason, it is important to have policies that directly attack the source of high-end rents. Reducing the purchasing power of those at the top leaves more room for expanding the purchasing power of everyone else, without adding to inflation pressures.

Combating inflation by taming high-end rents

There is no better place to begin the discussion of the politics of curbing high-end rents than the financial sector, which is the basis of many of the country's most bloated incomes. Here is it worth bringing the back the analogy of successful counterfeiters to get a better understanding of the economics.

The immediate effect of eliminating hundreds of billions of dollars of waste in the financial sector through a financial transactions tax and cracking down on abuses by the industry would be similar to the effect of shutting down a massive counterfeiting operation. The counterfeiting operation both directly employs people to print money and get it into circulation. It also indirectly employs people based on the spending of the counterfeiters. Exposing the bills as counterfeits will put all these people out of work. Nonetheless, shutting down counterfeiters is still considered to be good economic policy. The assumption is that the people now employed as a result of the fake bills will instead be reemployed in the real economy.

Eliminating waste in finance that isn't facilitating the working of the productive economy has the same impact as shutting down counterfeiters. It should lead to clear benefits as a whole, even if there are short-term costs as people need to adjust to an economy where they are not dependent on the spending of the counterfeiters or high-flyers in the financial industry.

This can be true even in a financial center like New York City. In addition to the jobs lost by people employed in the industry, there would also be jobs loss among the hundreds of thousands of people employed serving their meals, cleaning their houses, caring for their kids, and providing a whole range of other services. But the flip side of this situation is that the demand for housing, and therefore the cost, would be dramatically reduced. Suppose that rents in the city fell by 30 to 40 percent, as the Wall Street crew was no longer able to pay outlandish prices for condominiums and apartments. This would allow many people to move to the city who might otherwise never have been able to afford it. That should provide a huge boost to other industries, since they will be able to attract more workers. Also, lower rents will free up tens of billions of dollars a year from the budgets of people who already live in the city. These people will have more money to spend on a whole range of goods and services, filling much of the gap created by the drop in spending from the Wall Street crew.

It is likely that even in the case of New York City, most people who do not work in the financial industry end up as winners by reducing the waste in the industry. It is unambiguously the case that the rest of the country comes ahead by having less of its savings effectively taxed away by the financial industry.[108]

Of course, the politics of targeting waste in the financial industry will be difficult. Just as autoworkers would resist a trade pact that is likely to lead to wide-scale job loss in the auto industry, the financial industry will resist any proposal to reduce its income. But the financial industry has representatives in the places of power. Top officials in administrations of both parties are drawn from the financial industry. For Treasury Secretary, George W. Bush installed Henry Paulson, a former Goldman Sachs CEO; Bill Clinton installed Robert Rubin, also a former Goldman Sachs CEO; and Barack Obama installed Jack Lew, formerly a top executive at Citigroup. The top ranks of all three administrations were chockfull of representatives of the financial industry who would do everything in their power to block efforts to eliminate waste there. After all, we're talking about their friends' incomes, not autoworkers' paychecks.

The power of the financial industry will make it difficult to enact measures at the national level to tax financial transactions or to break up too-big-to-fail banks. But that hardly means that progressives should not continue to draw attention to the waste and high-end rents. Also, it would be possible for states with major financial centers (e.g., New York and Illinois) to impose modest financial transactions taxes on the trades that take place there. But since these trades can migrate fairly easily to other financial centers within the country, the taxes would have to be considerably lower than the levels that would be possible nationally.

It is possible to take other, more direct action at the state level to reduce other sources of waste in the sector. For example, any state (or set

---

108 The prospects of London in the post-Brexit era may provide insights into the plight of a financial center after the industry has been downsized. London is virtually certain to lose jobs in the financial industry under a Brexit, but it remains to be seen whether the net effect will be positive or negative for people not working in the industry. While the media are reporting declines in house prices as bad news, the opposite is true for Londoners (or potential Londoners) who don't own a house or condo. The prospect of lower rent and the possibility of paying less for a house in the future is unambiguously good news for them.

of states) can establish a low-cost retirement system that is available for contributions from the state's workers. Illinois is implementing such a system in 2017, and California was debating a similar plan in the summer of 2016.[109] A national pension system would be better, but it may be necessary for a number of states to take the lead.

States may also be able to set up low-cost services in other areas to compete with the financial industry. For example, a number of proposals for a postal banking system would provide basic banking services to low- and moderate-income households (Office of the Inspector General of the United States Postal Service 2014). States may be able to follow this model, perhaps with the cooperation of the Postal Service. States may also be able to provide lower-cost auto insurance and reduce unnecessary costs associated with buying and selling homes.

In addition, state and local government can act to ensure that they are not wasting money in their pensions by paying high fees to hedge funds and private equity funds that don't produce returns that beat the market. An important step to ensure this outcome is increased transparency. All contracts entered into by these pensions should be publicly available and show what the pensions paid to hedge fund and private equity fund managers and what returns the funds received. There can be real value in setting examples. If a progressive state like Vermont or California required that all terms be public, then other states might be shamed into following the example. The same could be the case if places like San Francisco or New York City went this route. And university endowments can also provide leadership in this area. There is no excuse for throwing away public money by paying high fees to the financial industry that are not justified by the returns they produce. The first step for avoiding this situation is public disclosure.

Finally, it is important to simplify the tax code in order to reduce the size of the tax avoidance industry. Allowing firms to issue non-voting shares of stock as an alternative to paying the corporate income tax is perhaps the best way to bring about corporate tax simplification. Companies would be allowed to issue a number of shares that is roughly

---

109 Illinois' law can be found in Illinois General Assembly (2015).

proportionate to the percentage of the corporate income that it expected to pay. This policy could be enacted by states that have corporate income taxes. If states followed this practice, they would likely both be reducing their own enforcement costs and setting a model that could be copied elsewhere.

If issuing shares were offered as an alternative to the corporate income tax at the national level it is difficult to believe there would not be some companies who now pay their taxes that would welcome the option of this simpler alternative. If any substantial number of companies went in their direction it could put pressure on the ones that didn't. Certainly it would be hard to explain why, if they actually are paying the taxes they owe, they would not prefer a simple mechanism that could save them a considerable amount of money in compliance costs. The first step is of course making the issuing of shares an option, which allows for the obvious question: what's wrong with giving people a choice?

Alternatives to patents and copyrights

The pharmaceutical, entertainment, and software industries can be expected to fight just as hard as the financial industry to keep in place the protections that ensure their profitability. But here, too, the market is our friend.

These industries, as currently structured, depend on an incredibly inefficient system of government-imposed monopolies. These monopolies make items that would otherwise be cheap, like prescription drugs and medical equipment, incredibly expensive. They also make it expensive to get recorded music, movies, and software — all items which could otherwise be transferred at zero cost. The goal of a reform strategy is to expose the enormous waste associated with these monopolies and to find mechanisms to allow increased production and use of non protected items. It is also important to block efforts by the government to extend the deeper reach of these monopolies to the rest of the world through trade agreements like the Trans-Pacific Partnership.

In the case of prescription drugs and medical equipment, consumers tend to have little appreciation of the extent to which patent monopolies raise prices because they have become so used to paying high prices and are unaware that high-quality generic versions are selling in, say India, for less than 1 percent of the U.S. price. These differences are incredible both at the level of the individual drug and also at the aggregate level. It is unlikely that even many economists are aware of the hundreds of billions of dollars of additional spending on drugs, tests, and medical equipment each year as a result of their protected status. This sum is far larger than what is at stake in most policy disputes.

One way to publicize these differences is to take advantage of them. Insofar as possible, people can attempt to buy generic versions of drugs in countries where they are available. In the case of some new drugs, which are priced at more than $100,000 for a course of treatment, it would be easy to cover the cost of an extended stay in India or other countries, bring along family members, and still have enormous savings. While this is far from an ideal way to receive medical care, it is certainly better than going without care or mortgaging a house and draining savings to cover the cost of medications. There is a basic principle that everyone should understand: drugs are cheap, but patents and other forms of protection make them expensive.

The other route is to increase the room for non-patent-supported R&D wherever possible. As noted in Chapter 5, it is not plausible that the country will flip over all at once from a system that relies on patent monopolies to one that relies on publicly funded research for prescription drugs and medical equipment. But publicly funded clinical trials could be a midway step. The government would contract with private companies, through a process of competitive bidding, to conduct clinical trials of chemicals that were either already in the public domain or to which the company bought the rights. The results would be publicly posted for doctors and researchers, and the drugs themselves would be available as generics once they had been through the FDA approval process so that anyone would be able to produce them.

This system of publicly funded clinical trials can be infinitely sliced and diced. There could public funding of trials in just some areas (for example, cancer drugs) which would require a relatively small portion of the funding now going to the National Institutes of Health. The payoff would be both the availability of a large amount of data on the effectiveness of the trials — possibly shaming drug companies into more disclosure of test results — and the possibility that some number of important new cancer drugs would be available at generic prices. The costs of clinical tests are low enough that a major foundation or a collaboration of smaller foundations could put up the necessary funding.[110] If this spending produced some number of effective drugs that were made available at generic prices, it could have a considerable impact.

There are many other ways that the process can be cut. For example, the government allows drug companies a six-month patent extension when they test a drug for pediatric uses. The government could instead pay for the testing itself (making the results public) and compare the implicit cost of a six-month patent extension with the cost of direct payment.[111] The point here is to get a foot in the door to allow a clear basis for comparing the efficiency of directly funded research with the current system of patent monopolies. It is likely that the patent monopoly system would flunk this test. It is likely that the drug industry knows that the patent monopoly system would flunk this test, which is why they will do everything in their power to ensure that such tests don't take place. One advantage in this effort is that the generic drug industry stands to benefit from weakening or eliminating patent monopolies. Insurers, in principle, also stand to benefit from the availability of low-cost drugs as well as medical tests. Even the major pharmaceutical companies could still profit through a system of publicly funded research, since they would likely be the major recipients of contracts. However, as long as these companies can make large profits under the current system, they will be

---

110 Doctors Without Borders is already engaged in a process along these lines with its Drugs for Neglected Diseases Initiative (http://www.dndi.org/). While this project has produced an enormous return on the money invested, it is explicitly targeted on diseases that primarily afflict poor people in the developing world. Therefore, it does little to affect thinking on the process of drug development in wealthy countries.

111 This idea was suggested to me by Jamie Love, the director of Knowledge Ecology International.

uninterested in a new route, regardless of the costs their system imposes on the country and the world.

There is a similar story on the enforcement of copyright monopolies. This is an increasingly archaic way of supporting creative work as the Internet makes it ever more difficult to prevent the transfer of unauthorized copies. This is the motivation for more punitive laws on copyright enforcement and increasing efforts to make third parties share in the cost of enforcement.

The answers in this case are both to resist repressive efforts at enforcement and to increase the availability of work not supported through copyrights. In terms of repressive efforts, the defeat of the Stop Online Piracy Act (SOPA) and the PROTECT IP Act (PIPA) were notable achievements. These laws would have required web intermediaries to police their sites for copyright violations. This is a big step up from current law, which already requires that companies side with claims by copyright holders, against their customers, and immediately remove material that is alleged to be in breach. The Trans-Pacific Partnership and other trade deals under discussion also increase the strength of copyright protection, imposing larger burdens on intermediaries.

Chapter 5 discusses a tax-credit system modeled on the charitable giving tax deduction as an alternative mechanism for supporting creative work. This can be implemented at the national level for an amount considerably smaller than the current cost of the charitable giving tax deduction. This would create a vast pool of funds to support creative work, which would almost certainly exceed the amount going to creative workers through the copyright system. As explained in that chapter, the condition for being eligible for receiving funding through the tax-credit system would be waving the right to get copyright protection for a limited period of time. This has the great virtue of being self-enforcing, since someone attempting to cheat the system by getting a copyright during their period of ineligibility would find that their claim was not enforceable.

While such a system could produce a large amount of creative work if it were implemented nationally, states or local governments could experiment with a similar tool. Suppose a city of 200,000 made available a credit of $50 per adult. To be eligible for the credit, a creative worker would not only have to forego copyright protection for a period of time, but he or she would also have to physically live in the city for at least eight or nine months of the year. Donations by three quarters of the population (a high share, but it's free, since the donor gets a full tax credit) would create a pool of $7.5 million to support creative workers.

Since these workers would be required to live in the city much of the year, they would have an incentive to perform their music or plays, conduct writing workshops, or perform other work that would both support them and increase their visibility to people deciding what to do with their tax credit. It is easy to envision a scenario in which this sort of influx brings in enough tourist revenue to more than cover the cost of the tax credit. Of course, this would be an easier proposition if a creative foundation were prepared to put up part of the cost.

In any case, this and many other mechanisms can increase the supply of material supported outside of the copyright system. As more free material becomes available, it will be more difficult and irrelevant to maintain copyright as we know it.

Reining in CEO pay: Getting corporations to serve their shareholders

Chapter 6 noted the explosion in CEO pay over the last four decades and argued that this was the result of a failed corporate governance structure, rather than the increased value that CEOs were providing to shareholders. The argument is that the corporate directors who most immediately determine CEO pay largely owe their jobs to top management. They have little incentive to ever challenge a CEO pay package since they risk angering the CEO and their fellow board members by pressing the issue. In contrast, virtually no director ever loses their job because of allowing an excessive pay package for CEOs and top management.

Insofar as this story accurately describes the rise in CEO pay, the appropriate political strategy involves making it easier for shareholders to exercise control over the company they are supposed to own. Chapter 6 proposes changes to corporate governance that alter the structure of incentives for corporate directors. For example, the directors could lose their annual stipend if a CEO pay package is voted down in a say-on-pay vote by shareholders. The pay for directors can also be structured in ways that give them a direct incentive for holding down CEO pay. For example, the directors can be allowed to share half of the savings from cutting CEO pay, as long as the company's stock performance was not harmed.

While changes in corporate governance rules could be implemented through Congress, this is not likely to happen anytime soon. However, it would be reasonable to push some changes as voluntary measures. For example, less than 3 percent of CEO pay packages are rejected by shareholders. This means that asking directors to voluntarily agree to an arrangement where they would surrender their pay in such cases is simply asking for a vote of confidence that they will not be in the bottom 3 percent of corporate boards. This is a rather low bar.

This also could be a situation where a few examples could prove very powerful. If the board of a major corporation accepted a rule whereby it agreed to forfeit its pay in the event that a say-on-pay initiative were defeated, it might shame other boards into following its lead. After all, why are these boards collecting their large salaries if they can't hold CEO pay to reasonable levels?

The other part of this chapter dealt with the run-up of pay of top executives in the nonprofit sector, which has paralleled the run-up in CEO pay. While the top executives of major universities and foundations are not getting paychecks in the tens of millions of dollars a year, it is not uncommon for their pay to cross $1 million, or more than 25 times the pay of the typical worker. As was noted in the chapter, this pay is largely subsidized by taxpayer dollars, since donations to these institutions are tax-exempt. This means that roughly 40 percent of their salaries came from taxpayers. In the case of a foundation or university president getting $1 million a year, effectively $400,000 is coming from taxpayers.

If taxpayers are paying the bill, it is reasonable to put limits on the top salaries that these institutions can pay. The President of the United States is paid $400,000 a year, which seems like a fair limit on the pay of people employed by tax-exempt institutions. Just to be clear, this is not limiting what nonprofit institutions can pay their presidents or other top officials. It is only limiting what they can pay them while getting a subsidy from taxpayers. This is a measure that also can be put in place at the state level. While the most important tax subsidy is allowing contributors to write off the donation on their taxes, most states exempt nonprofits from paying sales taxes and often property taxes. They could in principle make eligibility for this special tax treatment contingent on accepting limits on pay. As a practical matter, it is unlikely that states would have to worry much about nonprofits fleeing. Harvard is unlikely to leave Massachusetts even if it were forced to reduce its president's pay to $400,000 a year — the salary of the President of the United States — as a condition of special tax treatment.

Pressure on individual institutions by students, faculty, and alumni could prove effective. And some schools going this route would put pressure on others to follow. The fruit of lower pay for those at the top is lower tuition costs and more money available for other employees.

Protectionism for high-paid professionals

The last major form of rent discussed in this book is the pay of highly educated professionals, like doctors, dentists, and lawyers. These professionals are paid far more than their counterparts in other wealthy countries. As noted in Chapter 7, if doctors in the United States were paid the same as their counterparts in other wealthy countries it would save roughly $100 billion a year in health care costs.

It's not an accident that the pay of these workers has not been put under pressure by globalization. It was the result of deliberate policy decisions to largely protect these highly educated workers from foreign and even domestic competition. In the case of doctors, foreign-trained doctors are largely excluded from practicing medicine in the United States.

The issues with domestic forms of protection in highly paid professions are likely to become more serious as technology makes it possible for many relatively complex tasks to be performed by professionals with lower levels of training. For example, advances in diagnostic technology may allow nurse practitioners to make diagnoses of most conditions with the same or better accuracy than most doctors. However, if doctors are allowed to determine standards of care, then they are likely to leave in place regulations that effectively force people to see general practitioners or even highly paid specialists when a much lower paid professional could perform the work equally well.

If our trade negotiators treated doctors and other highly paid professionals the same way they treated manufacturing workers, then trade agreements would have been written to make it as easy as possible for smart, ambitious kids in Mexico, India, and other developing countries to study to meet U.S. standards. They then would be able practice their profession in the United States in the same way as someone born and educated in the United States. The fact that manufacturing workers face competition from low-paid workers in the developing world and doctors and other highly paid professionals don't has nothing to do with the inherent dynamics of globalization: it is about the differences in the power of these groups.

Ideally, we would start to change trade deals so that we did see this sort of competition at the high end. It would lead to the same sorts of gains from trade that we get from buying cheaper clothes and car parts from abroad. However, in this case, the impact would be to reduce inequality rather than increase it.

It is not likely that our trade agenda will be taken over by avid free traders anytime soon, but there are other mechanisms that can help to bring about similar outcomes. One is measures that make it easier for patients to take advantage of the lower prices for major medical procedures in other countries. There are many high-quality facilities in countries like India that charge prices that are often less one-tenth the prices in the United States. Since the cost of some of these procedures runs into the hundreds of thousands of dollars in the United States, and they are usually not done on an emergency basis, patients could travel for their surgery (and even bring along family members) and still have large savings.

While this practice is not likely to be promoted at the national level due to the power of the doctors' lobby, there is no reason that a state couldn't take advantage of this opportunity for cost savings. States could offer their Medicaid patients the option to get major operations overseas, while splitting the savings, as an alternative to having procedures done in the United States. They could also write rules for insurers to facilitate such arrangements. In addition, a solid international licensing system for medical facilities would be helpful for ensuring quality standards, as would clear rules on malpractice. Allowing more people to take advantage of low-cost health care in other countries will directly put downward pressure on prices in the United States by reducing demand. It can also have the beneficial political effect of allowing people to see first-hand that the quality of care in many other countries is comparable to that in the United States.

In principle, it would be possible to make similar arrangements with Medicare. The cost of providing health care to our retirees is more than twice as much per person as in other wealthy countries. This creates the potential for large gains if Medicare beneficiaries are given the opportunity to use their Medicare to buy into health care systems in other countries. The gap between the cost of providing care under the Medicare system and the cost of providing health care through another country's health care system could be shared between the beneficiary and the U.S. government. This would also reduce the demand for domestic medical services while educating people about the quality of health care in other countries.

Here also the doctors' lobbies will furiously fight the idea of globalizing Medicare. While it would be hard to overcome their resistance, it is a case where the doctors are clearly the enemies of globalization and relying on old-fashioned protectionism to maintain their bloated pay. If doctors were treated the same way as textile workers and autoworkers in trade pacts, they would face massive job loss and plunging paychecks.

There are similar, if less dramatic stories, with the other highly paid professions. There are enormous potential gains from opening them up to international competition. It is only the political power of these relatively highly paid workers that prevents them from being subject to the same sort of international completion as their less highly paid counterparts.

Adding it all up

All of the changes outlined in the previous chapters are not likely to happen anytime soon. But the point of this book is that the distribution of income can be hugely altered by restructuring the market to produce different outcomes. This doesn't dismiss the value of tax and transfer policies, but if the market is rigged to redistribute ever more income upward, it will be difficult to design tax and transfer policies to reverse this effect. And if the rigging efforts are never challenged, then they will impose an ever greater burden on those trying to reduce inequality through tax and transfer policy.

Table 8-1 shows the range of the gains from restructuring the market. The total comes to almost $2 trillion in additional income in 2016 in the low-end case, $3.7 trillion in the high-end case. Expressed as units of SNAP spending (**Figure 8-1**), the low-end amount is equal to 27.1 units and the high-end amount just under 50. In short, there is a lot of money at stake here.

This calculation requires several important qualifications. First, more than half of these potential gains are associated with full-employment policy. The high-end number is based on a projection of GDP that assumes the 2008 crash either never happened or that we responded to it quickly and aggressively enough to quickly restore GDP back to its potential. Of course, that didn't happen, and we can't rewrite the past. The result of the crash and subsequent policy failures has to been to permanently reduce potential GDP, both as a result of a lower capital stock and also due to some people likely permanently leaving the labor force. The lower figure, which assumes that we can make up half of the gap between the pre-crash projection of potential GDP and actual output, is more realistic but still optimistic.

The second qualification is that not all of this money would be transferred from the rich to everyone else. For example, if we increased GDP back to its potential, some of the gains would go the 1 percent. And even if a disproportionate share of the additional output from getting back to full employment goes to people lower down on the income distribution, the share going to the top 1 percent will not be zero. The same would hold true for all of the potential gains from eliminating rents. Not all the benefits will go to those lower down in the income distribution, even if the bulk does.

TABLE 8-1

Gains from restructuring markets

(billions of 2016 dollars)

	Low	High
Adopting a full-employment policy	$1,115	$2,300
Eliminating financial sector waste	$460	$636
Ending patent/copyright monopolies	$217	$434
Reforming corporate governance	$90	$145
Ending protection of highly paid professions	$100	$200
Total	$1,982	$3,715

Source and notes: Author's calculations; see text.

FIGURE 8-1

Gains from restructuring markets, in units of SNAP spending

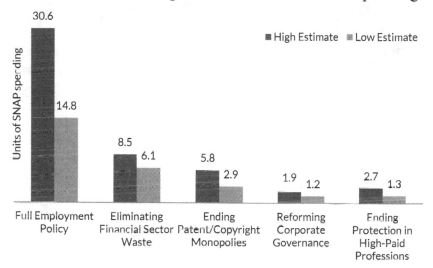

Source and notes: Author's calculations; see text.

Finally, there is likely to be some interactive effect that would go in the right direction from the standpoint of reducing inequality. For example, more than 470,000 physicians are specialists in the United States (Kaiser Family Foundation 2016), and the vast majority earn over $250,000 a year. They account for roughly a quarter of high-end earners in the United States (SSA 2016b). Reducing the ratio of specialists to primary care physicians down to the level that holds in other countries and bringing their average pay down closer to $200,000 (also more in line with other wealthy countries), would put downward pressure on the wages of high-end earners more generally. A sharp reduction in the number of high-paying jobs would have a substantial impact on the high end of the labor market just as the loss of manufacturing jobs has an impact on the labor market for non-college-educated workers more generally. For this reason, some of the estimates in Table 8-1 may actually understate how much eliminating rents may reduce income inequality.

For all the qualifications, there should be little doubt that there is potential to have a large impact on the distribution of income through economically plausible restructurings of the market. The gainers in the top 1 percent have structured the market over the last four decades in ways that increase their share of income. This restructuring can be reversed.

Chapter 9

Rewriting the Narrative on Economic Policy

The standard framing of economic debates divides the world into two schools. On the one hand, conservatives want to leave things to the market and have a minimal role for government. Liberals see a large role for government in alleviating poverty, reducing inequality, and correcting other perceived ill-effects of market outcomes. This book argues that this framing is fundamentally wrong. The point is that we don't have "market outcomes" that we can decide whether to interfere with or not.

Government policy shapes market outcomes. It determines aggregate levels of output and employment, which in turn affect the bargaining power of different groups of workers. Government policy structures financial markets, and the policy giving the industry special protections allows for some individuals to get enormously rich. Government policy determines the extent to which individuals can claim ownership of technology and how much they can profit from it. Government policy sets up corporate governance structures that let top management enrich itself at the expense of shareholders. And government policy determines whether highly paid professionals enjoy special protection from foreign and domestic competition.

Pretending that the distribution of income and wealth that results from a long set of policy decisions is somehow the natural workings of the market is not a serious position. It might be politically convenient for conservatives who want to lock inequality in place. It is a more politically compelling position to argue that we should not interfere with market outcomes than to argue for a system that is deliberately structured to make some people very rich while leaving others in poverty.

Pretending that distributional outcomes are just the workings of the market is convenient for any beneficiaries of this inequality, even those who consider themselves liberal. They can feel entitled to their prosperity by virtue of being winners in the market, yet sufficiently benevolent to share some of their wealth with the less fortunate. For this reason, they may also find it useful to pretend that we have a set of market outcomes not determined by policy decisions.

But we should not structure our understanding of the economy around political convenience. There is no way of escaping the fact that levels of output and employment are determined by policy, that the length and strength of patent and copyright monopolies are determined by policy, and that the rules of corporate governance are determined by policy. The people who would treat these and other policy decisions determining the distribution of income as somehow given are not being honest. We can debate the merits of a policy, but there is no policy-free option out there.

This may be discomforting to people who want to believe that we have a set of market outcomes that we can fall back upon, but this is the real world. If we want to be serious, we have to get used to it.

References

Alichi, A. et al. 2016. "Income Polarization in the United States."
Washington, D.C.: IMF. IMF Working Paper, WP/16/121.
http://www.imf.org/external/pubs/ft/wp/2016/wp16121.pdf.

American Bar Association (ABA). 2013. "Total National Lawyer Counts,
1878–2013." Chicago, Ill.: ABA.
http://www.americanbar.org/content/dam/aba/administrative/market
_research/total_national_lawyer_counts_1878_2013.authcheckdam.pdf.

American Dental Association (ADA). 2015a. "Income, Gross Billings, and
Expenses: Selected 2014 Results From the Survey of Dental Practice."
Chicago, Ill.: ADA.
http://www.ada.org/~/media/ADA/Science%20and%20Research/HPI
/Files/HPIData_SDPI_2014.ashx.

American Dental Education Association (ADEA). 2014. "The Canadian
Experience With Reciprocal Agreements Based on Accreditation."
Washington, D.C.: American Dental Education Association.
http://www.adea.org/WorkArea/DownloadAsset.aspx?id=25645.

American Medical Association (AMA). 2016. "IMGs in the United States."
Chicago, Ill.: AMA. http://www.ama-assn.org/ama/pub/about-
ama/our-people/member-groups-sections/international-medical-
graduates/imgs-in-united-states.page.

Anis, Aslam H. et al. 2005. "When Patients Have to Pay a Share of Drug Costs: Effects on Frequency of Physician Visits, Hospital Admissions and Filling of Prescriptions." *CMAJ*, Vol. 173, No. 11. http://www.cmaj.ca/content/173/11/1335.short?cited-by=yes&legid=cmaj;173/11/1335.

Angel, James et al. 2015. "Equity Trading in the 21st Century: An Update." *Quarterly Journal of Finance (QJF)*, Vol. 5, No. 1, pp. 1550002-1–1550002-39. http://EconPapers.repec.org/RePEc:wsi:qjfxxx:v:05:y:2015:i:01:p:1550002-1-1550002-39.

Appelbaum, Eileen and Rosemary Batt. 2014. *Private Equity at Work: When Wall Street Manages Main Street*. New York, N.Y.: Russell Sage Foundation. https://www.russellsage.org/publications/private-equity-work.

_____. 2016. "Are Lower Private Equity Returns the New Normal?" Washington, D.C.: Center for Economic and Policy Research. http://cepr.net/publications/reports/are-lower-private-equity-returns-the-new-normal.

Baker, Dean. 2002. "The Run-Up in Home Prices: Is it Real or Is it Another Bubble?" Washington, D.C.: Center for Economic and Policy Research. http://cepr.net/publications/reports/the-run-up-in-home-prices-is-it-real-or-is-it-another-bubble.

_____. 2008. *Plunder and Blunder: The Rise and Fall of the Bubble Economy*. Oakland, Calif.: Berrett-Koehler.

_____. 2016. "Rents and Inefficiency in the Patent and Copyright System: Is There a Better Route?" Washington, D.C.: Center for Economic and Policy Research. Working Paper. http://cepr.net/images/stories/reports/rents-inefficiency-patents-2016-08.pdf?v=2.

Baker, Dean and Nicole Woo. 2012. "States Could Save $1.7 Billion Per Year With Federal Financing of Work Sharing." Washington, D.C.: Center for Economic and Policy Research. http://cepr.net/publications/reports/states-could-save-17-billion-per-year-with-federal-financing-of-work-sharing.

Bakija, J., A. Cole, and B. Heim. 2012. "Jobs and Income Growth of Top Earners and the Causes of Changing Income Inequality: Evidence From U.S. Tax Return Data." Manuscript, Williams College.

Barnhart, Scott W, Michael F. Spivey, and John C. Alexander. 2000. "Do Firm and State Antitakeover Provisions Affect How Well CEOs Earn Their Pay?" *Managerial and Decision Economics*, Vol. 21, No. 8, pp. 315–28.

Beauchamp, Zack. 2016. "If You're Poor in Another Country, This Is the Scariest Thing Bernie Sanders Has Said." Vox.com, April 5. http://www.vox.com/2016/3/1/11139718/bernie-sanders-trade-global-poverty.

Bebchuck, Lucian Arye and Yaniv Grinstein. 2005. "The Growth of Executive Pay." Cambridge, Mass.: Harvard Law School. John M. Olin Center's Program on Corporate Governance Discussion Paper No. 510.

Bebchuck, Lucian Arye and Jesse Fried. 2006. *Pay Without Performance: The Unfulfilled Promise of Executive Compensation*. Cambridge, Mass.: Harvard University Press.

Bertrand, Marianne and Sendhil Mullainathan. 2001. "Are CEOs Rewarded for Luck? The Ones Without Principles Are." *Quarterly Journal of Economics*, Vol. 116, No. 3, pp. 901 32.

Bessen, James. 2005. "Open Source Software: Free Provision of Complex Public Goods." Harpswell, ME: Research on Innovation. Working Paper. http://papers.ssrn.com/sol3/papers.cfm?abstract_id=588763.

Bessen, James E. and Michael J Meurer. 2014. "The Direct Costs From NPE Disputes." *Cornell Law Review*, Vol 99, No. 387.

Bessen, James E., Jennifer Ford, and Michael J. Meurer. 2012. "The Private and Social Costs of Patent Trolls." *Regulation*, Vol. 26, Winter 2011–2012.

Boldrin, Michele, Juan Correa Allamand, David K. Levine, and Carmine Ornaghi. 2011. "Competition and Innovation." *Cato Papers on Public Policy*, Vol. 1, pp. 109–63.

Boldrin, Michele and David D. Levine. 2013. "The Case Against Patents." *Journal of Economic Perspectives*, Vol. 27, No. 1, pp. 3–22.

Bordo, Michael and Andrew Filardo. 2005. "Deflation in a Historical Perspective." Basel, Switzerland: Bank for International Settlements. BIS Working Paper No 186. http://www.bis.org/publ/work186.pdf.

Bumiller, Elisabeth. 1996. "Ascap Asks Royalties From Girl Scouts, and Regrets It." *New York Times*, December 17. http://www.nytimes.com/1996/12/17/nyregion/ascap-asks-royalties-from-girl-scouts-and-regrets-it.html.

Bureau of Economic Analysis (BEA). 2016. "National Income and Product Accounts." Washington, D.C.: BEA.

Bureau of Labor Statistics (BLS). 2014. "Occupational Outlook Handbook: Healthcare, Dentists." Washington, D.C.: BLS. http://www.bls.gov/ooh/healthcare/dentists.htm.

_____. 2016a. "Labor Force Statistics From the Current Population Survey." Washington, D.C.: BLS. http://www.bls.gov/cps/.

_____. 2016b. "27-3020 News Analysts, Reporters and Correspondents." Washington, D.C.: BLS. http://www.bls.gov/soc/2010/soc273020.htm.

_____. 2016c. "Table 1. Median Usual Weekly Earnings of Full-Time Wage and Salary Workers by Sex, Quarterly Averages, Seasonally Adjusted." Washington, D.C.: BLS.

Burns, Natasha and Simi Kedia. 2003. "Do Executive Stock Options Generate Incentives for Earnings Management? Evidence From Accounting Restatements." Cambridge, Mass.: Harvard Business School. Working Paper.

Burman, Leonard et al. 2016. "Financial Transaction Taxes in Theory and Practice." *National Tax Journal*, Vol. 69, No. 1, pp. 171–216. http://www.brookings.edu/~/media/research/files/papers/2016/02/29-financial-transaction-taxes-in-theory-practice-gale/burman-et-al_-ntj-mar-2016-%282%29.pdf.

Cecchetti, Stephen G. and Enisse Kharroubi. 2012. "Reassessing the Impact of Finance on Growth." Basel, Switzerland: Bank of International Settlements. BIS Working Paper No 381. http://www.bis.org/publ/work381.pdf.

Center for Responsive Politics. 2016a. "Top Interest Groups Giving to Members of Congress, 2016 Cycle." Washington, D.C.: Center for Responsive Politics. https://www.opensecrets.org/industries/mems.php. Accessed 2016-07-18.

_____. 2016b. "Interest Groups." Washington, D.C.: Center for Responsive Politics. https://www.opensecrets.org/industries/. Accessed 2016-07-18.

Centers for Medicare and Medicaid Services (CMS). 2010. "Total Personal Health Care Spending by Gender and Age Group, Calendar Years 2002, 2004, 2006, 2008, 2010." Woodlawn, Md.: CMS. https://www.cms.gov/Research-Statistics-Data-and-Systems/Statistics-Trends-and-Reports/NationalHealthExpendData/Downloads/2010GenderandAgeTables.pdf.

_____. 2014. "NHE Projections 2014-2024—Tables." Balitmore, Md.: CMS. https://www.cms.gov/Research-Statistics-Data-and-Systems/Statistics-Trends-and-Reports/NationalHealthExpendData/Downloads/Proj2014Tables.zip.

_____. 2015. "2015 Medicare Trustees Report, Table V.D1." Woodlawn, Md.: SSA. https://www.cms.gov/research-statistics-data-and-systems/statistics-trends-and-reports/reportstrustfunds/downloads/tr2015.pdf.

Center on Budget and Policy Priorities. 2016. "Policy Basics: Introduction to the Supplemental Nutrition Assistance Program (SNAP)." Washington, D.C.: Center on Budget and Policy Priorities. http://www.cbpp.org/research/policy-basics-introduction-to-the-supplemental-nutrition-assistance-program-snap.

Centers for Medicare and Medicaid Services (CMS). 2014. "National Health Expenditure Data, Historical (2013)." Baltimore, Md.: CMS.

Cohen, Wesley M., Richard R. Nelson, and John P. Walsh. 2000. "Protecting Their Intellectual Assets: Appropriability Conditions and Why U.S. Manufacturing Firms Patent (or Not)." Cambridge, Mass.: National Bureau of Economic Research. Working Paper 7552.

Commonwealth Fund. 2006. "Spending on Physician Services per Capita in 2004." New York, N.Y.: Commonwealth Fund. http://www.commonwealthfund.org/interactives-and-data/chart-cart/chartbook/multinational-comparisons-of-health-systems-data--2006/s/spending-on-physician-services-per-capita-in-2004.

Congressional Budget Office (CBO). 2011. "Options for Changing the Tax Treatment of Charitable Giving." Table 4. Washington, D.C.: CBO. https://www.cbo.gov/sites/default/files/112th-congress-2011-2012/reports/10-18-charitableTestimony.pdf.

_____. 2015a. "Temporary Assistance for Needy Families: Spending and Policy Options." Washington, D.C.: CBO. https://www.cbo.gov/sites/default/files/114th-congress-2015-2016/reports/49887-TANF.pdf.

_____. 2015b. "Cost Estimate: H.R. 880, American Research and Competitiveness Act of 2015." Washington, D.C.: CBO. https://www.cbo.gov/publication/49964.

_____. 2016. "The Budget and Economic Outlook: 2016 to 2026."
Washington, D.C.: CBO.
https://www.cbo.gov/sites/default/files/114th-congress-2015-
2016/reports/51129-2016Outlook.pdf.

Cooper, Richard A. 2008. "The U.S. Physician Workforce: Where Do
We Stand?" Paris, France: OECD. http://www.oecd.org/els/health-
systems/41500843.pdf.

Core, John E., Robert W. Holthausen, and David F. Larcker. 1999.
"Corporate Governance, Chief Executive Officer Compensation, and Firm
Performance." *Journal of Financial Economics*, Vol. 51, No. 3, pp. 371–406.

Cronqvist, Henrik and Rüdiger Fahlenbrach. 2012. "CEO Contract
Design: How Do Strong Principals Do It?" Geneva, Switzerland: Swiss
Finance Institute. Research Paper No. 11–14.

Davies, Richard and Belinda Tracey. 2014. "Too Big to Be Efficient? The
Impact of Implicit Subsidies on Estimates of Scale Economies for Banks."
Journal of Money, Credit and Banking, Vol. 46, No. s1, pp. 219–53.
http://onlinelibrary.wiley.com/doi/10.1111/jmcb.12088/full.

Dechezlepretre, Antoine et al. 2016. "Do Tax Incentives for Research
Increase Firm Innovation? An RD Design for R&D." Cambridge, Mass.:
National Bureau of Economic Research. Working Paper 22405.
http://www.nber.org/papers/w22405.

Desbiens, Norman A. and Humberto J. Vidaillet. 2010. "Discrimination
Against international Medical Graduates in the United States Residency
Program Selection Process." *BMC Medical Education*, Vol. 10, No. 5.
http://www.ncbi.nlm.nih.gov/pmc/articles/PMC2822781/.

Dill, Michael J. and Edward S. Salsberg. 2008. "The Complexities of
Physician Supply and Demand: Projections Through 2025." Washington,
D.C.: Association of American Medical Colleges.
https://members.aamc.org/eweb/upload/The%20Complexities%20of%
20Physician%20Supply.pdf.

Economic Policy Institute. 2012. "Hourly Wages of All Workers, by Wage Percentile, 1973–2011 (2011 Dollars)." Washington, D.C.: Economic Policy Institute. http://www.stateofworkingamerica.org/chart/swa-wages-table-4-4-hourly-wages-workers/.

Education Commission for Foreign Medical Graduates. 2015. "IMG Performance in the 2015 Match." Philadelphia, Pa.; Education Commission for Foreign Medical Graduates. http://www.ecfmg.org/news/2015/03/27/img-performance-in-the-2015-match/.

Epstein, Gerald and Juan Antonio Montecino. 2016. "Overcharged: The High Cost of High Finance." New York, N.Y.: Roosevelt Institution. http://www.peri.umass.edu/236/hash/fd100f263f6805db4562d7816b2 25e5f/publication/711/.

Federal Reserve Bank of New York. 2010. "Consumers' Quantitative Inflation Perceptions and Expectations in the Euro Area: An Evaluation." New York, N.Y.: Federal Reserve Bank of New York. https://www.newyorkfed.org/medialibrary/media/research/conference /2010/consumer/FerrucciFRBNY.pdf.

Federal Reserve Board. 2009. "Press Release: 2009 Banking and Consumer Regulatory Policy." Washington, D.C.: Federal Reserve Board. https://www.federalreserve.gov/newsevents/press/bcreg/20091112a.h tm.

_____. 2015. "Flow of Funds Accounts, Table L.117, Line 26 and Line 27." Washington, D.C.: Federal Reserve Board.

Federal Trade Commission (FTC). 2010. "Pay-for-Delay: How Drug Company Pay-Offs Cost Consumers Billions." Washington, D.C.: FTC. https://www.ftc.gov/sites/default/files/documents/reports/pay-delay-how-drug-company-pay-offs-cost-consumers-billions-federal-trade-commission-staff-study/100112payfordelayrpt.pdf.

Fernandes, Nuno et al. 2009. "Are US CEOs Paid More? New International Evidence." Paper presented at the European Finance Association, Bergen, Norway, 2009.
http://papers.ssrn.com/sol3/papers.cfm?abstract_id=2159119.

Food and Drug Administration (FDA). 2015. "Generic Competition and Drug Prices." Silver Spring, Md.: FDA.
http://www.fda.gov/AboutFDA/CentersOffices/OfficeofMedicalProdu ctsandTobacco/CDER/ucm129385.htm.

Footman, Katharine et al. 2014. "Cross-Border Health Care in Europe." Copenhagen, Denmark: European Observatory on Health Systems and Policies, World Health Organization.
http://www.euro.who.int/__data/assets/pdf_file/0009/263538/Cross -border-health-care-in-Europe-Eng.pdf.

Freeman, Richard B. 2006. "Does Globalization of the Scientific/Engineering Workforce Threaten U.S. Economic Leadership?" Cambridge, Mass.: National Bureau of Economic Research.
http://www.nber.org/chapters/c0207.pdf.

Fujisawa, Rie and Gaetan Lafortune. 2008. "The Remuneration of General Practitioners and Specialists in 14 OECD Countries: What Are the Factors Influencing Variations Across Countries?" Paris, France: OECD.
http://www.oecd.org/health/health-systems/41925333.pdf.

Gallini, Nancy T. 2002. "The Economics of Patents: Lessons From Recent U.S. Patent Reform." *Journal of Economic Perspectives*, Vol. 16, No. 2, pp. 131–54.

Gallu, Joshua et al. 2010. "Rattner Settles With SEC on Kickbacks as Cuomo Sues." Bloomberg, November 18.
http://www.bloomberg.com/news/articles/2010-11-18/sec-sues- steven-rattner-in-new-york-for-kickbacks-with-politcal-consultant.

Gandel, Stephen. 2016. "Marissa Mayer's Payday Is Even More Insane Than You Think." *Fortune*, July 26.
http://fortune.com/2016/07/26/marissa-mayers-verizon-yahoo-pay/.

Gittleman, Maury and Morris M. Kleiner. 2013. "Wage Effects of Unionization and Occupational Licensing Coverage in the United States." Cambridge, Mass.: National Bureau of Economic Research. Working Paper 19061. http://www.nber.org/papers/w19061.

Gokhale, Ketaki. 2015. "The Same Pill That Costs $1,000 in America Sells for $4 in India." Bloomberg, December 28. http://www.bloomberg.com/news/articles/2015-12-29/the-price-keeps-falling-for-a-superstar-gilead-drug-in-india.

Government Accountability Office (GAO). 2014. "Large Bank Holding Companies: Expectations of Government Support." Washington, D.C.: GAO, July, pp. 14–612.

Hall, Bronwyn H. and Rosemarie Ham Ziedonis. 2001. "The Patent Paradox Revisited: An Empirical Study of Patenting in the U.S. Semiconductor Industry, 1979-1995." *RAND Journal of Economics*, Vol. 32, No. 1, pp. 101–28.

Hall, Matthew et al. 2011. "The Geography of Immigrant Skills: Educational Profiles of Metropolitan Areas." Washington, D.C.: Brookings Institution. http://www.brookings.edu/research/papers/2011/06/immigrants-singer.

Handke, Christian. 2011. "Economic Effects of Copyright: The Empirical Evidence so Far." Commissioned Paper Prepared for The Committee on the Impact of Copyright Policy on Innovation in the Digital Era. Washington, D.C.: National Academies of the Sciences.

Hook, Alison. 2007. "Sectoral Study on the Impact of Domestic Regulation on Trade in Legal Services." Paris, France: OECD, World Bank. http://www.oecd.org/site/tadstri/40778871.pdf, p. 7.

Hurtado, Patricia. 2016. "JPMorgan's 'London Whale' Surfaces to Say '12 Loss Not His Fault." Bloomberg, February 22. http://www.bloomberg.com/news/articles/2016-02-23/jpmorgan-s-london-whale-surfaces-to-say-12-loss-not-his-fault.

Iacono, Corey. 2016. "Bernie Sanders' Trade Policies Would Make
Billions Poor." *Newsweek*, April 11. http://www.newsweek.com/bernie-
trade-policies-would-make-billions-poor-446292.

Illinois General Assembly. 2015. "Bill Status of SB2758 98th General
Assembly." Springfield, Ill.: Illinois General Assembly.
http://ilga.gov/legislation/billstatus.asp?DocNum=2758&GAID=12&G
A=98&DocTypeID=SB&LegID=78572&SessionID=85.

Ingraham, Christopher. 2016. "One Striking Chart Shows Why Pharma
Companies Are Fighting Legal Marijuana." *Washington Post*, July 13.
https://www.washingtonpost.com/news/wonk/wp/2016/07/13/one-
striking-chart-shows-why-pharma-companies-are-fighting-legal-
marijuana/?tid=pm_business_pop_b/.

International Federation of Health Plans. 2012. "2012 Comparative Price
Report, Variation in Medical and Hospital Prices by Country." London,
U.K.: International Federation of Health Plans.
http://static.squarespace.com/static/518a3cfee4b0a77d03a62c98/t/51d
fd9f9e4b0d1d8067dcde2/1373624825901/2012%20iFHP%20Price%20
Report%20FINAL%20April%203.pdf.

International Monetary Fund (IMF). 2010. "A Fair and Substantial
Contribution by the Financial Sector." Washington, D.C.: IMF.
https://www.imf.org/external/np/g20/pdf/062710b.pdf.

_____. 2014. "How Big Is the Implicit Subsidy for Banks Considered Too
Big to Fail?" Washington, D.C.: IMF. 2014 Global Financial Stability
Report, Chapter 3.

_____. 2016. "Report for Selected Countries and Subjects." Washington,
D.C.: IMF.
http://www.imf.org/external/pubs/ft/weo/2016/01/weodata/weore
pt.aspx?pr.x=20&pr.y=13&sy=2004&ey=2021&scsm=1&ssd=1&sort=c
ountry&ds=.&br=1&c=924&s=BCA_NGDPD&grp=0&a=.

Jaffe, Adam B. 2000. "The U.S. Patent System in Transition: Policy
Innovation and the Innovation Process." *Research Policy*, Vol. 29, No. 4–5,
pp. 531–57.

Kaiser Family Foundation. 2013. "2013 Survey of Americans on the U.S. Role in Global Health." Washington, D.C.: Kaiser Family Foundation. http://kff.org/global-health-policy/poll-finding/2013-survey-of-americans-on-the-u-s-role-in-global-health/.

_____. 2016. "Total Professionally Active Physicians, April 2016." Washington, D.C.: Kaiser Family Foundation. http://kff.org/other/state-indicator/total-active-physicians/?currentTimeframe=0&sortModel=%7B%22colId%22:%22Location%22,%22sort%22:%22asc%22%7D.

Kessler, Glenn. 2013. "Annotating Obama's 2006 Speech Against Boosting the Debt Limit." *Washington Post*, January 15. https://www.washingtonpost.com/blogs/fact-checker/post/annotating-obamas-2006-speech-against-boosting-the-debt-limit/2013/01/14/aa8cf8c4-5e9b-11e2-9940-6fc488f3fecd_blog.html.

Katari, Ravi and Dean Baker. 2015. "Patent Monopolies and the Costs of Mismarketing Drugs." Washington, D.C.: Center for Economic and Policy Research. http://cepr.net/documents/publications/mismarketing-drugs-2015-04.pdf.

Kleiner, Morris M. et al. 2014. "Relaxing Occupational Licensing Requirements: Analyzing Wages and Prices for a Medical Service." Cambridge, Mass.: National Bureau of Economic Research. Working Paper 19906. http://www.nber.org/papers/w19906.

Kleiner, Morris M. and Robert T. Kudrle. 2000. "Does Regulation Affect Economic Outcomes? The Case of Dentistry." *Journal of Law and Economics*, Vol. 43, No.2, pp. 547–82. http://www.jstor.org/stable/10.1086/467465?seq=1#page_scan_tab_contents.

Kleiner, Morris M. and Kyoung Won Park. 2010. "Battles Among Licensed Occupations: Analyzing Government Regulations on Labor Market Outcomes for Dentists and Hygienists." Cambridge, Mass.: National Bureau of Economic Research. Working Paper 16560. http://www.nber.org/papers/w16560.

Kocieniewski, David. 2011. "But Nobody Pays That; At G.E. on Tax Day, Billions of Reasons to Smile." *New York Times*, March 25. http://query.nytimes.com/gst/fullpage.html?res=9E07E5DE1131F936 A15750C0A9679D8B63.

Kovacs, Eszter et al. 2014. "Licensing Procedures and Registration of Medical Doctors in the European Union." *Clinical Medicine*, Vol. 14, No. 3, pp. 229–38. http://www.clinmed.rcpjournal.org/content/14/3/229.long.

Landes, William M. and Richard A. Posner. 2004. "The Political Economy of Intellectual Property Law." Washington, D.C.: AEI Brookings Joint Center for Regulatory Studies.

Lane, Charles. 2016. "The Sanders-Pope 'Moral Economy' Could Hit the Income Inequality Fight." *Washington Post*, April 13. https://www.washingtonpost.com/opinions/the-sanders-pope-francis-moral-economy-could-hurt-the-income-inequality-fight/2016/04/13/8007b80a-01ae-11e6-9203-7b8670959b88_story.html.

Lanjouw, Jean O. 1998. "The Introduction of Pharmaceutical Product Patents in India: 'Heartless Exploitation of the Poor and Suffering'?" Cambridge, Mass.: National Bureau of Economic Research. Working Paper 6366.

Lanjouw, Jean O. and Josh Lerner. 2001. "Tilting the Table? The Use of Preliminary Injunctions." *Journal of Law and Economics*, Vol. 44, No. 2, pp. 573–603.

Lanjouw, Jean O. and Mark Schankerman. 2001a. "Characteristics of Patent Litigation: A Window on Competition." *RAND Journal of Economics*, Vol. 32, No. 1, pp. 129–51.

_____. 2001b. "Enforcing Intellectual Property Rights." Cambridge, Mass.: National Bureau of Economic Research. Working Paper 8656.

Laugesen, Miriam J. and Sherry A. Glied. 2008. "Higher Fees Paid To US Physicians Drive Higher Spending for Physician Services Compared to Other Countries." *Health Affairs*, Vol. 30, No. 9, pp. 1647–56. http://content.healthaffairs.org/content/30/9/1647.full.html.

Lerner, Joshua. 1995. "Patenting in the Shadow of Competitors." *Journal of Law and Economics*, Vol. 38, No. 2, pp. 463–95.

Lerner, Josh and Jean Tirole. 2000. "The Simple Economics of Open Source." Cambridge, Mass.: National Bureau of Economic Research. Working Paper 7600.

Lerner, Josh and Robert P. Merges. 1998. "The Control of Technology Alliances: An Empirical Analysis of the Biotechnology Industry." *Journal of Industrial Economics*, Vol. 46, No. 2, pp. 125–56.

Levitt, Marty Jay. 1993. *Confessions of a Union Buster*. New York, N.Y.: Crown Publishing. https://www.amazon.com/Confessions-Union-Buster-Marty-Levitt/dp/0517583305.

Liu, Crocker H. and David Yermack. 2007. "Where Are the Shareholders' Mansions? CEOs' Home Purchases, Stock Sales, and Subsequent Company Performance." Tempe, Ariz.: W. P. Carey School of Business, Arizona State University.

Love, Brian J. 2013. "An Empirical Study of Patent Litigation Timing: Could a Patent Term Reduction Decimate Trolls Without Harming Innovators?" *University of Pennsylvania Law Review*, Vol. 161, pp. 1309–59.

Magee, Stephen P. et al. 1989. *Black Hole Tariffs and Endogenous Policy Theory: Political Economy in General Equilibrium*. Cambridge, U.K.: Cambridge University Press.

Major, Lindsey & Africa. 2014. "Partner Compensation Survey." Washington, D.C.: Major, Lindsey & Africa.

Malmendier, Ulrike and Geoffrey Tate. 2008. "Superstar CEOs." Cambridge, Mass.: National Bureau of Economic Research. Working Paper 14140.

Marriage, Madison. 2016. "BlackRock Slammed Over Too Many Votes for High Pay." *Financial Times*, May 22. http://www.asyousow.org/wp-content/uploads/2016/05/20160524-Financial-Times-BlackRock_slammed_over_too_many_votes.pdf.

Marshall, Ric and Linda Eling Lee. 2016. "Are CEOs Paid For Performance? Evaluating the Effectiveness of Equity Incentives." New York, N.Y.: MSCI. https://www.msci.com/documents/10199/91a7f92b-d4ba-4d29-ae5f-8022f9bb944d.

Martin, Andrew. 2010. "Bank of America to End Debit Overdraft Fees." *New York Times*, March 9. http://www.nytimes.com/2010/03/10/your-money/credit-and-debit-cards/10overdraft.html.

Matheson, Thornton. 2011. "Taxing Financial Transactions: Issues and Evidence." Washington, D.C.: IMF. IMF Working Paper WP/11/54. https://www.imf.org/external/pubs/ft/wp/2011/wp1154.pdf.

Matoo, Aaditya and Randeep Rathindran. 2006. "How Health Insurance Inhibits Trade in Health Care." *Health Affairs*, Vol. 25, No. 2, pp. 358–68. http://content.healthaffairs.org/content/25/2/358.long.

Mayer, Gerald. 2004. "Union Membership Trends in the United States." Ithaca, NY: Cornell University, ILR School. http://digitalcommons.ilr.cornell.edu/cgi/viewcontent.cgi?article=1176&context=key_workplace.

McNeil, Douglas G. Jr. 2015. "Curing Hepatitis C, in an Experiment the Size of Egypt." *New York Times*, December 15. http://www.nytimes.com/2015/12/16/health/hepatitis-c-treatment-egypt.html.

Medley, Bill. 2013. "Riegle-Neal Interstate Banking and Branching Efficiency Act of 1994." Washington, D.C.: Federal Reserve Board. http://www.federalreservehistory.org/Events/DetailView/50.

Mishel, Lawrence and Jessica Schieder. 2016. "Stock Market Headwinds Meant Less Generous Year for Some CEOs." Washington, D.C.: Economic Policy Institute. http://www.epi.org/publication/ceo-and-worker-pay-in-2015/.

Mitchell, Karlyn and Nur M Onvural. 1996. "Economies of Scale and Scope at Large Commercial Banks: Evidence From the Fourier Flexible Functional Form." *Journal of Money, Credit and Banking*, Vol. 28, No. 2, pp. 178–99.
http://econpapers.repec.org/article/mcbjmoncb/v_3a28_3ay_3a1996_3ai_3a2_3ap_3a178-99.htm.

Munnell, A.H. et al. 2011. "A Role for Defined Contribution Plans in the Public Sector." Chestnut Hill, Mass.: Trustees of Boston College, Center for Retirement Research. http://crr.bc.edu/wp-content/uploads/2011/04/slp_16-508.pdf.

Nash, Kent D. and L. Jackson Brown. 2012. "The Market for Dental Services." *Journal of Dental Education*, Vol. 76, No. 8, pp. 973–86. http://www.jdentaled.org/content/76/8/973.full.

National Academy for Social Insurance. 1998. "Evaluating Issues in Privatizing Social Security: Report of the Panel on Privatization of Social Security." Washington, D.C.: National Academy of Social Insurance.

National Association for Law Placement (NALP). 2015. "First-Year Associate Salaries at Large Law Firms Have Become Less Homogenous, Though $160,000 Continues to Define the Top of the Market." Washington, D.C.: NALP. http://www.nalp.org/2015_assoc_salaries.

National Science Foundation. 2012. "Business Research and Development and Innovation: 2012." Arlington, Va.: National Science Foundation. http://www.nsf.gov/statistics/2016/nsf16301/#chp2, Chapter 2.

New Zealand Ministry of Business, Innovation, and Employment. 2015.
"Economic Modelling on Estimated Effect of Copyright Term Extension
on New Zealand Economy." Wellington, New Zealand: New Zealand
Ministry of Business, Innovation, and Employment.
https://www.tpp.mfat.govt.nz/assets/docs/TPP%20-
%20Analysis%20of%20Copyright%20term%20extension,%20explanator
y%20cover%20note.pdf.

Nuñez, Daniela. 2006. "Survey Finds Close Ties Between Drug
Companies and Patient Groups." Consumers Union, Safe Patient Project,
October 30. http://safepatientproject.org/posts/2257-
survey_finds_close_ties_between_drug_companies_and_patient_groups.

O'Neil, Michael. 1999. "Rubin, Greenspan & Summers: The Committee
to Save the World." *Time*, February 15.
http://content.time.com/time/covers/0,16641,19990215,00.html.

OECD. 2014. "OECD Health Statistics 2014 - Frequently Requested
Data." Paris, France: OECD. http://www.oecd.org/els/health-
systems/oecd health-statistics-2014-frequently-requested-data.htm.

_____. 2015. "Health Expenditure and Financing." Paris, France: OECD.
http://stats.oecd.org/Index.aspx?DataSetCode=SHA.

_____. 2016. "Benefits and Wages: Statistics." Paris, France: OECD.
http://www.oecd.org/els/benefits-and-wages-statistics.htm.

Office of the Inspector General of the United States Postal Service. 2014.
"Providing Non-Bank Financial Services for the Underserved." Arlington,
Va.: Office of the Inspector General of the United States Postal Service.
https://www.uspsoig.gov/sites/default/files/document-library-
files/2015/rarc-wp-14 007 0.pdf.

Orszag, Peter R., and Joseph E. Stiglitz. 2001. "Rethinking Pension
Reform: Ten Myths About Social Security Systems." Washington, D.C.:
World Bank. In *New Ideas About Old Age Security: Toward Sustainable Pension
Systems in the 21st Century*, eds. Robert Holzmann and Joseph E. Stiglitz,
pp. 17–56.

Pollack, Andrew. 2016. "Makers of Humira and Enbrel Using New Drug Patents to Delay Generic Versions." *New York Times*, July 15. http://www.nytimes.com/2016/07/16/business/makers-of-humira-and-enbrel-using-new-drug-patents-to-delay-generic-versions.html.

Prequin. 2014. "2014 Preqin Global Private Equity Report." London, U.K.: Prequin. https://www.preqin.com/docs/samples/The_2014_Preqin_Global_Private_Equity_Report_Sample_Pages.pdf.

PricewaterhouseCoopers. 2015. "2015 Patent Litigation Study: A Change in Patentee Fortunes." New York, N.Y.: PricewaterhouseCoopers. https://www.pwc.com/us/en/forensic-services/publications/assets/2015-pwc-patent-litigation-study.pdf.

Quigley, Timothy J., Craig Crossland, and Robert J. Campbell. 2016. "Shareholder Perceptions of the Changing Impact of CEOs: Market Reactions to Unexpected CEO Deaths, 1950–2009." *Strategic Management Journal*, Vol. 29, March.

Radelet, Steven and Jeffrey Sachs. 2000. "The Onset of the East Asian Financial Crisis." In *Currency Crises*. Chicago, IL: University of Chicago Press. http://www.nber.org/chapters/c8691.pdf.

Rappaport, Edmund. 1998. "Copyright Term Extension: Estimating the Economic Values." Washington, D.C.: Congressional Research Service. Report 98-144E.

Ray, Rebecca, Milla Sanes, and John Schmitt. 2013. "No-Vacation Nation Revisited." Washington, D.C.: Center for Economic and Policy Research. http://cepr.net/publications/reports/no-vacation-nation-2013.

Ringel, Jeanne S. et al. 2002. "The Elasticity of Demand for Health Care: A Review of the Literature and Its Application to the Military Health System." Santa Monica, Calif.: RAND Corporation. http://www.rand.org/pubs/monograph_reports/MR1355.html.

Rob, Rafael and Joel Waldfogel. 2004. "Piracy on the High C's: Music Downloading, Sales Displacement, and Social Welfare in a Sample of College Students." Cambridge, Mass.: National Bureau of Economic Research. Working Paper 10874.
http://www.nber.org/papers/w10874.

Rosnick, David. 2013. "Reduced Work Hours as a Means of Slowing Climate Change." Washington, D.C.: Center for Economic and Policy Research. http://cepr.net/publications/reports/reduced-work-hours-as-a-means-of-slowing-climate-change.

Sahay, Ratna et al. 2015. "Rethinking Financial Deepening: Stability and Growth in Emerging Markets." Washington, D.C.: IMF. IMF Staff Discussion Note.
http://www.imf.org/external/pubs/ft/sdn/2015/sdn1508.pdf.

Salganik, Matthew J, Peter Sheridan Dodds, and Duncan J. Watts. 2006. "Experimental Study of Inequality and Unpredictability in an Artificial Cultural Market." *Science*, Vol. 311, pp. 854–56.
https://www.princeton.edu/~mjs3/salganik_dodds_watts06_full.pdf.

Schankerman, Mark. 1998. "How Valuable Is Patent Protection? Estimates by Technology Field." *RAND Journal of Economics*, Vol. 29, No. 1, pp. 77–107.

Schankerman, Mark and Ariel Pakes. 1986. "Estimates of the Value of Patent Rights in European Countries During the Post-1950 Period." *Economic Journal*, Vol. 96, No. 384, pp. 1052–76.

Scherer, F.M. 2009. "The Political Economy of Patent Policy Reform in the United States." *Journal on Telecommunications and High Technology Law*, Vol. 7, No. 2, pp. 167–216.

Shapiro, Carl. 2001. "Navigating the Patent Thicket: Cross Licenses, Patent Pools, and Standard Setting." Berkeley, Calif.: University of California, Berkeley, Haas School of Business. SSRN Working Paper.

Shue, Kelly and Richard Townsend. 2016. "Growth Through Rigidity: An Explanation for the Rise in CEO Pay." Cambridge, Mass.: National Bureau of Economic Research. Working Paper 21975. http://www.nber.org/papers/w21975.

Seward, Zachary M. 2016. "This Is How Much a Bloomberg Terminal Costs." *Quartz*, May 15. http://qz.com/84961/this-is-how-much-a-bloomberg-terminal-costs/.

Sharp, L.K. et al. 2002. "Specialty Board Certification and Clinical Outcomes: The Missing Link." *Academic Medicine*, Vol. 77, No. 6, pp. 534–42. http://journals.lww.com/academicmedicine/Abstract/2002/06000/Specialty_Board_Certification_and_Clinical.11.aspx.

Social Security Administration (SSA). 2014a. "Master Beneficiary Record, 100 Percent Data; and U.S. Postal Service Geographic Data." Woodlawn, Md.: SSA.

_____. 2015a. "Social Security Annual Statistical Supplement. SSA Publication 12-11700, pp 5.100, 5.101." Woodlawn, Md.: SSA.

_____. 2015b. "Table V.A2.—Social Security Area Population on July 1 and Dependency Ratios." Woodlawn, Md.: SSA. https://www.ssa.gov/oact/TR/2015/V_A_demo.html#271410.

_____. 2015c. "Fast Facts & Figures About Social Security, 2015." Woodlawn, Md.: SSA. https://www.socialsecurity.gov/policy/docs/chartbooks/fast_facts/2015/fast_facts15.html.

_____. 2016a. "Detailed Reports on the Financial Outlook for Social Security's Old-Age, Survivors, and Disability Insurance (OASDI) Trust Funds." Woodlawn, Md.: SSA. https://www.ssa.gov/oact/tr/.

_____. 2016b. "Wage Statistics for 2014." Woodlawn, Md.: SSA. https://www.ssa.gov/cgi-bin/netcomp.cgi?year=2014.

Stange, Kevin M. 2013. "How Does Provider Supply and Regulation Influence the Health Care Market? Evidence From Nurse Practitioners and Physicians Assistants." Cambridge, Mass.: National Bureau of Economic Research. Working Paper 19172.
http://www.nber.org/papers/w19172.

Stewart, James. 2013. "Bad Directors and Why They Aren't Thrown Out." *New York Times*, March 29.
http://www.nytimes.com/2013/03/30/business/why-bad-directors-arent-thrown-out.html.

Sullivan, Margaret. 2013. "The Times Is Working on Ways to Make Numbers-Based Stories Clearer for Readers." *New York Times*, October 18.
http://publiceditor.blogs.nytimes.com/2013/10/18/the-times-is-working-on-ways-to-make-numbers-based-stories-clearer-for-readers/?hp&_r=0.

The Telegraph. 2011. "ECB President Jean-Claude Trichet 's Leaving Speech: In Full." *The Telegraph*, October 19.
http://www.telegraph.co.uk/finance/financialcrisis/8837055/ECB-president-Jean-Claude-Trichet-s-leaving-speech-in-full.html.

Thrift Savings Plan (TSP). 2015. "Administrative Expenses." Washington, D.C.: Federal Retirement Thrift Investment Board.
https://www.tsp.gov/planparticipation/administrative/administrativeExpenses.shtml.

Trading Economics. 2016. "China Foreign Exchange Reserves 1980-2016." Trading Economics, September 2.
http://www.tradingeconomics.com/china/foreign-exchange-reserves.

Transparent California. 2016. "Transparent California: Salaries." Las Vegas, Nev.: Nevada Policy Research Institute.
http://transparentcalifornia.com/.

U.S. Census Bureau. 2014. "American Community Survey (ACS)." Suitland, Md: U.S. Census Bureau. http://www.census.gov/programs-surveys/acs/data.html.

_____. 2015. "Projections of the Size and Composition of the U.S. Population: 2014 to 2060, Figure 5." Suitland, Md.: U.S. Census Bureau. https://www.census.gov/content/dam/Census/library/publications/2015/demo/p25-1143.pdf.

U.S. Copyright Office. 1998. "The Digital Millennium Copyright Act of 1998." Washington, D.C.: U.S. Copyright Office. http://www.copyright.gov/legislation/dmca.pdf.

U.S. Government Publishing Office (GPO). 2012. "Public Law 112-211, 112th Congress." Washington, D.C.: U.S. GPO. https://www.gpo.gov/fdsys/pkg/PLAW-112publ211/html/PLAW-112publ211.htm.

U.S. Patent and Trademark Office (USPTO). 2011. "Duration of Copyright." Washington, D.C.: USPTO. http://www.copyright.gov/circs/circ15a.pdf.

_____. 2015. "2701 Patent Term [R-07.2015]." Alexandria, Va.: USPTO. http://www.uspto.gov/web/offices/pac/mpep/s2701.html#sect2701.

U.S. PIRG. 2013. "Twenty Top Generic Drugs Delayed by Industry Payoffs." Washington, D.C.: U.S. PIRG. http://www.uspirg.org/news/usp/twenty-top-generic-drugs-delayed-industry-payoffs.

Verizon. 2016. "Basic International Rates." New York, N.Y.: Verizon. http://www.verizon.com/home/phone/international/basicinternational rates/?pos=1.

Waldfogel, Joel. 2010. "Music File Sharing and Sales Displacement in the iTunes Era." *Information Economics and Policy*, Vol. 22, No. 4, pp. 306–14. http://www.sciencedirect.com/science/article/pii/S0167624510000260.

_____. 2011. "Bye, Bye, Miss American Pie? The Supply of New Recorded Music Since Napster." Cambridge, Mass.: National Bureau of Economic Research. Working Paper 16882. http://www.nber.org/papers/w16882.

Warner, Kris. 2012. "Protecting Fundamental Labor Rights: Lessons From Canada for the United States." Washington, D.C.: Center for Economic and Policy Research. http://cepr.net/publications/reports/protecting-fundamental-labor-rights.

Washington Post. 2012. "Salary Gaps and Doctor Shortages." Washington, D.C: Washington Post. https://www.washingtonpost.com/business/salary-gaps-and-doctor-shortages-growing/2012/02/10/gIQAPkZM4Q_graphic.html.

Weissman, Jordan. 2016. "Bernie Sanders' Bizarre Idea of Fair Trade." Slate.com, April 5. http://www.slate.com/blogs/moneybox/2016/04/05/bernie_sanders_is_the_developing_world_s_worst_nightmare.html.

Westerholm, Russell. 2013. "Top 10 Highest Paid Private College Presidents; Why Harvard's Leader Is Nowhere Close To Top." University Herald, December 16. http://www.universityherald.com/articles/6244/20131216/top-10-highest-paid-private-college-presidents-why-harvards-leader-is-nowhere-close-to-top.htm.

Winston, Clifford et al. 2011. First Thing We Do, Let's Deregulate All the Lawyers. Washington, D.C.: Brookings Institution Press. http://www.brookings.edu/research/books/2011/firstthingwedoletsderegulateallthelawyers.

Williams, Heidi L. 2010. "Intellectual Property Rights and Innovation: Evidence From the Human Genome." Cambridge, Mass.: National Bureau of Economic Research. Working Paper 16213.

Woolhander, Steffie et al. 2003. "Costs of Health Care Administration in the United States and Canada." *New England Journal of Medicine*, No. 349, pp. 768–775.
http://www.nejm.org/doi/full/10.1056/NEJMsa022033#t=articleResults.

World Salaries. 2016. "International Average Salary Income Comparison, Dentist Salary." World Salaries.
http://www.worldsalaries.org/dentist.shtml.

Worstall, Tim. 2016. "Bernie Sanders Sure Doesn't Know Much About Trade." *Forbes*, April 6.
http://www.forbes.com/sites/timworstall/2016/04/06/bernie-sanders-sure-doesnt-know-much-about-trade/.

Yermack, David. 2005. "Flights of Fancy: Corporate Jets, CEO Perquisites, and Inferior Shareholder Returns." New York, N.Y.: Stern School Business, New York University.
http://portal.idc.ac.il/en/main/research/caesareacenter/annualsummit/documents/yermak.pdf.

Zakaria, Fareed. 2016. "Barack Obama Is Now Alone in Washington." *Washington Post*, September 1.
https://www.washingtonpost.com/opinions/barack-obama-is-now-alone-in-washington/2016/09/01/4d2e1348-7080-11e6-9705-23e51a2f424d_story.html.

Appendix

This Appendix includes Table 6-1, referenced on page 136.

TABLE 6-1

Directors of the 100 largest publicly traded companies in the U.S. who have previously held positions in government

Firm	Name	Government Agency	Government Position
Apple Inc.	Albert Gore Jr.	White House	Vice President
McKesson	Wayne Budd	Department of Justice	Associate Attorney General
UnitedHealth Group	Gail Wilensky	Centers for Medicare and Medicaid Services	Administrator
CVS Health	Nancy-Ann Deparle	White House	Deputy Chief of Staff for Policy
General Motors	Michael Mullen	Joint Chiefs of Staff	Chairman
Ford Motor Company	William Kennard	FCC (1997–2001), Embassy to European Union (2009–2013)	Chairman, Ambassador
Ford Motor Company	Jon Huntsman	State of Utah	Governor
AT&T	Richard Fisher	Federal Reserve Bank of Dallas	President
AT&T	Laura D'Andrea Tyson	Department of State	Secretary of State Foreign Affairs Policy Board
AT&T	William Kennard	FCC (1997–2001), Embassy to European Union (2009–2013)	Chairman, Ambassador
AT&T	Glenn Hutchins	Federal Reserve Bank of New York	Director
General Electric	Mary Schapiro	Securities and Exchange Commission	Chairman

TABLE 6-1

Directors of the 100 largest publicly traded companies in the U.S. who have previously held positions in government

Firm	Name	Government Agency	Government Position
General Electric	Peter Henry	Federal Reserve Bank of New York	Member of Economic Advisory Panel
AmerisourceBergen	Jane Henney	Food and Drug Administration	Commissioner
Verizon	Donald Nicolaisen	Securities and Exchange Commission	Chief Accountant
Verizon	Rodney Earl Slater	Department of Transportation	Secretary
Chevron	Linnet Deily	Office of the U.S. Trade Representative	Deputy Representative
Chevron	Jon Huntsman	State of Utah	Governor
Costco	Daniel Evans	U.S. Senate	Senator (R-WA)
Kroger	Susan Phillips	Board of Governors of Federal Reserve System	Governor
Amazon	Jamie Gorelick	Department of Justice	Deputy Attorney General
Walgreens	William Foote	Federal Reserve Bank of Chicago	Chairman of the Board
Walgreens	David Brailer	Department of Health and Human Services	National Coordinator for Health Information Technology
Walgreens	Leonard Schaeffer	Centers for Medicare and Medicaid Services	Administrator
Express Scripts Holding	William Roper	Centers for Disease Control	Director
Express Scripts Holding	Woodrow Myers	New York City Department of Health and Mental Hygiene	Commissioner
Express Scripts Holding	Roderick Palmore	Department of Justice	Assistant U.S. Attorney for Northern District of Illinois
Express Scripts Holding	Elder Granger	Department of Defense	Deputy Director and Program Executive Officer of the TRICARE Management Activity
JPMorgan Chase	Laban Jackson	Federal Reserve Bank of Cleveland	Director
JPMorgan Chase	Linda Bammann	Freddie Mac	Director
Boeing	Kenneth Duberstein	White House	Chief of Staff
Boeing	Susan Schwab	Office of the U.S. Trade Representative	Representative
Boeing	Edmund Giambastiani	Joint Chiefs of Staff	Vice Chairman
Bank of America	Susan Bies	Board of Governors of Federal Reserve System	Governor
Bank of America	Monica Lozano	Board of Regents of University of California	Board Member
Wells Fargo	John Stumpf	Federal Reserve Board	Member of Financial Advisory Council

TABLE 6-1

Directors of the 100 largest publicly traded companies in the U.S. who have previously held positions in government

Firm	Name	Government Agency	Government Position
Wells Fargo	Cynthia Milligan	Omaha Branch of Kansas City Federal Reserve	Director
Wells Fargo	Federico Pena	Department of Energy	Secretary
Wells Fargo	James Quigley	Securities and Exchange Commission	Member of Advisory Committee on Improvements to Financial Reporting
Wells Fargo	Elaine Chao	Department of Labor	Secretary
Wells Fargo	Elizabeth Duke	Federal Reserve Board	Chair of Committee on Consumer and Community Affairs, Member of Committee on Bank Supervision and Regulation, Member of Committee on Board Affairs
Wells Fargo	Suzanne Vautrinot	U.S. Air Force	Major General and Commander, 24th Air Force, Air Forces Cyber and Air Force Network Operations
Citigroup	Eugene McQuade	Freddie Mac	Director
Citigroup	Joan Sperro	Department of State	Under Secretary, Economics, Business and Agricultural Affairs
Citigroup	Diana Taylor	State of New York	Superintendent of Banks
Citigroup	Ernesto Zedillo	President of Mexico	President
Citigroup	Anthony Santomero	Federal Reserve Bank of Philadelphia	President
Phillips 66	Marna Whittington	State of Delaware	Secretary of Finance
IBM	Joan Sperro	Department of State	Under Secretary, Economics, Business and Agricultural Affairs
IBM	Shirley Ann Jackson	U.S. Nuclear Regulatory Commission	Chairman
Valero Energy	Donald Nickles	U.S. Senate	Senator (R-OK)
Valero Energy	Deborah Majoras	Federal Trade Commission	Chair
Valero Energy	Susan Kaufman Purcell	Department of State	Member, Policy Planning Staff
Procter & Gamble	Ernesto Zedillo	President of Mexico	President
Procter & Gamble	Francis Blake	Department of Energy	Deputy Secretary
State Farm Insurance	Dan Arvizu	Department of Energy	Director, National Renewable Energy Laboratory
State Farm Insurance	Christopher DeMuth	Office of Management and Budget	Administrator for Information and Regulatory Affairs
State Farm Insurance	Allan Landon	Board of Governors of Federal Reserve System	Governor
State Farm Insurance	Gary Perlin	World Bank	CFO

TABLE 6-1

Directors of the 100 largest publicly traded companies in the U.S. who have previously held positions in government

Firm	Name	Government Agency	Government Position
State Farm Insurance	Susan Phillips	Board of Governors of Federal Reserve System	Governor
Comcast	Kenneth Bacon	Fannie Mae	Executive Vice President
Target	Kenneth Salazar	Department of the Interior	Secretary
Johnson & Johnson	A. Eugene Washington	Centers for Disease Control	Employee
Johnson & Johnson	D. Scott Davis	Federal Reserve Bank of Atlanta	Chairman
Johnson & Johnson	Mark McClellan	Centers for Medicare and Medicaid Services	Administrator
MetLife	R. Glenn Hubbard	Council of Economic Advisors	Chairman
MetLife	Carlos Gutierrez	Department of Commerce	Secretary
MetLife	William Kennard	FCC (1997–2001), Embassy to European Union (2009–2013)	Chairman, Ambassador
Archer-Daniels Midland	Francisco Sanchez	Department of Commerce	Under Secretary for International Trade
Marathon Petroleum	John Snow	Department of Treasury	Secretary
Marathon Petroleum	B. Evan Bayh	U.S. Senate	Senator (R-IN)
Marathon Petroleum	John Surma	Federal Reserve Bank of Cleveland	Deputy Chair of Board of Directors
Freddie Mac	Nicholas Retsinas	Department of Housing and Urban Development	Assistant Secretary for Housing, Federal Housing Commissioner
Freddie Mac	Richard Hartnack	Federal Reserve Bank of San Francisco	Director
Freddie Mac	Anthony Williams	Department of Agriculture	CFO
Freddie Mac	Raphael Bostic	Department of Housing and Urban Development	Assistant Secretary for Policy Development and Research
PepsiCo	Richard Fisher	Federal Reserve Bank of Dallas	President
United Technologies	Christine Todd Whitman	Environmental Protection Agency	Administrator
United Technologies	Lloyd Austin	U.S. Army	Vice Chief of Staff
United Technologies	Richard Myers	U.S. Air Force	Chairman of the Joint Chiefs of Staff
Aetna	Jeffrey Garten	Department of Commerce	Under Secretary for International Trade
Aetna	Frank Clark	Chicago Board of Education	President
Aetna	Molly Coye	California Department of Health Services	Director

TABLE 6-1

Directors of the 100 largest publicly traded companies in the U.S. who have previously held positions in government

Firm	Name	Government Agency	Government Position
Aetna	Olympia Snowe	U.S. Senate	Senator (R-ME)
UPS	Kevin Warsh	Board of Governor of Federal Reserve System	Governor
AIG	Peter Fisher	Department of Treasury	Under Secretary for Domestic Finance
AIG	Theresa Stone	Federal Reserve Board of Richmond	Director
Prudential Financial	George Paz	Federal Reserve Bank of St Louis	Chairman
Prudential Financial	Sandra Pianalto	Federal Reserve Bank of Cleveland	President
Intel Corp	Charlene Barhefsky	Office of the U.S. Trade Representative	Representative
Intel Corp	Reed Hundt	Federal Communications Commission	Chairman
Humana	David Jones	Jefferson County Board of Education	Chairman
Cisco	Kristina Johnson	Department of Energy	Under Secretary for Energy
Pfizer	Joseph Echevarria	Presidential Commission on Election Administration	Member
FedEx	Shirley Ann Jackson	U.S. Nuclear Regulatory Commission	Commissioner
FedEx	Susan Schwab	Office of the U.S. Trade Representative	Representative
FedEx	John Inglis	National Security Agency	Deputy Director
Caterpillar	Susan Schwab	Office of the U.S. Trade Representative	Representative
Caterpillar	Jon Huntsman	State of Utah	Governor
Lockheed Martin	James Ellis	Air Force	Commander, U.S. Strategic Command
Lockheed Martin	Joseph Ralston	NATO	Commander, U.S. European Command and Supreme Allied Commander Europe
Lockheed Martin	James Loy	Department of Homeland Security	Deputy Secretary
Lockheed Martin	Bruce Carlson	National Reconnaissance Office	Director
Coca-Cola Co.	Helene Gayle	Centers for Disease Control	Director, National Center for HIV, STD, and TB Prevention
Coca-Cola Co.	Alexis Herman	Department of Labor	Secretary
Coca-Cola Co.	Samuel Nunn	U.S. Senate	Senator (D-GA)
Coca-Cola Co.	Richard Daley	City of Chicago	Mayor

TABLE 6-1

Directors of the 100 largest publicly traded companies in the U.S. who have previously held positions in government

Firm	Name	Government Agency	Government Position
HCA Holdings	Nancy-Ann Deparle	White House	Deputy Chief of Staff for Policy
Tyson Foods	Mike Beebe	State of Arkansas	Governor
Delta Airlines	Shirley Franklin	City of Atlanta	Mayor
Delta Airlines	Francis Blake	Department of Energy	Deputy Secretary
Delta Airlines	Thomas Donilon	National Security Council	National Security Advisor
Nationwide Mutual	Diane Koken	State of Pennsylvania	Insurance Commissioner
Johnson Controls	Jeffrey Joerres	Federal Reserve Bank of Chicago	Director
Johnson Controls	Dennis Archer	City of Detroit	Mayor
Honeywell International	D. Scott Davis	Federal Reserve Bank of Atlanta	Chairman of the Board
Honeywell International	Judd Gregg	U.S. Senate	Senator (R-NH)
Honeywell International	George Paz	Federal Reserve Bank of St Louis	Chairman of the Board
Honeywell International	Linnet Deily	Office of the U.S. Trade Representative	Representative
Massachusetts Mutual Life Insurance	Patricia Diaz Dennis	Department of State	Assistant Secretary for Human Rights and Humanitarian Affairs
Massachusetts Mutual Life Insurance	Marc Racicot	State of Montana	Governor
Massachusetts Mutual Life Insurance	Cathy Minehan	Federal Reserve Bank of Boston	President
Massachusetts Mutual Life Insurance	Laura Sen	Federal Reserve Bank of Boston	Director
Oracle	Michael Boskin	Council of Economic Advisors	Chairman
Oracle	Leon Panetta	Department of Defense	Secretary
Morgan Stanley	Erskine Bowles	White House	Chief of Staff
Morgan Stanley	Donald Nicolaisen	Securities and Exchange Commission	Chief Accountant
Morgan Stanley	Judith Miscik	Central Intelligence Agency	Deputy Director for Intelligence
Morgan Stanley	Alistair Darling	Her Majesty's Treasury	Chancellor of the Exchequer
Cigna	Jane Henney	Food and Drug Administration	Commissioner
Cigna	David Vitale	Chicago Board of Education	President
Allstate	Thomas Wilson	Federal Reserve Bank of Chicago	Deputy Chair
INTL FCStone	John Fowler	Department of Transportation	General Counsel
American Express	Charlene Barhefsky	Office of the U.S. Trade Representative	Representative

TABLE 6-1

Directors of the 100 largest publicly traded companies in the U.S. who have previously held positions in government

Firm	Name	Government Agency	Government Position
American Express	Anne Lauvergeon	French Presidency	Deputy Chief of Staff
American Express	Michael Leavitt	Department of Health and Human Services	Governor
Gilead Sciences	John Cogan	Department of Labor	Assistant Secretary for Policy
General Dynamics	Lester Lyles	U.S. Air Force	Vice Chief of Staff
General Dynamics	John Keane	U.S. Army	Vice Chief of Staff
General Dynamics	James Mattis	U.S. Marine Corps	Commander, U.S. Central Command
General Dynamics	Rudy deLeon	Department of Defense	Deputy Secretary
General Dynamics	Peter Wall	British Army	Chief of the General Staff
ConocoPhillips	Charles Bunch	Federal Reserve Bank of Cleveland	Chairman
ConocoPhillips	Richard Armitage	Department of State	Deputy Secretary
World Fuel Services	John Manley	Commodity Futures Trading Commission	Chief Accountant
Mondelez International	Charles Bunch	Federal Reserve Bank of Cleveland	Chairman
Exelon	Nicholas Debenedictis	Pennsylvania Department of Environmental Resources	Secretary
Exelon	Anthony Anderson	Federal Reserve Bank of Chicago	Director
Exelon	Richard Mies	U.S. Navy	Commander, U.S. Strategic Command
Twentieth Century Fox	Viet Dinh	Department of Justice	Assistant Attorney General for Legal Policy
Twentieth Century Fox	Robert Silberman	Department of Defense	Assistant Secretary of the Army
Deere & Co.	Michael Johanns	U.S. Senate	Senator (R-NE)
Tesoro	Susan Tomasky	Federal Energy Regulatory Commission	General Counsel
Time Warner	William Barr	Department of Justice	Attorney General
Time Warner	Deborah Wright	New York Department of Housing Preservation and Development	Commissioner
Time Warner	Carlos Gutierrez	Department of Commerce	Secretary

Source and notes: Annual reports of listed companies.

Dean Baker is Co-Director of the Center for Economic and Policy Research (CEPR) in Washington, D.C., which he founded in 1999 with Mark Weisbrot. His areas of research include housing and macroeconomics, intellectual property, Social Security, Medicare, and European labor markets. He is the author of several books, including *Getting Back to Full Employment: A Better Bargain for Working People* (with Jared Bernstein), *The End of Loser Liberalism: Making Markets Progressive, The United States Since 1980, Social Security: The Phony Crisis* (with Mark Weisbrot), and *The Conservative Nanny State: How the Wealthy Use the Government to Stay Rich and Get Richer.* His blog, Beat the Press, provides commentary on economic reporting. He received his B.A. from Swarthmore College and his Ph.D. in Economics from the University of Michigan.

Made in the USA
San Bernardino, CA
27 October 2018